HOW DARE YOU!

Peter Foster

GWPF

ISBN 978-1-8380655-0-8

Set in Minion and Adelle.
Cover and illustrations by Cartoons by Josh www.cartoonsbyjosh.
com
Printed by KDP.
Published by The Global Warming Policy Forum.
www.thegwpf.com.

To the memory of my friend Jim Doak

There's room for them all to do well in this place, that's the thing. There's plenty of demand for their talents. Because here they are, right at the centre of things, with the whole universe to plan and control and advise and entertain. And they have the satisfaction of knowing that they are indispensable. For what would the universe be without this concentration of moral and intellectual power in the metropolis? Mere chaos. Undifferentiated interstellar gas. Nothing.

– *Sweet Dreams* by Michael Frayn

Contents

VIRTUE-SIGNALLER-IN-CHIEF

Preface: a Thatcherite skeptic in Trudeaupia

As I write this preface, the world is experiencing economic tur moil due to lockdown policies imposed as a result of the coronavirus pandemic. Obviously, none of the hundred or so columns in this collection, which is a selection from pieces I wrote for the *National Post* between 1998 and 2019, deals with COVID-19, but they are all relevant to the issue of economic recovery in its wake.

When COVID-19 hit, the global economy was already being challenged from other directions, including, and perhaps most significantly, from calls to deal with an alleged "Climate Crisis." In the fall of 2019, London was disrupted by the protests of a radical climate group called Extinction Rebellion, whose movement spread rapidly round the world. Canada was the site of numerous such protests but was already undergoing a crisis of the rule of law, brought on by radical climate activism and muddled climate policy. Rail lines across the country had been blocked by protesters. Pipelines were held up in the courts and by direct action. Draconian legislation proposed by the Liberal government of Justin Trudeau had introduced further obstacles to fossil fuel development. Megaprojects had been cancelled. Petroleum-rich Alberta was at political boiling point.

The coronavirus will pass when a vaccine is developed, but the battle to kill fossil fuels will continue, only now it will represent even more of a threat to ravaged economies, and in particular that of Canada. Thus it is important to understand the origins of the demonization of fossil fuels, and how it represents more than a threat merely to prosperity. It is an assault on freedom, and even the environment. That is what this collection is about.

Many of the columns selected here deal with the issues that were coming home to roost before COVID-19 hit: radical environmental thuggery, the corruption of science, climate policy folly, and the perils of corporate appeasement (that is, appeasement by corporations). Certainly Canada's unresolved aboriginal problems are important, and these problems were highlighted during yet another spate of worldwide protests (which ignored COVID-19's social distancing rules) about alleged "systemic racism" in the wake of the killing of a black man, George Floyd, by a Minneapolis police officer.

Perhaps more significant – both for Canada and the world – was how aboriginal grievances had been manipulated by a large and growing group of national and international environmental non-governmental organizations, ENGOS. These entities are in turn agents of a larger Global Governance Agenda. That Agenda has its ideological home in the UN, and is supported by virtually every government and international bureaucracy on earth. It has also been backed by foundations based on capitalist fortunes, by radical billionaires, and by rent seekers and "useful idiots" in the business community who do not seem to realize – to use Lenin's famous phrase – that they are knitting the rope for their own hanging.

Environmental hysteria has been with us for more than half a century, but it has risen to new heights of frenzy in the past couple of years, most recently in the elevation by those promoting The Agenda of a Swedish schoolgirl named Greta Thunberg. Thunberg is an emotionally disturbed child who has been disgracefully exploited, and is perhaps the most prominent example of what might be called pre-traumatic stress disorder, a state of deliberately induced acute environmental anxiety.

I write a good deal here about eco child abuse and the use of children as pawns in the fight to bring industrial society under tighter central political control. Meanwhile I suspect that few of the young people marching under the symbol of Extinction Rebellion understand that they are part of a movement that could be robbing them of their future. Indeed, they have been persuaded that unless they kill fossil fuels, they will have no future.

I do not wish to make Greta suffer more than she already has, but I have used her now-famous challenge at the UN in the fall of 2019 – "How dare you!" – as the title of this collection because it reflects the self-righteous authoritarian intolerance of the climate industrial complex and its mouthpieces.

The COVID-19 crisis has slowed the climate juggernaut but its promoters remain resolute in their desire to kill fossil fuels. The Secretary General of the UN, António Guterres, declared in the midst of the crisis that government relief funds should not be directed towards fossil fuel companies but only to their green counterparts. In Canada, the government of Justin Trudeau linked corporate relief to climate commitments. When Extinction Rebels cut off access to the Bank of England last fall, its Canadian-born Governor, Mark Carney, had no arguments with the protesters. He was due to leave the Governorship to become the United Nations Special Envoy for Climate Action and Finance, and had been a key figure in pressuring investors to "divest" from coal, oil and natural gas.

However, one surprise factor that severely undermined Guterres' demands, and Trudeau's and Carney's proposed strong-arming, was the release, on Earth Day 2020, of a movie, *Planet of the Humans*. It projected a devastating critique of wind, solar and biofuel "alternative" energy, and exposed the frauds, hypocrites and charlatans who promote it, including Al Gore and Bill McKibben. It represented a more than inconvenient truth because it was backed by radical left-liberal Oscar-winning documentary maker Michael Moore. Written and directed by Moore's associate Jeff Gibbs, the film still reflected anti-capitalist, anti-human climate alarmism and the view that people were "cockroaches." However, it caused a furor among climate True Believers, even though its apostasy did not extend to asking whether alarmist climate science might be as corrupt as its most prominent peddlers.

I have been following energy, climate and related issues for a long time. When, in 1998, Terry Corcoran invited me to write a twice-weekly column on the FP Comment page in Conrad Black's new *National Post*, I had written eight books, five of which focussed on energy and energy politics. These included books on the Pierre Trudeau-era energy policy disasters of the National Energy Program (*The Sorcerer's Apprentices*) and state oil company Petro-Canada (*Self-Serve: How Petro-Canada pumped Canadians Dry*). The title of the

Petrocan book summed up my reservations about Canada's "Natural Ruling Party" and its bureaucratic cohorts, so if one of the objectives of the new National Post was to get rid of the Liberal government in Ottawa, I had solid credentials for the job. And we certainly did help oust them, at least from 2006 to 2015.

The damaging consequences of the economic nationalism of the first Trudeau Liberals hung over the 1980s in Canada. During the same period, Margaret Thatcher was doing a remarkable job of rescuing my native Britain from economic and political decline. It would become ever more clear to me – especially after the election of Pierre Trudeau's son, Justin, in 2015 – that I had been an ideological outlier in Canada, a "Thatcherite in Trudeaupia." I love Canada, but Canada is not synonymous with the Liberal Party.

My journalism and book research had refined an ideological perspective that was in distinct contrast to the left-liberal/Liberal conventional wisdom that represented – and continues to represent – the dominant stream of political opinion in Canada and much of the Western world (A former Governor-General of Canada once said that I didn't write "like a Canadian." What she meant was that I didn't write like a Liberal).

It was clear well before the new *Post* was launched that the left had adopted radical environmentalism as its justification for more political power. The new rationale for Global Governance in the cause of Global Salvation was the alleged need to impose "sustainable development" in the face of projected catastrophic man-made climate change. The objective now wasn't merely to control the oil industry, as it had been under the first Trudeau government, it was to kill it, which presented more than a minor problem for a country with the world's third largest petroleum reserves, and for a world whose growth had been, and still was, fossil fuelled.

One of editor Terry Corcoran's most important initiatives at FP Comment was to create a journalistic haven (I hesitate to use the term "safe space") for critics of climate science and policy. This provided both a podium and a stockade against constant *ad hominem* attacks. It is surely significant that the arguments of skeptics against impending catastrophe and counterproductive policy are rarely if ever addressed directly. Instead, skeptics are screamed down as "deniers," or shills for Big Oil.

By the time I came to the new *Post* I had been working for some years on a broader examination of the left-liberal worldview, and why the same damaging – often disastrous – policies keep coming back in mutated form, like viruses. The result was my ninth book, *Why We Bite the Invisible Hand: The Psychology of Anticapitalism*, which I published in 2014. It is very much a companion volume to the columns reproduced here.

I consider it my enormous good fortune, and indeed an honour, that this book is being published by the Global Warming Policy Forum. The Forum is the campaigning arm of the London-based Global Warming Policy Foundation, the educational think tank set up by Lord Nigel Lawson, a former Chancellor of the Exchequer, to combat disinformation and bad policy on climate. I had contacted Dr. Benny Peiser, the GWPF's director, because I wanted to reach their cartoonist "Josh," whose brilliant graphic take-downs of climate fraud and folly embellish the GWPF's website. I told Benny that I wanted Josh to illustrate a collection of my *Post* columns that I was planning to self-publish. Benny, to my surprise and delight, offered to publish it. The publication would be handled by Andrew Montford, the GWPF's deputy director and publishing guru, whose writing on his Bishop Hill blog and in two fine books on the Climategate scandal I had admired. Working with Andrew and Josh has been a pleasure.

One additional reason for gratitude was that I knew that when Lord Lawson had written a devastating analysis of the climate issue, *An Appeal to Reason: A Cool Look at Global Warming*, he had had immense trouble finding a publisher. When he did eventually get the book out, he was vehemently smeared by mainstream media reviewers, who ignored his substantive arguments and variously described him as an arrogant "public school Tory grandee," "one of the few remaining serious people who argue against the current consensus on global warming," and a "Grumpy Old Denier." Thanks to his creation of the GWPF, my own path to publication has been almost embarrassingly easy. The failure of temperatures to rise in line with alarmist models has not lowered outrage against skeptics. Indeed it has amplified it; but if I receive just a small part of the opprobrium directed at Lord Lawson, I shall consider it a badge of honour.

Once the COVID crisis is over, it is essential that business be as innovative, efficient and productive as possible in order to mend the economic damage that the pandemic – and pandemic policy – has done to lives and livelihoods. It cannot afford the burden of a bogus "Climate Crisis" and The Agenda's myriad related tentacles, which seek to force a transition to a "carbon-neutral economy" as part of a deliberately poorer, freedom-constrained and globally-governed world.

I have divided this collection into sections. I kick off with a series of columns on perhaps the most prominent – and mendacious – of alarmists, Al Gore. I continue with columns on the broad theme of the climate derangement. Then comes a section on the "Climateers," other key figures pushing the climate Agenda. This is followed by columns on the particular insanities of Trudeaupian Canada. Then I have sections on eco child abuse and hysteria over biodiversity. There follow sections dealing with ENGOs and their vicious US-funded attacks on Canadian resource companies, particularly in the forest industry and the Alberta oilsands. Finally I have segments dealing with the subversive concepts of "sustainable development" and "corporate social responsibility" and how, and why, the much-heralded green transition simply isn't happening, and indeed can't.

One of the good things about a collection of columns is that readers can dive in anywhere, particularly when all the columns deal with one grand theme. I have made minor editing changes to some of the columns, and truncated others to avoid repetition, although some repetition is inevitable, even essential. I take full responsibility for all examples of thoughtcrime contained herein.

Finally, I want to record that the *Post* has been an important part of my journalistic life, and I relish having been invited to contribute along with Terry Corcoran and other friends and kindred spirits including Larry Solomon, Bill Watson, Philip Cross, Jack Mintz, Kevin Libin, Joe Oliver, Steve McIntyre, Ross McKitrick and Rex Murphy. I wish to thank the *National Post*, for allowing me to reproduce these columns, and in particular Elena Novikova, for dealing so efficiently with the permissions process. I am also deeply grateful to one of my literary heroes, Michael Frayn, for his kind permission, via his agent, Carol Heaton, to allow me to reproduce a paragraph from his wonderful novel, *Sweet Dreams*, as the epigraph to this book. That paragraph speaks volumes. This is one of them.

Peter Foster
Toronto. June 2020

1

The Goracle

I start this selection with a number of columns on former US vice-president Al Gore. Not only has he been the highest-profile prophet of impending climate catastrophe, he is a satirist's dream.

An Inconvenient Truth, the Oscar-winning movie about his climate crusade, profoundly influenced an entire generation. Indeed, it was forced on schoolchildren, thus contributing to pre-teen traumatic stress disorder. He also shared the Nobel Peace Prize with the Intergovernmental Panel on Climate Change, the IPCC, for promoting an issue that has spawned nothing but international disharmony. Far too few people have noted the irony.

Crazy Al-Gore-ithms

28 April 2006

Vanity Fair's May, 2006, "Green Issue" lies somewhere between hilarious and terrifying. Never mind the disconnect between so much doom and gloom amid all the glossy ads for bling and Botox, it's the glorification of intellectual vapidity and clinical alarmism.

The issue's cover features a green-tinted Julia Roberts as woodland nymph standing vacuously behind secular enviro-saints George Clooney, Robert F. Kennedy Jr. and – the real star of the show – Al Gore (Ms. Roberts, we are informed somberly inside, takes a metal cup when she goes out for coffee and "religiously" returns grocery bags to the store for a nickel).

The Kryptonite shading reminded me that there has always been something slightly extraterrestrial about Gore. Even his name, which seems more appropriate as one word – Algor – makes him sound like an enemy of Superman. However, Gore's complex psyche makes him very human indeed. In fact, he is almost a case study of the psychological demons that seem to drive so much radical environmentalism.

Former presidential candidate Gore is now Hollywood's flavour of the month, largely due to the ecstatic reception that his documentary, *An Inconvenient Truth*, received earlier this year at the Sundance Film Festival. The film is based, somewhat improbably, on a presentation on global warming that Gore has allegedly given more than 1000 times. The title of the film says it all. He thunders self-righteously as a guardian of "The Truth" against the forces of evil/commercial self-interest. That is, George W. Bush. But if President Bush should be criticized for anything recently, it is surely for sounding too much like Al Gore. Paradoxically, meanwhile, Gore's guardianship of the truth involves him telling endless whoppers.

Gore's *Vanity Fair* contribution, a "Green Essay" entitled "The Moment of Truth," spews the kind of apocalyptic mush that first polluted the noosphere via his monumentally unbalanced 1992 book, *Earth in the Balance*. Science simply doesn't come into it.

Humans are melting glaciers. Polar bears are drowning. Great sheets of polar ice threaten to raise sea levels by 20 feet. Species are being exterminated wholesale. Acid seas threaten to dissolve shellfish. And, most grandiosely, "We are ...altering the balance of energy between our planet and the rest of the universe."

So perhaps Krypton does come into it after all.

Why do "our leaders" not take these threats seriously? Why can't they hear the voices that reverberate around Gore's overheated cranium? Too inconvenient? Or...are they mere tools of Big Oil and Big Coal?

Gore associates himself and his environmental cause with the fights against slavery and fascism. Both Churchill and Abraham Lincoln are recruited to stand behind him. However, the policy details of Gore's global masterplan are conspicuously absent, apart from his desire for a vague environmental "Marshall Plan." In a recent article in *The Wall Street Journal,* he claimed that all that is required to save the world is for some central authority to determine the "right" prices for resources and commodities. Then you simply climb aboard the hybrid Algorwagon, let your mind go and wait for Utopia. Not only, according to Gore, will the environment be mended, but so will HIV/AIDS, global poverty, Darfur, family dysfunction and the democratic deficit.

"Ultimately," writes Gore, "it is not about any scientific discussion or political dialogue; it is about who we are as human beings."

And here we may at last agree. Among our less attractive psychological traits, human beings tend to be conformist hypocrites. We have a slim intuitive grasp of science and an even slimmer grasp of economics. We tend to demonize our opponents and attribute base motives to them (imagine me thinking that Al Gore primarily lusts after political power!), and we tend to overestimate our intelligence and problem-solving ability.

Global warming may indeed be taking place, but the contribution of mankind remains uncertain. What is certain is that the kind of draconian action that lurks beneath Gore's bromides will have little or no effect apart from delivering the world into something that looks very much like the fascism that he so frequently condemns.

This man almost became president of the United States. He may run again in 2008. Now that's really scary.

Al Gore's convenient agitprop
7 June 2006

An Inconvenient Truth is a propaganda masterpiece. In the documentary about Al Gore's crusade to educate the world on the horrors of man-made climate change, we observe the stolid former Veep presenting his paradoxically slick message – complete with sophisticated visuals, heavily doctored graphics and misleading props – to rapt audiences. The presentation is interwoven with his personal story and shots of his global travels in pursuit of his environmental White Whale. As with Captain Ahab, however, travel seems to narrow Gore's mind. Whether he is at the North Pole, the South Pole or in the Amazon, he is open to only one conclusion: Apocalypse Soon. Unless, that is, we listen to him. All this, meanwhile, is interspersed with the stock shots of belching smokestacks, hurricanes, collapsing ice shelves and, for some reason, molten lava.

Gore comes across as earnest and yet surprisingly self-effacing and witty, and his rhetoric is as blatant as his science is warped. Much of what he claims to be the "truth" is either downright false or hysterically speculative, such as the claim that current rates of extinction are 1000 times historical levels. Gore treats all opponents as apostates who are either servants of naked self-interest – the "carbon lobby" – or else suitable cases for psychological treatment, "in denial" about the truth that has colonized his brain.

His most egregious nose-stretcher is that there is no scientific disagreement with his point of view. Equally ridiculous is his claim that skepticism is somehow a product of a manipulated "corporate" media. In fact, Gore's film has been greeted with an almost complete lack of media skepticism. Just look at the fawning reviews in *The Globe and Mail*, *The Toronto Star* and even *The National Post*. All swallow without question the alleged scientific consensus/media bias line.

The route to Gore's better world is vague, but passes through dangerous waters. His "solution" – as skimmed over in the movie – seems to involve nothing more than a painless global One-Tonne Challenge, which will be facilitated by new technologies promoted by wise governments. Anybody who objects to this approach, suggesting perhaps that we might examine the fruits of government wisdom in the past, is to be dismissed as an "ideologue."

Gore claims that climate change is, above all, a moral problem, but any search for scientific truth that starts with immoveable moral conviction is severely hampered, if not fatally flawed. Part of his rhetoric is to compare his own moral crusade with not just the fight against fascism but the struggles to end slavery or give women the vote. He regards himself as the environment's Ghandi, Nelson Mandela and Martin Luther King. In fact, beneath its glib exterior, Gore's message contains a great threat to freedom and prosperity.

Al Gore's assault on reason

1 June 2007

The title of Al Gore's latest book, *The Assault on Reason*, says it all. Illogicalities, *non sequiturs*, false analogies, fallacies and *ad hominems* tumble forth in profusion from its pages.

Meanwhile one's Spidey sense feels that something sinister lurks beneath the noble words and the plethora of quotations from Great Men. The book has one obvious target, but isn't piling on to George W. Bush a little like flogging a dead duck?

Dubya has certainly had his share of issues. In particular, he is in deep doo-doo in Iraq. But according to Gore, the President is intent on using the war against terror as an excuse to overturn the US Constitution and set up a corporate plutocracy as part of a plot to achieve world "domination."

Gore foams and bubbles about the absence of Weapons of Mass Destruction and about torture at Abu Ghraib, whose horrors increase with the length of the book (On page 150, 90% of its inmates are declared to be innocent. By page 208, that figure has grown to 99%). Gore rails about the incompetence that failed to pick up the warnings of 9/11, or respond adequately to the ravages of Hurricane Katrina. These are legitimate political issues, but his solution to this welter of government incompetence is more and bigger government! The galvanizing factor that will transmute self-interest and incompetence into collective wisdom is the "climate crisis."

"In rising to meet this challenge," declares Gore, "we too will find self-renewal and transcendence and a new capacity for vision to see other crises in our time that cry out for solutions: 20 million HIV/AIDS orphans in Africa alone, civil wars fought by children, genocides and famines, the rape and pillage of our oceans and forests, an extinction crisis that threatens the web of life, and tens of millions of our fellow humans dying every year from easily preventable diseases."

One would like to see the organization chart for such an ambitious initiative. Oh, hang on, we already have one. It's called the United Nations.

Gore spends the first half of his book in a conventional left-liberal assault on wealth and power. His peculiar bugbear is that democracy has been subverted by the decline of the printed word – which allegedly facilitated discourse – and the rise of television, a "one-way" medium that is controlled by evil corporations in league with the Bush White House. Politics is now all about raising the cash for 30-second commercials.

But isn't a newspaper pretty much "one-way?" As is a book. Sure, you can scribble "BS!" in the margins, but you soon run out of space with a book like this.

According to Gore, what makes media corporations so lethal is that they can control the programming and the agenda. Thus, presumably, you would never find Al Gore appearing on, say, Jon Stewart or David Letterman. And you'd never find the publishing subsidiary of a giant corporation (say Penguin) publishing a book by him. OK, well maybe the theory falls down there.

But what makes them really sinister is that they have the insights of professional media manipulators at their disposal. So, let's say they were to publish a book by a guy whose physique now resembles that of Orson Welles or Marlon Brando in their latter years; they'd print a much younger and slimmer picture on the dust jacket, making him look like Superman in civvies. The manipulation! But I digress...

Anyway, this control over the media explains why George W. Bush was able to lie about weapons of mass destruction with no expectation of being caught, why he is now able to maintain a high popularity rating, and why nobody has ever heard, or complained about, Abu Ghraib. But hang on again. George Bush's ratings are in the basement, and Abu Ghraib could not possibly have evoked more adverse coverage. So doesn't that suggest that Gore's thesis of a massive threat to free speech from a plutocratically-manipulated media is, well, crap? Except, that is, in the threat that he presents himself. Gore constantly calls for more discussion and public input, but when it comes to man-made climate change, he declares the debate closed. Questioning of theories – sorry, Inconvenient Truths – about man-made climate change can come only from a Bush White House that gets all its views from ExxonMobil.

The suggestion that there can be no intellectually honest opposition to Gore's alarmism is disturbing, to say the least. Even more worrying is his bizarre claim that merely to posit opposing views amounts to "censorship." But then that's the sort of mindset you're bound to finish up with if you genuinely believe that your opponents are trying to "destroy the habitability of our planet and ruin the prospects of every generation that follows ours."

In fact the scientific consensus – even if it did exist – wouldn't answer the much more fundamental issues of the lack of economic and political consensus. Gore declares glibly that "we know what to do." Tell that to the warring factions ahead of the upcoming G8 summit.

The lust for power is astonishingly successful in hiding itself from itself, and projecting its darkest desires on to others. Gore even warns against those who claim to have exclusive possession of the truth!

My favourite Martian

4 July 2007

Mars ain't the kind of place to raise your kids. In fact it's cold as hell...

–Elton John, *Rocket Man*

Elton John won't be performing at next Saturday's *Live Earth* series of concerts, reportedly the biggest charitable music event ever. However, like Elton's *Rocket Man*, the concerts' main promoter, Al Gore, has invoked life – or rather its absence – on another planet.

In a piece in last Sunday's *New York Times*, Gore suggested that Venus is a valid reference point for the dangers of the enhanced greenhouse effect, a.k.a. man-made climate change. Earth's average temperature is a balmy 59 degrees (Fahrenheit), that of Venus a metal-melting 867 degrees. Is that difference due to being closer to the sun? Of course not, says Gore. Venus is three times hotter on average than Mercury, which is practically sitting on the sun! The culprit? "It's the carbon dioxide."

We might note, however, that there have been no reports that X-ray surveys of Venus's cloud-enshrouded surface have uncovered the remnants of coal-fired power plants or suv factories. Venus's carbon dioxide is thought to come entirely from its volcanoes, indicating the awesome power of natural forces. That presumably isn't the conclusion Gore wants us to draw.

The Venus reference is important for reasons beyond its typical attempt to use factoids to stoke hysteria. I have long thought that Al Gore is in fact an extraterrestrial in disguise. There were too many other-planetary references in his *Times* piece for this to be any longer in doubt.

One of Gore's more earthling rhetorical techniques is to marshal the voices of the noble dead to his cause. In last Sunday's column, he elicited the unlikely support of Ronald Reagan, who once said "I occasionally think how quickly our differences would vanish if we were facing an alien threat from outside this world."

Given that Gore is a prime example of psychological "projection" (he accuses George Bush of being obsessed with power and world domination!), should we perhaps call in the *Men in Black*? I have little trouble envisioning a scenario in which Will Smith and Tommy Lee Jones confront Gore, whereupon he morphs into something with an exoskeleton.

Live Earth certainly represents a gathering of space cadets. It might be called *An Inconvenient Truth: The Musical*. Apart from Gore, its main organizer is Kevin Wall, an LA-based distributor of digital concerts. Wall, a veteran organizer of awareness-raising shindigs such as *Live Aid* and *Live 8*, claims that he was inspired to join *Live Earth* by seeing Gore's documentary. He subsequently changed his life by trading in his Mercedes for a Lexus Hybrid. Despite his admiration for Gore, Wall refers to him as "Rhythm," and acknowledges that he is "a little stiff." But then what do you expect when your inner alien is straining to escape?

Another straw in the solar wind: Gore reportedly wanted to turn out the lights all over Britain for a brief period at the time of the concert. Was this really an attempt to signal to his home planet? As it turned out, the plot was foiled when the operators of the National Grid pointed out that the power surge when the lights were switched back on might disrupt the entire system, possibly flat-lining hospital patients on life-support.

Live Earth's hypocrisy seems a little out of this world, too. Its stars are among the largest individual consumers of energy on Earth. They are, however, reportedly being given "green counselling." Those of a Jacobin temperament have an extraordinary urge to consume their own, and sure enough Greater Moralists have rounded on *Live Earth*'s fellow pop poseurs. Saint Bob Geldof raised a discordant note when he suggested the concert was pointless because "We are all f–king conscious of global warming." Roger "Talking 'Bout My Co-Generation" Daltrey, lead singer of *The Who*, noted that the concert would represent a waste of fuel. Matt Bellamy, front man for a band called *Muse*, described it as "private jets for climate change." Case in point, Madonna, who will headline the show in London, reportedly emitted 440 tonnes of carbon dioxide on her *Confessions* tour last year.

Live Earth has inevitably spawned a welter of "carbon offsets" to compensate for its very existence. Still, perhaps all the artists can get together to record inspirational titles such as "Do they know it's the Apocalypse?" or "Hybrids are not enough."

While *Live Aid* and *Live 8* perpetuated the flawed notion that the underdeveloped world's problems are rooted in a failure to redistribute the wealth generated in the West, we might still believe that their promoters' and participants' hearts were in the right place. *Live Earth* has much more dubious political underpinnings. One of the less-publicized is its role in boosting another run by Gore for the White House. Go to AlGore.org and you will find the "2008 Grassroots Draft Campaign," motto: "The People, Not the Powerful '08."

I hope that Will and Tommy Lee are keeping their weapons charged.

Gore and peace
13 October 2007

Al Gore just won the Nobel Peace Prize the same week as a British court established that his Oscar-winning documentary, *An Inconvenient Truth*, contained nine glaring scientific errors. Still, the Peace Prize – which was awarded to Gore jointly with the UN's Intergovernmental Panel on Climate Change, the IPCC – isn't about science. Moreover, Gore is by no means an anomaly when it comes to Peace Prizewinners being peddlers of nonsense, tellers of lies, or even promoters of political strife.

The winner of the 2004 award, Kenyan environmentalist Wangari Maathai, claimed that HIV had been created by Western scientists as a form of biological warfare. Rigoberta Menchu Tum, a Guatemalan activist, won the 1992 prize on the basis of an autobiography that was subsequently found to be severely economical with truth. And what can one say about the late Yasser Arafat being a recipient?

According to the Nobel committee's citation, the prize was

awarded to Gore and the IPCC "for their efforts to build up and disseminate greater knowledge about man-made climate change, and to lay the foundations for the measures that are needed to counteract such change." But what does that have to do with peace? Alfred Nobel, in his 1895 will, wrote that the Peace Prize would be awarded to the person who, in the preceding year, "shall have done the most or the best work for fraternity between nations." One of the greatest causes of current international disagreement is climate-change policy, or lack thereof. Moreover, if addressing climate change is designed to promote peace, how would you explain the fact that North American ethanol subsidies led, via higher corn prices, to Mexico's "tortilla riots." In fact, by sowing policy discord and demonizing the "consumer society," climate change activists have both joined cause with, and provided further ammunition for, violent anti-Western sentiment.

Meanwhile, the claim that Gore and the IPCC are in the "knowledge" business is surely wide of the mark. They both deal in scientific speculation, but it is worth pointing out that their projections are wildly at variance. Gore talks in his movie about sea levels rising 20 feet. The latest IPCC projection is for a rise of between 3 and 23 inches by the end of this century. Such a mammoth discrepancy would surely confirm that the science is far from "settled."

But let's forget the dodgy science. According to the Nobel committee, Gore "is probably the single individual who has done most to create greater worldwide understanding of the measures that need to be adopted." In fact, Gore's trademark is to combine apocalyptic visions with vague "Marshall Plan" solutions that will somehow magically not fall prey to the incompetence, corruption and threat to individual freedoms that grand central plans always involve.

As for the IPCC, this prize exposes what claims to be a scientific organization as the activist institution that it is, spinning the complex and carefully hedged reports of its thousands of scientific contributors into blatantly political "Summaries for Policymakers."

Significantly, in its report last April, the IPCC promoted the notion of "climate-change conflict," suggesting that stressed humans would fight like rats for dwindling resources. The genocide in Darfur was described as such a conflict, implying that the killing might be blamed as much on driving suvs in Lethbridge or Indianapolis as on murderous Islamic militants. Gore too identifies the "real culprit" for Darfur as the fact that "the us emits a quarter of the world's greenhouse gases."

Hence Al Gore's and the ipcc's idea of peace involves demonization of Western lifestyles and promoting the belief that, until we change, we deserve to be attacked morally, and perhaps even physically. It's a funny basis for a Peace Prize.

Climate scientology

9 August 2017

Among the egregious misrepresentations in Al Gore's Oscar-winning 2006 movie *An Inconvenient Truth* was the claim that there were exactly zero scientific papers questioning projected catastrophic man-made global warming. Therefore, Gore continued, the amount of media coverage given to skepticism was entirely disproportionate. In fact, the mainstream media had already mostly wrapped itself in the capacious cape of the climate crusade, but for Gore even one scintilla of skepticism was one scintilla too many.

Well, the word is in from left-liberal peer movie reviewers about Gore's follow-up movie, *An Inconvenient Sequel: Truth to Power*, and it's two righteous thumbs up! While they admit it's a bit of a snoozer, there is not a trace of doubt that *An Inconvenient Truth* – a masterpiece of alarmist agitprop inflicted on an entire generation of schoolchildren – was bang on, and that weather is indisputably getting worse. Meanwhile the transition to a low-carbon economy is proceeding apace, whatever roadblocks thrown by the likes of that Neanderthal denier Donald Trump.

Peer review of climate science has rightly come under attack for often being warped by ideology and government funding. Left-liberal peer film review apparently involves no fact checking at all.

Then again, as Gore relentlessly claims, we are dealing with a "moral issue," thus any questioning is clearly funded by ExxonMobil and/or the Koch brothers, and puts you on the side of slave-traders and those who supported apartheid and would have denied women the vote. Record temperatures or any example of extreme weather mean the scientific case is closed.

But have – as Gore's first movie predicted – the snows of Kilimanjaro disappeared, along with all summer sea ice in the Arctic? Has there been a decline in polar bear populations due to a spate of drownings?

No, no and no. In the earlier movie, Gore confidently announced that carbon capture and storage was "A big solution you're going to hear a lot more about." It's been an expensive disaster. Still, didn't the flooding in Lower Manhattan caused by Superstorm Sandy in 2012 vindicate Gore's catastrophist insight? Hadn't he presented a simulation of Lower Manhattan underwater? Well yes, but Gore's computer inundation was due to the land ice of Greenland and/or Antarctica suddenly, and massively, dropping into the world's oceans and raising sea levels 10 or 20 feet. The devastation caused by Sandy was due to the coincidence of a severe storm and high tides. It had happened before. Sea levels subsequently went back to where they had been previously.

An Inconvenient Sequel is not so much a sequel as a rehash. Same old shots of earth from space. Same old "Nature hike through the Book of Revelation," although now "every storm is different." One significant – and disturbing – development highlighted in *Sequel* is that Gore has trained thousands of True Believers to spread the Gorespel of climate scientology.

"Talking truth to power" is the perpetual self-appointed mission for left liberals, who believe that they have a monopoly on truth and virtue while their greedy, short-sighted obstructionist opponents have a stranglehold on power. The movie's actual alleged example involves Gore – Michael Moore-style – entering the Trump Tower and disappearing into an elevator. He has claimed that he spent months trying to persuade Trump to see the light. One doubts that Trump could stand Gore for minutes, let alone months.

The former Veep is portrayed in the movie as a significant power broker at the 2015 Paris climate conference, working the phones in order to find some way to bribe India to use more solar power. He claims India had just seen monsoon rains not witnessed in a thousand years. In fact, 2015 was a year of below average rainfall.

The peer movie reviewers also swallowed Gore's claim that wind and solar are becoming ever more economically viable. Never mind the *Toronto Star* falling for Gore's "hard evidence," even *The Wall Street Journal*'s reviewer gushed that "he brings good news along with the litany of tempests and record temps – the growth of wind and solar power on exponential curves that were unimaginable a decade ago." But according to the International Energy Agency – which, as a global bureaucracy, is gung-ho for bureaucratic climate policies – wind and solar will account for no more than 3% per cent of global energy use in the year 2040. Some transition.

Gore's "hard evidence" on solar consists of one chart showing the declining cost of solar panels, and another off-the-chart chart (he doesn't use a mechanical hoist to dramatically point to the top this time) showing the growth of solar installations in Chile. In fact, Chile disastrously overstimulated investment in solar capacity, which, without corresponding transmission infrastructure, led to the price of solar electricity dropping to zero. Facts schmachts.

By far the most significant development in energy in the past decade, which of course is mentioned nowhere in the movie, is the revolution in fracking, which has led to a surge in US oil and natural gas production, and lower global prices, which has been a boon to manufacturing and job creation. Ironically, it is also the gas boom that has been largely responsible for the US leading the world in reducing carbon dioxide emissions. In the real world, where truth isn't magically absorbed from a cinema seat, the transition is in terrible trouble. Ontario is among the classic examples. And how has Premier Kathleen Wynne dealt with the problem of soaring costs (for zero benefits)? By shoving the bill onto future generations. You remember, those about whom Wynne, Gore and left-liberal peer movie reviewers claim to be so morally concerned.

2
Climate crazy

Any movement with Al Gore as its Messiah is fundamentally deranged and ripe for skewering. Policies to control the climate tend to be perverse and/or contradictory and/or hypocritical and/or illogical and/or pointless, except as tools of "virtue signalling." For more than two decades I have followed these bizarre trends and their influence on the politicians, institutions, celebrities, scientists, businessmen and billionaires who have climbed – or been forced – aboard the doomster bandwagon.

The Climate Mind

21st Century Climate Science
As taught at St Greta's School for Emergencies

The madness of eco-crowds
23 May 2007

One of my favourite books is *Memoirs of Extraordinary Popular Delusions and the Madness of Crowds*. Written more than 150 years ago by Charles Mackay, it provides a necessary reminder of mankind's periodic tendency to go collectively off its rocker.

I was reminded of the book while listening to a CBC report that featured some earnest soul suggesting that a piece of marble falling off Toronto's First Canadian Place might be due to climate change.

"In reading the history of nations," writes Mackay, "We find that whole communities suddenly fix their minds upon one object, and go mad in its pursuit; that millions of people become simultaneously impressed with one delusion, and run after it, till their attention is caught by some new folly."

Extraordinary Delusions is filled with accounts of great public manias, from the South Sea Bubble and Tulipomania to widespread belief in witches and apocalyptic prophesies. Which brings us to current apocalyptic environmental forecasts and the almost universal call for centrally coordinated global mobilization to "do something." Now.

It is not that climate change is not a fact, or that humans may not be having a more-than-marginal impact upon it. It is not even that the science is far less certain than radicals claim. It is that these beliefs have come to be considered an all-consuming "truth." Everything is suddenly seen through a climate change prism. This perspective warps the view from the highest levels of government to the smallest communities. With regards to the latter, another report on the CBC last week focused on a small English village, Ashton Hayes, which is attempting to become "carbon neutral" to fight climate change. My mind instantly went to another British village, the one in the recent comedy *Hot Fuzz*. In that movie, a hotshot policeman – who is so good at his job that he makes his colleagues look bad – is dispatched to an allegedly sleepy, crime-free hamlet that does, however, have an extraordinary number of "accidents."

It emerges that a cabal of influential villagers – obsessed with winning the award for prettiest village in England – are not above murdering anybody who might threaten their home's picturesque status. Similarly, Ashton Hayes – which has become a point of pilgrimage for eco-warriors/worriers (and is described by the *Financial Times* of London as being like a "green-tinged Lourdes") – doesn't sound so much admirable as creepy, with roaming teams of eco-auditors, and social pressure to stop such wasteful practices as sending individual Christmas cards. Again according to the *Financial Times*: "Refuse recycling rates have replaced village cricket as the jealously fought competitive sport between rival villages." When it comes to real sport, meanwhile, the village has a carbon-neutral soccer team.

Sounds like a nightmare to me, although organizers claim that there is no "finger pointing" at anybody who refuses to sign on to the eco-moralization of virtually every form of activity, from leaving on the coffee machine to taking holiday flights.

Apparently, more than 30 other British communities have joined Ashton Hayes on the *Via Dolorosa* to carbon neutrality. One would love to hear what the half of the village that hasn't signed on to this mania thinks of it, and what kind of pressures they feel from their Puritan neighbours.

There have been myriad examples of manias and delusions since Mackay's book. Malthusian obsessions with resource depletion and projections of starvation have raised their head with astonishing regularity in the past century and a half. Not long after Mackay wrote, there was concern that the Industrial Revolution might grind to a halt for want of coal. Pundits have confidently predicted the exhaustion of petroleum virtually since its discovery. Meanwhile there have always been seers and charlatans around to point the way to salvation. Significantly, however, some of the most truly apocalyptic events of the past 150 years have been linked to following their diktats.

Although believing that man-made climate change is causing pieces of marble to fall off buildings is perhaps at the outer limits of mania, global warming is now claimed by pundits and the mainstream media to be behind every extreme weather event, from Parisian heat waves to Hurricane Katrina.

"Men, it has been well said," wrote Mackay, "think in herds; it will be seen that they go mad in herds, while they only recover their senses slowly, and one by one."

The man who doubted Al Gore
29 August 2009

Dealing with acolytes of the Al Gore school of climate change (that is, virtually every government on earth, plus the chattering and scribbling classes of the entire Western and developing worlds) reminds me of a classic series of illustrations by Australian-born British cartoonist H.M. Bateman.

Bateman's *Man Who...* series depicted people falling about, jaws dropping and eyes popping, while the surrounding buildings literally shook, as some poor fool made a monumental social gaffe. They included *The Man Who Missed the Ball on the First Tee at St. Andrews*, and *The Man Who Lit His Cigar Before the Royal Toast*.

If one were to think of current candidates for the most disastrous of faux pas, surely none could be greater than *The Man Who Expressed Skepticism About Catastrophic Man-made Global Warming*. Mouths inevitably gape, and eyes roll at such a dimwit's failure to grasp that there is "consensus" on the issue. Indeed, to dissent is seen not merely as evidence of mental deficiency but moral turpitude.

I once attended a dinner party thrown by a corporate executive who – like his guests – was astonished at my apostasy, which was met by the requisite mime show of shock from other guests, who knew nothing about climate science. The following day my host sent me a newspaper clipping about melting Arctic ice. That, presumably, would put me straight.

Earlier this year I wrote an article for *The Walrus* magazine on the great Scottish philosopher and father of economics Adam Smith. I made a passing reference to the fact that Smith, as a student of the scientific method, might be skeptical about the notion that any science was "settled." A letter was subsequently published in which a correspondent replied, somewhat testily: "[W]hat special qualifications does Foster have to assess the validity of climate change theory? ...[W]e are being told by people who have spent their whole lives studying climate change that we need to be concerned, and that's good enough for me."

I entirely appreciate the correspondent's point. We rely on authority for the vast majority of what we believe, but global warming theory does not rank as knowledge of the same order as whether Iceland exists or the moon is made of green cheese. My reason for believing in the existence of Iceland is that a conspiracy to conjure it out of geographical thin air is passing unlikely. Lunar cheese theory surely requires no refutation. Anthropogenic global warming is different. Far from being an established fact, it is a hypothesis whose allegedly disastrous consequences will occur in the distant future. It also comes attached to considerable political and financial advantages for its promoters.

It conforms neatly to the view – long and fondly promoted by fans of Big Government – that capitalism is essentially shortsighted and greed-driven. This stance is not merely appealing to activist politicians and bureaucrats, it is pure gold for the vast and growing army of radical environmental lobby groups, whose very *raison d'être* – and fundraising – are closely related to the degree to which Mother Nature is seen to be "endangered." It is also appealing to rent-seeking businessmen who see the profit potential in successfully negotiating the vast and growing array of government controls and subsidies.

Most ordinary people reasonably imagine in the face of such a weight of "authority" that the case must be closed. It isn't. For a start, the weight of authority is based on the political doctoring of studies that are in any case designed to countenance no other conclusion than that man-made carbon dioxide drives climate change. Moreover, the very fact that the theory's promoters are so reluctant to actually engage in scientific debate (No time to talk. Must act!) is highly suspicious.

Still, once you get people believing in "authority," then you're pretty much home and dry. Authority relieves us of the anxiety of uncertainty and the pain of thought. If the issue can also be portrayed as "moral" (millions of poor people dying from Biblical droughts and floods!), then to question it is not merely cause for rejection but censure. Skeptics must be either crackpots, monsters or in the pay of Big Oil.

I recently had what I tried to make a level-headed exchange with somebody who was visibly agitated at my daring to quote science, facts and sources in support of my skepticism. This person – dredging up material from the conventional noosphere – finally told me that I was like "a holocaust denier," or somebody who believed in UFOs! Their conviction, like *The Walrus* correspondent, was based on the fact that "Nobel prize winners" had declared that catastrophic global warming was a fact.

Now it's certainly true that Al Gore has a Nobel prize, but it is equally certain that it isn't for science. The nations of the world are currently involved – ahead of the next giant climate shindig in Copenhagen in December – in rancorous discussions about sharing the economic self-mutilations that are claimed to be needed as part of a successor to the egregiously-failed Kyoto Accord. No issue has more divided the rich and poor, and pitted the West against India and China.

In case you need reminding, the Nobel that Al Gore shared with the Intergovernmental Panel on Climate Change (IPCC) was for Peace. Mentioning that massive incongruity should cause people's eyes to roll, or maybe even buildings to shake.

Alice in UN Climate Land
12 March 2010

"No, no!' said the Queen. "Sentence first – verdict afterwards."

"Stuff and nonsense!" said Alice loudly. "The idea of having the sentence first!"

"Hold your tongue!' said the Queen, turning purple.

"I won't!" said Alice.

"Off with her head!" the Queen shouted at the top of her voice. Nobody moved.

"Who cares for you?" said Alice, (she had grown to her full size by this time.) "You're nothing but a pack of cards!"

The United Nations has decided to follow the Red Queen's approach when it comes to recent mounting scandals over its Intergovernmental Panel on Climate Change, the IPCC: exoneration first, review afterwards!

On Wednesday, the UN and the IPCC announced an "independent" review of the IPCC's operations by the InterAcademy Council (IAC). Never heard of it? Doesn't matter. The verdict is already in.

UN Secretary General Ban Ki-moon declared "Let me be clear: the threat posed by climate change is real...Nothing that has been alleged or revealed in the media recently alters the fundamental scientific consensus on climate change."

Ban, who has admitted making climate change his focus, declared on Wednesday that the 2007 IPCC report had contained a "very small number of errors." But shouldn't the exact number of errors be a matter for the review? Assuming that Ban had no knowledge, for example, of the egregious projection of the disappearance of Himalayan glaciers by 2035, why should he assume that there are not numerous similar howlers of which he is unaware?

The smell of whitewashed rat is overwhelming.

The InterAcademy Council is an NGO that is about as independent from the UN system as Tweedledum was from Tweedledee. It is an "umbrella group" for National Academies of Sciences, and was set up in 2000 specifically to advise the UN and the World Bank.

In 2009, the National Academies of the G8 countries issued a statement claiming that "climate change is happening even faster than previously estimated." But where did they get their information if not from the IPCC that their "umbrella group" is now meant to be reviewing?

The IAC is in fact deeply embedded in the UN's anti-market "sustainability" agenda. It has produced many reports with typical salvationist titles such as "Inventing a Better Future" and "Lighting the way." When it produced a study of African agriculture, one of its main recommendations was to set up "agricultural centres of excellence."

Bureaucracy first, development afterwards.

The IAC has in fact admitted the problem of finding independent reviewers. Its co-chair Robbert Dijkgraaf noted that the review needed people with knowledge of climate science who weren't too close to the IPCC. "Clearly you cannot be the reviewer and the reviewed at the same time," he said. IPCC functionary Christopher Field acknowledged that "almost anybody who has been involved in climate science has some connection with the IPCC."

To achieve any credibility, such a review would have to recruit scientists such as MIT's Richard Lindzen and the University of Colorado's Roger Pielke, Jr. If no such well-credentialled skeptics are included, the review will rightly be suspected as a whitewash.

As for the vaunted objectivity of scientists, last week, a leaked series of emails between leading academics at Stanford University revealed a plan to mount "an outlandishly aggressively partisan" attack on climate skeptics. The emails were full of paranoid demonization of "well-funded, merciless enemies." Renowned alarmist Stephen Schneider invoked McCarthyism. In fact, it is skeptics who have been subjected to a witch hunt. The Stanford emails compared them to those who "would deny the reality of the law of gravity." Those involved in this email exchange are all members of the US National Academy of Sciences.

The notion of "official" climate reviews has already been tainted by the UK's Stern Review, which emerged as a blatantly skewed political document designed to support UK policy. More recently, the official review of the Climatic Research Unit of the University of East Anglia – from which the Climategate emails were liberated – was involved in controversy when two of its members were revealed to hold flagrantly alarmist views.

Still, there is some humour in this, as befits a Wonderland-ish situation. The IAC is headquartered in Amsterdam. One of the 2007 IPCC report's "very small number or errors" was to double the amount of the Netherlands that lies below sea level.

At Wednesday's press conference, neither IPCC head Rajendra Pachauri nor Ban took questions. It was not reported whether they subsequently disappeared down a rabbit hole. It will be fascinating to see how long the IPCC's house of cards survives repeated scandals, which grow ever "curiouser and curiouser."

Moral boiling oil for "deniers"

29 January 2015

Al Gore once suggested that since climate change is a "moral issue," it is "beyond politics." You must not question "settled" science or policy "consensus." You must check your brain at the door, and obey the dictates of, er, politicians.

Moral issues are ultimately about how we treat each other. Those such as Gore who espouse grim Biblical projections of droughts, floods and plagues of insects, all caused by the malign hand of industrial capitalist man, claim that they are only "speaking up for" poor people both now and in the future. They stand against "intergenerational tyranny."

But even if one discounts the possibility that these sentiments are reflections of H.L. Mencken's trenchant observation that the desire to save the world is almost invariably a false front for the urge to rule it, then that still leaves the question of whether catastrophic projections are likely to be true, and the policies proposed likely to be effective.

If anybody doubts that such questions lead to moral opprobrium, check out the online comments on my most recent column. That piece noted that the claim that 2014 was the "hottest year on record" was highly uncertain (as now confirmed by the British Meteorological Office) or, if true, not particularly surprising. I also refuted the notion that for 13 of the past 15 years to be "the hottest years on record" was no more astronomically implausible after a period of warming (man-made or otherwise) than that a person would be taller as an adult than a child.

My reward for these observations was a tsunami of moral outrage. I am apparently not just scientifically ignorant but plain stupid. I am in the pay of the fossil fuel industry, or at least trying to drum up more advertising for the *Post* from the Canadian Association of Petroleum Producers. One commentator even suggested that I was probably also opposed to gay rights.

The fundamental "moral" assumption behind all this *sturm und drang* is that fossil fuels – which are above all a proxy for capitalism – are "unsustainable" and thus morally "bad." This assumption is well challenged in a recent book, *The Moral Case for Fossil Fuels*, by Alex Epstein.

Epstein does an excellent job of outlining the astonishing benefits that the development of coal, oil and natural gas have delivered to mankind: improving health, lengthening lives, and facilitating a vast expansion in both material welfare and leisure possibilities. He also notes, with copious data, that fossil fuel development has – contrary to conventional wisdom – gone along with a cleaner environment (China will get there eventually, once it embraces freedom). He explains clearly and logically why wind, solar and biofuels are technological dead ends. He lays out convincingly why attempting to force these technologies on developing countries amounts to a death sentence.

It is sometimes said that Canada has a "moral obligation" to support global initiatives. Stephen Harper has pointed out that he will not support any treaty that pointlessly damages the Canadian economy or fails to include the leading emitters, particularly China. But how, in any case, could there be any moral obligation to sign onto a global agreement that is not merely bad for future generations, who need fossil fuels to flourish, but that destroys wealth and damages freedom right now? It is particularly morally reprehensible to recommend more and bigger versions of policies that have already caused hardship and suffering. Obvious examples are the impact of biofuel policy on food prices, and how the subsidization of expensive and unreliable wind and solar power has driven the very poorest members of Western societies into "fuel poverty."

Nevertheless, "authority," itself a moral concept, has been successfully captured, and the ethical high ground has been seized by those who prefer to pour rhetorical boiling oil on those who question them rather than engage in rational debate.

Epstein does a fine job of exposing how professional doomsters such as Gore, Paul Ehrlich, James Hansen and Bill McKibben have been as mendacious as they have been wrong. But the really fascinating issue is the moral mindset that makes these thundering Jeremiahs – and their acolytes – seemingly impervious to rational arguments and objective evidence. Thus the one area where Epstein's book may fall short is in making the case promised in the title. Making a practical, rational case is not synonymous with making a moral case, or at least one that will convert diehard opponents.

Morality is based on feelings, which means that it doesn't make people think very clearly or logically. In fact, it often stops them from thinking at all. That makes moral psychology one of the most fascinating – and contentious – of the social sciences. Epstein's book is well worth reading on its own terms, but it raises issues that demand much further and deeper analysis of our "moral sentiments." The Catch-22 lies in the fact that, due to the nature of morality, such analysis is likely to be ignored, or angrily refuted.

And now I stand ready for my next dose of boiling oil.

Will Pachauri's karma run over IPCC dogma?

25 February 2015

Rajendra Pachauri's resignation this week as head of the Intergovernmental Panel on Climate Change, the IPCC, after sexual harassment allegations, was instantly and inevitably followed by claims that this in no way reflected on the IPCC's credibility.

To be sure, when you look at the long list of Pachauri's disingenuities and evasions, you might be inclined to ask why one more (alleged) example of sleaziness would make any difference. Still, all those other economies with the truth were in a noble cause: saving the planet from capitalism. It's difficult to claim that sexting (texting explicit sexual messages) might play any role in sustainable development.

Pachauri, 74, resigned on Tuesday following charges by an unnamed 29-year-old female researcher at his organization, The Energy and Resources Institute (TERI), based in Delhi. She claims that he sent her "unwanted" and "graphic" emails, texts, and WhatsApp messages.

Admittedly, this doesn't appear to reach the levels of abuse inflicted by other leading members of the international community, such as the serially priapic Dominique Strauss-Kahn, former head of the IMF, but there is some irony in Pachauri being nabbed via social media, which has circulated so much hysterical climate porn.

It was also intriguing to see Pachauri's attempt at what might be called "The Climategate diversionary manoeuvre." Forget the incriminating communications; the important thing is that they were "hacked" by "cyber criminals." Who did it, and who paid them? Could it be the evil fossil fuel industry?

Unfortunately for Pachauri, another woman has come forward alleging that she and other female employees were also subject to the old goat's advances. This second woman said that she complained to TERI's administrative head, who told her that she may have misread Pachauri's "warmth." When the woman resigned to study abroad, she claimed that Pachauri warned her about the range of his influence.

The reported unwillingness of TERI's administrator to address the women's complaints speaks to the very relevant tendency of institutions to protect their own. Dissent is silenced. Complaints are hushed. The IPCC is no different. Indeed, given its place within the corrupt UN system, it is likely much worse.

When, in 2005, IPCC hurricane expert Dr. Chris Landsea went to Pachauri to complain that another prominent IPCC scientist/mouthpiece, Kevin Trenberth, had misrepresented Landsea's findings during a widely publicized news conference, Pachauri brushed him off. Dr. Landsea resigned, noting that the IPCC process had been "subverted and compromised."

When Indian scientists pointed out that IPCC projections of the Himalayan glaciers disappearing by 2035 were nonsense, Pachauri attacked their "voodoo science." Then it was revealed that it was the melting projections that were voodoo, and had come off the top of the head of a scientist who wound up working for...Pachauri!

"Glaciergate" also confirmed that Pachauri's claim that everything in IPCC reports was "peer-reviewed" was monumental bunk. A subsequent review of the IPCC by the InterAcademy Council, an organization of national science academies, accused Pachauri of political advocacy. The review was buried without trace.

Pachauri's resignation letter on Tuesday, aptly described by blogger Donna Laframboise as a "two-page love letter to himself," moved from effrontery to gag-worthiness with its claim that "For me the protection of Planet Earth, the survival of all species and sustainability of our ecosystems is more than a mission. It is my religion and my dharma."

Dharma is all about cosmic order and obligation. Perhaps karma – reaping what you sow – is more appropriate. Given that Pachauri's hobbies include writing novels featuring the soft-porn adventures of an Indian climate expert, the harassment charges do not exactly come as a surprise. The question now is whether – to paraphrase that classic bumper sticker – Pachauri's karma will run over the IPCC's dogma. That 18-year global average temperature "hiatus" leaves the dogma sitting in the middle of the road (although Pachauri has claimed that it can afford to sit on the white line scratching itself for

"30 or 40 years, at least"). Meanwhile is it not embarrassing for the IPCC to have its leader of 13 years admit that he was motivated not by scientific objectivity but by religion?

Media defenders of the faith – led by the *Guardian* and the BBC – came out strongly, brandishing the IPCC's "thousands of scientists," its government support, and its Nobel Peace Prize. The BBC snootily recorded that Pachauri had in fact been the favoured candidate of the "US Bush administration," which reportedly didn't like Pachauri's predecessor's "willingness to tell governments what he believed to be the unvarnished truth – that human activities were contributing dangerously to climate change." So there.

When the BBC is calling you a patsy for the Bush administration, you know you're being thrown under the climate bus.

The contents of those sexts are bound to be titillating. It might have been possible to apply smoke, mirrors and lipstick to Climategate emails such as the famous "trick to hide the decline," by suggesting that "trick" meant a mathematical fix rather than outright fraud, but one suspects that Pachauri's emails might be a little more difficult to obfuscate. As one observer wryly noted, we're likely talking about "fifty shades of green."

Writhing on the Marrakech Express

20 October 2016

A lame 1980s-style music video called "Save the World" is about to become compulsory viewing among skeptics of climate alarmism. It features a German pop star named Bernadette La Hengst, dressed as a green fairy, along with a man dressed as, well, a green fairy, doing a very poor imitation of Ziggy Stardust.

The duo float in space against a backdrop of the earth. The man warbles the English version, samples of whose earnest lyrics include "There is no right, in the wrong climate" and "Sharing your things instead of producing…Talk to your neighbours about something to lend. Instead of a client, you'll get a new friend." The song's chorus, and bottom line, is "Say goodbye to lethargy. Save the world with this melody."

These are the kind of facile sentiments you might expect from an eco-indoctrinated eighth grader, but the intriguing thing about the video is the identity of the male warbler. He is Nick Nuttall, head of communications for the United Nations Framework Convention on Climate Change, UNFCCC, which is about to hold yet another cast-of-thousands climate conference in Marrakech.

It's not that singing, dancing and posturing are unusual down at the UNFCC. Two years ago, before the climate conference in Lima, its head, Christiana Figueres – who has admitted that she wants a global revolution – choreographed a surprise dance routine to Beyoncé's *Move Your Body*.

However, Nuttall's performance is particularly newsworthy because he is the man who just turned down media accreditation to the Marrakech conference for Ezra Levant's *Rebel Media*, on the grounds that Levant and his staff espouse "advocacy journalism," or, more precisely, the wrong kind of advocacy.

On Tuesday night, Nuttall, a former Environment and Technology Correspondent for *The Times* of London, was interviewed about his decision on the CBC's *As It Happens* by Carol Off.

Struggling to explain himself, Nuttall said that he had looked at *Rebel Media*'s website, and it seemed to be just a platform for "this chap Ezra...I can't remember his surname. I don't live in Canada so I don't know." He said they got all sorts of applications from people who "purport" to be journalists with "axes to grind." He said that the *Rebel Media* website "was pushing a particular point of view. It made me wonder how it was funded, who backs it." Thus he slimily implied that Levant might just be one of those fictional fronts for the fossil fuel industry conjured up by climate fanatics. But while Levant has certainly stoutly defended Canada's "Ethical Oil," and fracking, he doesn't seem to front for anybody's opinions but his own.

Carol Off soon had Nuttall in a hole, whereupon he proceeded to keep digging. He declared that *Rebel Media* was all "Anti-refugee, anti-climate, anti this, anti that, and I just didn't think it was appropriate in terms of better understanding of the public in terms of climate issues." It didn't represent "balanced reporting."

So, Off suggested calmly, Levant was being rejected because Nuttall didn't like his point of view?

Oh no, writhed the UN flack. It was just that Levant's view was so "personal." Off hit him with the clip of journalists breaking into applause when agreement was reached at the most recent UN conference in Paris. Didn't that indicate media bias?

Nuttall continued desperately to sing, dance and dig. Maybe they did have "a moment of cheering," he admitted, but they weren't going to go back to their desks and "become zombies in favour of some soft, beautiful, world of climate change." Whatever that meant. He claimed those journalists would hold governments to account, but he clearly meant for following the UN agenda, not questioning it.

Off noted that Levant also held governments to account, whereupon Nuttall attempted to draw her into condemnation of the feisty right-wing broadcaster. Off, to her credit, was having none of it.

Nuttall then waffled on about the complexity of the world, and the sad state of investigative journalism, before suggesting that he didn't think Levant was being "helpful." Off quietly pounced. So to be accredited to the UN you had to be seen as "helpful"?

Nuttall was now flailing, and referred to "inflammatory headlines" in which Levant had described climate change as a "crock of something or other."

Off then asked him if turning down *Rebel Media* hadn't given Levant's position more publicity. Nuttall admitted that was one of the reasons he had been reluctant to be interviewed. He said that all sorts of people had told him how adept Levant was at using this kind of thing to "generate more money from crowd funding to keep his website going. I hope those people who listen to this interview might think twice."

I suspect they will, and promptly increase their donations. Was there any way Nuttall might be convinced to change his mind about Levant? Nuttall said that he had received letters from "serious Canadian journalist associations" asking him to rethink his decision, "so I'm really thinking about it."

You bet he is. Perhaps Nuttall's most egregious error was to tell Off he would let Levant interview him, so that Levant could produce a "decent" report about climate change.

We can't wait.

Climate crusaders lost in space
18 August 2017

Climate derangement syndrome has claimed another celebrity astrophysicist, Neil DeGrasse Tyson, "science communicator" and host of the 2014 TV series *Cosmos: A Spacetime Odyssey*.

Last month, Stephen Hawking, author of *A Brief History of Time*, declared that Donald Trump's withdrawal from the Paris agreement meant that Earth could become like Venus, where it rains sulphuric acid and temperatures reach 250 degrees Celsius. Roy Spencer, a climate specialist at the University of Alabama, pointed out that Venus has 93 times as much atmosphere and 22,000 times as much carbon dioxide as Earth, so we shouldn't be too worried about it raining acid any time soon.

Now comes DeGrasse Tyson, claiming that climate science is as certain and predictable as next week's solar eclipse. He tweeted: "Odd. No one is in denial of America's Aug 21 total solar eclipse. Like Climate Change, methods & tools of science predict it."

DeGrasse Tyson's claim was immediately leaped upon by Nassim Nicholas Taleb, author of *Black Swan*, a classic work on probability, uncertainty and randomness. Taleb tweeted back "Thus (sic) guy is an intellectual fraud. Nonlinear domains like climate & markets != mechanics like solar eclipses. If it were true he wd be rich."

But we're talking something more serious here than forecasting the stock market. I asked Christopher Essex, professor of applied mathematics at the University of Western Ontario, and an expert on climate chaos, to comment. He said that circumstances for climate prediction are even worse than suggested by Taleb's legitimate concern over nonlinearity. "Tyson writes about using science to 'predict it.' But what is 'it?'" asked Essex. "'It' remains physically not so well-defined. An essential prerequisite for prediction is to know precisely what you are trying to predict. Eclipses satisfy this prerequisite, while climate does not."

Climate is complex and chaotic, quite unlike the Newtonian predictability of planetary motion, but DeGrasse Tyson doesn't seem to be very clear about that either.

His 13-part *Cosmos* series, first aired in 2014, was conceived as a successor to popular scientist Carl Sagan's 1980 series *Cosmos: A Personal Voyage*. With the aid of computer graphics, DeGrasse Tyson travels through space and time to present the very latest in science. However, the opening episode contains a major error, embodied in a graphic of how people understood the cosmos before Copernicus and Galileo.

The ancients believed that the Earth was the centre of the universe, and that everything moved around it, but *Cosmos* has the sun, moon and planets all revolving about the Earth in a circle. This is not what pre-Copernicans believed, because it's not what they saw. The sun and moon appear to circle the Earth regularly, but the planets do not, precisely because they circle the sun rather than the Earth. Viewed from earth they appear to wander back and forth in "epicycles." That was why they were called planets, from the Greek for "wanderers," and why navigational charts based on the Ptolemaic system were so complicated (although the planetary dance was indeed recorded and calculated with great precision, until a better theory came along).

The *Cosmos* graphic amounts to ignorance rather than misinformation, but Tyson's solar eclipse claim speaks to the peculiar psychology of climate conviction: that the science is so "settled" that it is like Newtonian clockwork. Doubting impending catastrophe would be like being an eclipse denier!

An additional irony is that *Cosmos'* error about the movement of planets is followed by a segment on Giordano Bruno, the Dominican friar who was burned at the stake for embracing Copernicus' heliocentric theory, and for other heretical notions. DeGrasse Tyson sombrely bemoans the Catholic Church's "thought police", but seems incapable of contemplating the possibility of similar forces at work today in the Church of Climate.

Thomas Kuhn, in *The Structure of Scientific Revolutions*, pointed out that the advance of science is much messier than people think. Scientists adopt and commit to theoretical "paradigms," which then become fundamentally unquestionable, particularly once they have been "professionalized" and if there is a moral element involved.

Not only have governments poured tens of billions into confirming rather than testing the theory of CO_2-driven climate change, the resulting dire predictions are claimed by the likes of Al Gore to be the greatest moral issue of our time. The problem is that moralism eclipses any inclination to treat skepticism with the respect it deserves, however much you hate Donald Trump.

Last week, celebrity economist Paul Krugman suggested in the *New York Times* that climate skepticism was the fruit of an "Axis of Evil" that combines fossil fuel money (which is apparently much more corrupting than government funding), ideological rejection of any and all regulation, and contrarian egoism. Krugman wrote that he couldn't think of a single climate skeptic who was acting in anything but bad faith, but has he ever spoken to a climate skeptic? Then again, why would he bother? They're all evil.

DeGrasse Tyson, who *National Review* called "the dumbest smart person on Twitter," has suggested that the world needs a new kind of virtual state called "Rationalia" with a one-sentence constitution: "All policy shall be based on the weight of evidence." This is embarrassingly facile.

No sensible person "denies" climate change. The issues are whether it is outside the range of normal variation, what contribution humans might be making, and what prudent policies the situation demands. Rational examination is hardly helped by hysterical forecasts of Venusian concentrations of acid rain, or by pontification on the part of somebody who doesn't seem to understand the difference between an alarm clock and a thunderstorm.

Trump vs. the Climate Industrial Complex
3 November 2017

Donald Trump as saviour not just of American democracy but global freedom? One can imagine tall foreheads exploding everywhere at such a thought. Although he doesn't express it quite that strongly, this is one inevitable conclusion from Rupert Darwall's tremendous new book, *Green Tyranny: Exposing the Totalitarian Roots of the Climate Industrial Complex*. That's because Trump, by abandoning the Paris climate agreement, and reversing his predecessor's attempts to bypass Congress on environmental matters, has heaved a mighty wrench into the UN/EU-based thrust to impose global bureaucratic "governance" under the pretext of saving the world from climate catastrophe.

Beyond all the blather about Trump's presidency representing the triumph of redneck ignorance and deplorable racism – and whatever Trump's personal shortcomings – Darwall notes that one of the main reasons for his victory was that the American left had abandoned working people in pursuit of identity politics and radical environmentalism. "From being the voice of working people," writes Darwall, "the Democratic Party has become the political arm of the Climate Industrial Complex," an unholy alliance of bureaucrats, NGOs, green corporate rent-seekers and Silicon Valley "oligarchs." With additional funding (as they like to say on PBS) from a raft of mega-billion-dollar foundations built on capitalist success but seemingly dedicated to destroying capitalism.

Darwall wrote *Green Tyranny* as a sequel to his similarly incisive 2013 book, *The Age of Global Warming*, specifically to expand on the critical roots of environmental ideology and power-seeking in Europe, in particular Sweden and Germany. He also records how the issues of acid rain and "nuclear winter" were, in many ways, political trial runs for the great assault on freedom in the name of saving the world from climate change. In each case, a critical factor was the corruption of science by politicized scientists. The contributions of Sweden and Germany are complex but fascinating, since they originated in seemingly incompatible thrusts. "The politics of global warming originated in Sweden as a tool to promote nuclear power. Using wind and solar power to combat global warming originated in Germany, where the Greens had become a political force, thanks to popular opposition to nuclear power."

Soon, however, all the Eurolefties wound up on the same page. Their key strategy was, to paraphrase Leonard Cohen, first we take Berlin – and Bonn, and Stockholm, and Paris and London – then we'll take Manhattan, and Sacramento, and Washington.

The US was the overwhelming problem for the global governors because of its picky constitutional concerns about the separation of powers (significantly to counter potential tyranny) and the First Amendment (which is under attack in more areas than climate).

Canada doesn't play a major role in the book, but one can certainly see all the elements of the Climate Industrial Complex at work here, from US foundation-funded NGO campaigns against the oilsands, pipelines and the regulatory system, to the fact that three senior members of the federal cabinet, including Prime Minister Justin Trudeau, have executive assistants who formerly headed environmental NGOs. All part of what Darwall calls "a dense network of people defined by the same outlook, committed to the same goal, and, crucially, agreeing on the means of achieving it that operates as a monopoly provider of advice and expertise to governments."

Non-believers simply don't get invited to "join the conversation."

One can also see that Ontario's ever-mounting wind and solar disaster is merely a mirror of the very mother – or should we say "mutti" – of policy perversity: Germany's *Energiewende*. "Germany was going to export wind turbines and solar PV panels around the globe," notes Darwall. "Instead the 2000…renewable energy law spawned 100,000 profiteers and a gigantic solar industry in China." Similarly, Ontario policy was great for South Korea.

Darwall details how California leads the US in terms of destructive Europeanization with its "German energy policies, French labour regulation, Italian public debts, and a Scandinavian cost of living premium." Makes one wonder why Ontario and Quebec have yoked themselves to the fast deindustrializing state's cap-and-trade system.

The ever-growing conundrum is how the climate crusade continues despite the failure of climate models and the cratering of climate policies. Surely the most telling and ironic statistic is that over the period 1999–2012, German power stations increased emissions by 17.2 million metric tons, while their American counterparts cut theirs by ten times that amount. The main factor was fracking technology, which has absolutely nothing to do with green energy policy.

Darwall castigates German Chancellor Angela Merkel, who, as a scientist, must be well aware of the inevitable unreliability of wind and solar. Yet she has increasingly made policy via opinion poll, thus denting German competitiveness.

Sweden is important for more than punching far above its weight in promoting lousy policies based on dodgy science. It is, suggests Darwall, an extreme example of social democracy. The "social" swamps the "democracy" and dissent is asphyxiated, a phenomenon known as the "spiral of silence."

But then, in 2015, the US electorate spoke up, refusing to kowtow to the social democratic Bourbons and their plans to deindustrialize America. That is one big reason why Donald Trump – The antityrant! The voice of economic sanity! (at least in this case) – sits in the White House, and why Canadian climate policy looks even more ridiculous.

Carbon disclosure goes up in flames
5 February 2019

Last week, California utility PG&E filed for Chapter 11 bankruptcy protection in the face of an estimated US $30 billion of liabilities related to the disastrous California wildfires of 2017 and 2018.

The climate crusaders of the mainstream media have been atwitter with claims that PG&E represents the "first climate bankruptcy." That's because PG&E's power lines are believed to have sparked fires in dry vegetation. That dryness was allegedly the result of an extreme drought due to climate change brought about by fossil-fuelled industrial society and greedy, feckless oil and coal companies.

It's a stretch.

That climate change is an existential threat to companies' health has been a growing theme of the UN-based Climate Industry. The PG&E collapse will likely ramp up the already intense demands by climate activists for companies to confess that their business models fail adequately to reflect climate risk. Indeed PG&E has itself sought to blame climate change – that most nebulous and subversive of concepts – for its travails. But such a claim represents neither science nor policy guidance. It represents corporate desperation.

One of the most prominent promoters and facilitators of the disclosure of emissions and climate programmes is a London-based NGO named CDP (previously the Carbon Disclosure Project). One problem for CDP's credibility – and the whole notion that confessing to contrived carbon crimes is "just good business" – is that PG&E has been the very model of corporate climate concern. CDP has dubbed it "one of the leading companies in the world when it comes to openly sharing public information on greenhouse gas emissions, emissions reduction targets, and the implications of climate change for its business."

Fat lot of good it seems to have done them.

CDP's latest rankings note that PG&E's climate score for 2018 is "forthcoming" (due to "methodological changes," according to a CDP spokesperson), but the company's filing is available online. "PG&E has a long history of taking action to combat climate change," it declares. "Doing so is integral to our ongoing efforts to provide safe, reliable, affordable, and clean energy to customers. We remain focused on reducing our carbon footprint, advancing low-carbon policies for California and the nation, helping customers reduce their energy use with industry-leading tools and incentives, and addressing the need to adapt to changing climate conditions."

Perhaps they should have concentrated on trimming dead trees near transmission lines.

CDP claims that "By scoring businesses from A to D (minus), we take organizations on a journey through disclosure to awareness, management, and finally to leadership." Unfortunately, PG&E found itself leading the way into burning forests, personal tragedy and a potential conflagration of its balance sheet.

CDP rated the company "A minus" in 2017. If this disclosure ritual was meant to assure investors that PG&E was a sound investment, they were misled. Indeed, one wonders if a good lawyer might look at whether CDP is itself subject to legal action on that count.

Meanwhile the last thing that PG&E's problems justify is any redoubling of international climate conferences to conjure up more fake commitments. It is bordering on insanity to suggest that the way to deal with California wildfires is to force more solar panels on Burundi, windmills on Spain, or electric cars on China.

One of the strategic successes of the Climate Industry has been to conflate all natural disasters or extreme weather with man-made climate change. However, the notion that PG&E represents some kind of corporate climate tipping point is absurd. Businesses without sufficient insurance have been driven into bankruptcy by natural disasters since the Great Flood.

If climate bankruptcies are taken to include those caused by climate activism or perverse climate policies, then there are many companies in Alberta already made bankrupt by the Climate Industry's campaign to close off their expansion. And what about those alternative energy companies that went under when their subsidies were withdrawn?

California has always been renowned for the size and scope of its natural disasters. It has also faced energy crises in the past based on flawed regulation and deregulation, and the success of environmentalists in bringing power plant construction to a halt. The state's climate policies are considered the most "advanced" – that is, draconian and costly – in the US. Meanwhile PG&E has sought bankruptcy protection before as a result of perverse policies.

There is no doubt that California's wildfires in the past two years were the most deadly and destructive in the state's history, but their deadliness and destructiveness were not a function of being unprecedented in size, but of the fact that more people have – with state and municipal approval – been building more valuable property in wildfire-prone areas. Ill-thought-out fire-suppression policies have also increased the incidence of larger fires.

PG&E has been obliged by the state to run power lines to these new or growing wildfire-prone neighbourhoods, thus increasing the possibility of lines coming into contact with dry wood and sparking a fire. Although the company has been trying to minimize these risks, they appear to have been the source of many of the blazes. The other key factor in PG&E's need to seek bankruptcy protection is state laws that impose liability even where there has been no negligence.

One major *non sequitur* is that this fiasco requires corporations to line up for more monitoring of their emissions and climate programs, as CDP and its fellow self-appointed monitors might have us believe. But who, and what, exactly is CDP?

The Carbon Disclosure Project was reportedly founded in 2000 with money from Rockefeller Philanthropy Advisors (CDP did not respond to questions about its founders, backers or past chairpersons), which is closely linked to forces that have been trying to close down the Alberta oilsands and which also supports initiatives such as the late Maurice Strong's subversive *Earth Charter*. Carbon Disclosure's clever founding strategy was to drum up professed climate concern among big investors, who were already being softened up by radical NGO campaigns. In some cases – such as those of state-run or state-influenced pension funds – the institutions required no softening up.

CDP then began writing letters on behalf of these allegedly concerned investors to every public company on earth, starting with the 500 largest, demanding the disclosure of emissions and climate programs.

It took bravery to refuse to sign up. No executive wanted to be screamed down as a climate denier. It has been suggested that companies were merely "erring on the side of caution." They were actually erring on the side of hysteria.

CDP isn't a scientific organization. It has no political legitimacy (although it receives government money). Nobody gave it "social licence" except the big investors that allowed it to be their mouthpiece, and the companies that rashly agree to be rated. Moreover, its fundamental rationale – that climate concern is driven by investors – is bogus. While activist investors make lots of noise, and can proliferate climate resolutions at AGMs, average shareholders show little interest in applying pressure on directors to get out in front of the climate crusade.

Many companies have in fact resisted pressure to report their supposed climate risks. For example, "sustainable and responsible" activist investor Calvert Investments brought a motion to force Amazon to file with CDP, but the company resisted, with its shareholders' support. Amazon said it did not believe that "preparing an ad-hoc climate change report is an efficient use of time and resources." Truly responsible investors might find it more useful to pass motions asking companies to stop wasting money filling in the CDP's voluminous questionnaires.

Part of the genius of the CDP process is that it forces companies to address worst-case scenarios from the catalogue of alleged impending climate catastrophe, and then elaborate what those hypothetical disasters might do to their business. It is a classic case of "begging the question" – not so much "When did you stop beating your wife (or husband)?" as "If you were to beat them, what sort of injuries do you think they might suffer?" Responses could then be included in a study claiming dramatic evidence of potential spousal abuse, which would be dutifully reported by the media.

Typical was a story about CDP's 2018 rankings in last week's *Financial Post*. It began: "Quebecor executives considering worst-case scenarios that could befall their business as a result of climate change suggest buried internet infrastructure could be at risk from rising sea levels. At Molson Coors Brewing Co., meanwhile, management is thinking about how they'll make enough beer to meet consumer demand if competition heats up over scarce supplies of clean water."

Not to fault the reporter, who indeed noted these "worst-case scenarios," but it takes only a moment's reflection to realize how ludicrous it would be for Molson Coors to be genuinely concerned about running out of water, but then you have to feed the questionnaire beast the worst-case alarmism it demands.

Meanwhile, it seems bizarre that Canadian petroleum companies should line up to be ranked for carbon crime by an organization that is part of an agenda designed to close them down. In this year's rankings, Husky and Suncor scored "B"s. Enbridge and TransCanada scored "C"s. CNR and Encana sat bottom of the class with "D"s. Still, one encouraging sign is that last year both ExxonMobil and its Canadian subsidiary, Imperial Oil, stopped reporting.

CDP ranks such refusal under "F," for failure.

A careful reading of submissions shows that many companies see the most significant threat not from climate change but from climate-change policy. Loblaw's filing notes the obvious potential of damage from fires and floods, but also reports that "the Quebec Cap and Trade Regulation increases our energy costs…Carbon taxes on fuel and energy will have a direct impact on our business activity costs and also indirectly increase cost from our suppliers of services and goods."

PG&E was facing no shortage of climate-change policy risks and related financial burdens itself. It has to comply with California's Renewable Portfolio Standard, which requires the company to increase renewable energy to 33% of its total sales by the end of 2020, and to 50% by 2030. But it is increasingly obvious that the more wind and solar any system uses, the less reliable that system becomes, thus potentially greatly increasing costs, which PG&E acknowledges. According to the company's 2018 CDP filing, the cost of managing regulatory risks, compliance, and renewable energy procurement was a stunning US $2.4 billion. The company also notes the potentially high costs of California's cap-and-trade system (to which that of Quebec is linked).

CDP has inevitably expanded its bureaucratic tentacles into assessments of water and forestry too, and into the conflicted business of consulting for those it ranks. It also identifies a great swath of ranked companies as financial "supporters" or "premium supporters." (That's on top of the fees CDP charges to be an investor partner or a ranked company).

PG&E now has few friends in state governments, or courts, or among the general public. Emerging from bankruptcy protection is likely to be a long and complicated process. By contrast, CDP's business seems to be booming. But surely CDP should feel some of the heat from the fact that PG&E's lofty status as a climate discloser did nothing for its investors, employees or customers, or for the victims of those tragic wildfires. Indeed, it may have created a false sense of security. I asked CDP for their comments. They chose not to respond, so I guess they get an "F."

Bill Gates defies the climate malanthropists

22 February 2019

Market advocates since Adam Smith have claimed that policy advice from business should be treated with suspicion, and that the road to economic hell is paved with corporate welfare and "national champions." The "progressive" left have traditionally been much more harsh, claiming that big business sought only monopoly and plutocracy.

Ever since command of economic resources was, wrongly but usefully, deemed synonymous with political power, some of the greatest businessmen and philanthropists all time – such as John D. Rockefeller, Andrew Carnegie and Cornelius Vanderbilt – have been reflexively dubbed "Robber Barons."

A remarkable change has come over the left in recent decades. With the collapse of socialism (in fact, if not in theory), big business was no longer an automatic enemy. Indeed, it was to be co-opted as a partner in "social responsibility" and "sustainable development." Some of the world's wealthiest business people eagerly sought to start knitting the rope of Global Salvationism.

Meanwhile the modern counterparts of the Robber Barons might be called the Climate Barons, those billionaires and capitalist foundations that seek to kill the fossil-fuelled industrial age in order to save mankind from man-made environmental catastrophe, while making big bucks on subsidized renewables. While America's Koch brothers are ritually condemned as funding "denialism," a far more substantial group of "the rich" is supporting NGO thuggery and misinformation, and promoting lawsuits and other pressure tactics to euthanize fossil fuels. They also seek to hide the huge economic and social costs of the allegedly essential "transition to a low-carbon economy."

This group includes US billionaires Tom Steyer and Michael Bloomberg, and the British hedge-fund billionaires Jeremy Grantham and Chris Hohn. It includes a raft of multibillion-dollar foundations bearing names such as Rockefeller, Hewlett and Packard.

The Climate Barons present themselves as promoters of "Climate Philanthropy," but insofar as their promised low-carbon transition involves forcing the adoption of expensive and unreliable energy, they are both responsible for destroying jobs (Alberta being perhaps the most prominent victim), and exacerbating poverty in poor countries. Their activities might more accurately be described as Climate Malanthropy.

Here's the good news: the world's most prominent philanthropist, Bill Gates, has broken ranks.

Although the Microsoft co-founder still outsources his thinking on catastrophist science, he has acknowledged that intermittent wind and solar power are the last thing to be forced on poor countries. He has also castigated the Climate Barons' strategy of killing fossil fuels via financial pressure.

During a recent onstage Q&A at Stanford University, when interviewer Arun Majumdar, a "Google Scholar," suggested breezily that people were "optimistic" that the costs of renewables and battery storage were coming down, Gates got visibly agitated. "That is so disappointing," he said, castigating such feeble optimism. While he supported nuclear, he said battery technology was woefully deficient and renewables needed "a miracle." They certainly weren't the solution for India or Africa right now.

Gates also revealed that he had recently been at a New York conference of financiers backing the fashionable demand of "climate disclosure," whereby corporations are required to offer up highly unlikely climate-risk scenarios so as to unnecessarily worry investors and increase their cost of capital. Gates claimed that the idea that finance or investor pressure could provide a solution was "madness."

So, he said, was the demonization of electrical utilities. And where, he asked, would steel and plastic come from? What would power the airplanes? Most dramatically, he claimed that those who suggested that the climate problem was easy to solve were a bigger problem than climate "deniers".

It is intriguing to compare the Gates interview with another video, made around the same time, in which Majumdar also appears. It was touted as a "Giving Pledge Learning Session" designed to boost "Climate Philanthropy." One especially intriguing aspect was that Gates and his wife founded the Giving Pledge, in the vain hope of convincing people billionaires aren't evil. This video suggests that some just might be.

The video features hedge-fund billionaire Jeremy Grantham, who has established several climate foundations that spread alarmism and seek to silence deniers. The chair of Grantham's main climate foundation is Lord Nicholas Stern, author of 2006's outrageously perverted Stern Review (officially titled: *The Economics of Climate Change*). "Everybody needs to be in on this (transition)" said Grantham. Meaning everyone needs to agree with him.

Another Climate Baron making an appearance was Julie Packard, vice-chairman of the David and Lucile Packard Foundation, which has committed US $1 billion to climate over the past 10 years. And then there was Larry Kramer, head of the Hewlett Foundation, which has also devoted massive amounts to the climate-alarm crusade.

Chris Hohn, a British hedge-fund billionaire, asserts in the video that "solar and wind are cheaper than coal." He might try running that past Gates. Hohn also claimed that there is need for a "massive step up" in climate philanthropy, but we might note that such spending is pretty stepped up already. Hohn funds a charity called the Children's Investment Fund Foundation, CIFF, which oversees a portfolio of multiyear grant commitments worth more than US $800 million. Of that total, almost US $300 million is dedicated to climate change, more than 10 times the amount committed to "child protection." CIFF is also a big supporter of "carbon disclosure." It's hard to see what that has to do with children who are suffering poverty, malnutrition or abuse right now.

CIFF's website maintains that "A low carbon world will help secure a healthy and prosperous future for children." Again, Bill Gates – or indeed any reasonably objective observer – would disagree.

Now that Gates has seen the light on the difficulties – indeed absurdities – of the "transition," maybe he'll turn his analytical mind to just how "settled" climate science really is.

3
The climateers

Having already dealt with Al Gore, there now follows a selection of columns on other villains, ideologues, frauds, fools, poseurs and liars who have been – and continue to be – prominent in pushing the radical climate Agenda. As a country perennially inclined to an inferiority complex because of its mighty neighbour to the south, here is one area in which Canada can truly claim to "punch above its weight;" that is, inflict damage out of proportion to its size. The historical Canadian super-heavyweight champion is the late Maurice Strong, the first in our rogues' gallery.

Chairman Mo

Maurice Strong's Davos plot
29 January 1999

The pirate captain of spaceship Earth
3 June 2000

Mikhail Gorbachev's mystic world order
6 September 2000

Earth Council flees Costa Rica
12 May 2004

Strong's China plan
9 August 2008

Chairman Mo's little red website
13 November 2009

An icon with a very mixed record
30 November 2015

Maurice Strong's Davos plot
29 January 1999

Nine years ago, Maurice Strong – Fabian socialist and leading Canadian light in the United Nations wonkosphere – gave an interview in which he described the "plot" of a novel he had been mulling. The setting was the annual conference of the World Economic Forum (WEF) at the Swiss Alpine resort of Davos.

Rich countries are presented with an ultimatum by a "group of world leaders" to stop destroying the environment. When they refuse, "this group of world leaders form a secret society to bring about an economic collapse. It's February. They're all at Davos...They have positioned themselves in the world's commodity and stock markets. They've engineered, using their access to stock exchanges and computers and gold supplies, a panic. Then they prevent the world's stock markets from closing. They jam the gears. They hire mercenaries who hold the rest of the world leaders at Davos as hostages."

What was arresting – not to say spine-tingling – about Strong's plot was that he was, and remains, a leading player at the WEF, whose 29th annual get-together in Davos began yesterday.

Maybe Strong was just playing to his own stereotype – having a little mischievous fun with his reputation as an aspiring global dictator. Then again, maybe he was providing some unconscious insight into his power fantasies. Either way, his plot should make us think about what's really going on in the mountains this weekend.

The annual Davos schmoozefest projects a kaleidoscope of contradictions. A conference that trumpets "transparency," it ranks as perhaps the highest-profile series of secret meetings on the planet. To some, it appears a cabal of the world's great corporate interests, an elite conspiracy at which politicians receive their marching orders. To others it represents the epicentre of Strong's brand of electronic Rolodex socialism, where the Useful Idiots of the business community are co-opted into supporting subversive environmental and social agendas. Two years ago, American academic Samuel Huntington castigated "Davos Man" as an entirely unrepresentative member of

a white, educated, Western elite. Huntington appeared to think that
the archetypal "Davos Man" was Bill Gates (who will, of course, be
making an appearance again this year). In fact, Davos Man is much
more appropriately Maurice Strong or George Soros – doomsayers
who call for more central control in the name of saving the planet
from too much uncoordinated freedom.

The key to WEF thinking – that is, the not-so-secret agenda of the
organization – is that globalization requires corresponding "global
governance." WEF founder and president Klaus Schwab wrote in the
organization's 1998 annual report that the Asian crisis had "brought
a very salient question to the fore. How are we going to govern globalization? This will be a top collective priority as we move toward
the 21st century."

But who exactly is this "we" and who ever tasked it with setting
the world's collective priorities?

The main thrusts of the WEF agenda remain global redistribution and the claim that (relatively) free markets are (a) inherently
unstable, (b) dangerously depleting resources, and (c) destroying the
planet's environment.

Strong's latest WEF venture is something called "Trustees 21," yet
another attempt to co-opt legions of short-sighted (or scared) businessmen into adding their names to the next doorstop report claiming the end is nigh – and recommending myriad new interventionist
solutions. According to a WEF blurb about the project: "The single
most crucial factor determining our future in the new millennium
will be our capacity to manage global interdependence. Old systems
and traditional solutions are simply not enough and we need new
insights and fresh ideas..."

This continuous harping on "new" approaches invariably leads
back to the very old fixation on more central political control.

The same vague but ultimately sinister message can be found in
any number of related weighty tomes, from the Brundtland Commission's report through the Rio Summit's *Agenda 21* and beyond, in all
of which Strong was heavily involved.

For the real Davos Man, one of the worst pieces of news this year
came, ironically, from Davos. Not only had the Asian financial flu,

Russian collapse and the Brazilian crisis failed to bring down capitalism, but a WEF-sponsored survey revealed that 80% of CEOs worldwide are optimistic about the prospects for their companies over the next three years.

For Davos Man – who is consumed with tendentious pessimism – a rosy future presents less opportunity for plotting to save the world.

The pirate captain of spaceship Earth
3 June 2000

For those paranoid right wingers who claim that Maurice Strong is at the centre of a plot of take over the world, his autobiography – *Where on Earth are we Going?* – contains both bad news and good news. The bad news: you weren't paranoid after all. The good news: Strong's plan for "Managing the World without World Government" is laughably unworkable.

The book's most revealing chapter is the first, a "Report to the Shareholders, Earth Inc.," dated Jan. 1, 2031. In Maurice Strong's mental future, "The human tragedy is on a scale hitherto unimagined." There have been unprecedented extremes of weather. The North American prairies are experiencing their 10th year of drought. "[W]ater vendors with armed guards roam the streets of Los Angeles." Hundreds of thousands of people have just died in Washington from a heat wave. There are plagues of insects and rodents. Malaria has turned New Orleans into a "shrinking fortress held only with poisonous amounts of lethal pesticides."

In Strong's desire to compound future horrors (particularly in the United States), he has Florida both underwater and plotting to secede. Perhaps it's planning a political union with Atlantis. Meanwhile, despite the environmental horrors of the US, illegal immigrants are still "stumbling over the polar ice caps" to reach it. But not all is bleak. There's a good guy running Germany, a "benevolent dictator" seeking "to ensure that all Germans work together for the common good and share equitably in both the sacrifices and the benefits achieved." There are other "scattered islands of sanity and order." One such is Crestone, Colorado, "A community created as a spiritual retreat in recent materialistic times has proven a haven for the virtues of sustainability, harmony and ethical husbandry" (Strong is too modest to mention here that he founded the community, which is a little more complicated than he suggests). There are other bright spots. "Everywhere, indigenous people are rediscovering their traditional way of life." (Does he mean disease and poverty?) Order is being restored by "volunteer security corps." (Mmmm. Sounds like NGOs with guns). People have turned away from science and toward religion, and that's a good thing. But the brightest prospect, according to Strong, is that two-thirds of the world's already-diminished population may be wiped out, "...a glimmer of hope for the future of our species and its potential for regeneration."

A glimmer of hope?

Strong himself asks whether the chapter is "just sour fantasy, the dismal fiction of a doomsayer...the ravings of an activist with a hidden agenda." But just when it seems he is onto himself, he notes that his grim scenario is all "entirely plausible." To question his vision would be irresponsible. All Strong needs is the power to act. Now.

Strong is a man of amiable demeanour, considerable achievement and toxic ideas. He has led an amazing life. Born in abject poverty in Oak Lake, Manitoba, he ran away from home as soon as he could, pursuing a series of picaresque adventures as cabin boy, fur trapper, prospector and teenage financial wheeler dealer.

He claims he was haunted by the spectre of a capitalist economic system that – as conventional leftist wisdom would have it – had "broken down" during the Depression, which he suffered personally. As a boy, he had to eat dandelion and pigweed. He saw his father wrap his feet in rags before going out to the bush to cut wood. He witnessed his educated mother lose her mind.

Strong claims he was profoundly influenced by a newspaper story that literally blew across his path one day about the formation of the United Nations. Henceforth, he claims, he fixated on a career in international affairs.

At first, he was rejected for government service because of his lack of qualifications. He decided that since corporate stature opened doors, he would use business success as a route to public service. Before you could say Horatio Alger, he was running Power Corp. in Montreal. He used politically-connected Power as a springboard to Ottawa, where he created the Canadian International Development Agency, CIDA. Then he discovered the potential of the environment. "I knew there was a role for me to play here…I also began to sense one of the great underlying truths of environmental politics: the environment is supranational. It transcends the nation state. At the very least it has to be dealt with multilaterally."

The environment was the ultimate rationale for global control.

Dubbed "Captain of Spaceship Earth," Strong achieved apotheosis in 1972 when he chaired the United Nations Conference on the Human Environment in Stockholm. His second global coming was 20 years later, as head of the United Nations Conference on Environment and Development in Rio. He had certainly not been idle in the intervening period. His exploits included being the first head of state oil company Petro-Canada, undertaking a raft of roles within the UN, including African famine relief, and becoming involved in myriad messy business schemes.

Strong played Rio to the hilt, orchestrating the greatest collection of world leaders ever. He has relentlessly pursued power in the name of "saving the planet," but shouldn't he, of all people, know how power both obstructs and corrupts? He writes of "swinging the ever-cumbersome apparatus of government into action." He notes that "government officials know how to resist and often bury the initiatives of their political masters…" Of the UN, he writes "Petty politics and small-mindedness constantly interfere with [its] work." He admits that its personnel policies "always favour politics…over competence."

Moreover, Strong's distinctly spotty business record should surely have taught him the limits of management. Time and again, companies in which he has been involved have been mired in controversy or teetered on the point of bankruptcy. Time and again, he admits to neglecting his business affairs. And yet we are presumably to inter-

pret this as a mark of his selflessness rather than his lack of competence. His pretension is megalomanic, but he clearly feels up to the
task. "Well," he writes, "we are all gods now, gods in charge of our
own destiny, and gods can't be capricious."

Maurice Strong's modest proposal is to manage not just particular organizations and issues, but everything! "[W]e must devise a
new approach to co-operative management of the entire system of
issues," he writes. One can imagine this fantasy originating in an academic ivory tower, but how could a man of Maurice Strong's vast
experience hold it, unless he is advocating a system that is much less
co-operative than he would have people imagine?

Strong is not an intellectual, although he has 42 honorary degrees.
He borrows ideas as they serve his interventionist purpose. His vision
of environmental apocalypse is predicated on the conventional left-
liberal view that free markets are obsessed by the short term, and that
people are all giddy grasshoppers. He bemoans "a culture of materialism and self-gratification," as opposed, presumably, to one of mysticism and being forced to gratify others.

He trots out numerous sophistic rationalizations and non-
sequiturs. Some people once argued for slavery and child labour, and
even against traffic lights, hence anybody who doubts the need for
more global regulation is an ignorant reactionary, marked by preju-
dice and wicked self-interest. We already have lots of rules, writes
Strong, so why not more – a lot more – as "preconditions for freedom"?

Naturally, Strong bemoans "the gap" between rich and poor.
However, he reaches new heights of nonsense when he complains
about the enormous proportion of patents "controlled" in the developed countries, particularly the United States. So what does he want?
Frontal lobotomies for Western research scientists?

Strong's solution to Third World poverty is the same old tired,
failed socialist redistributionism, only now with a green twist. Strong
also promotes "global democracy," which would mean that the
inhabitants of poor countries – rather than standing with begging
bowls – could simply vote themselves the earnings of the developed
world. Strong's version of global democracy would also mean ditch-

ing the UN tradition of consensus in favour of something a little more forceful.

In terms of tactics for imposing Strong's better world – the final piece of the puzzle – the NGOs are crucial. He has spent years cultivating such organizations and funnelling public money to literally thousands of them. It is very clear which type of NGO Maurice Strong favours, since he claims that "business…tends to look on NGOs as ideological opponents to its own free enterprise notions." As tireless activists, NGOs can be used to manipulate agendas – as they were ahead of the 1992 Rio conference – and even encouraged to stage (or at least not condemned for staging) violent demonstrations.

Repeatedly, Strong obliquely refers to how – because of threatened environmental apocalypse – behaviour will have to be changed and transgressors punished. "The single greatest weakness of the existing international legal regime is the almost total lack of capacity for enforcement." To correct that, he wants the UN to be able to raise its own taxes on the "global commons" or via a "Tobin tax" on international capital transactions.

The next stop would inevitably be a full-time international police force or army. A force for good.

Mikhail Gorbachev's mystic world order
6 September 2000

That this week's State of the World Forum in New York should be treated with seriousness, even reverence, is stunning. Designed to run in parallel with the United Nations Millennium Summit, the forum is the epicentre for promoting a "New World Order," which has been code for coercive global government since Fabian socialist H.G. Wells wrote a book of the same name. Perhaps most bizarre is that the United Nations, about whose incompetence and ineptitude fresh revelations emerge daily, remains the focus for the forum's monstrous pretensions.

The forum is sponsored by the Gorbachev Foundation. You remember Mikhail Gorbachev; he's the man who hastened the Soviet Union's implosion by imagining he could reform it. For this we should be grateful, but it should hardly incline us to put faith in his wisdom or understanding. Nevertheless, eminent businessmen and politicians continue to rush to lend their names to a bunch of mystic-socialist waffle fronting an agenda to "manage" the bogeyman force of globalization. Globalization has taken over from capitalism as the catch-all for everything socialists don't like, especially freedom, private property and the inevitably unequal wealth that arises from them. Meanwhile, the Foundation's mysticism is typified by one of its three board members, Caroline Myss. Ms. Myss is a "medical intuitive – one who 'sees' illnesses in a patient's body by intuitive means."

My intuition smells a collectivist rat.

At the first such forum in 1995, Gorbachev said, without a trace of embarrassment: "We have to reinvent the paradigm of our existence to build a new civilization." Gorbachev's call to "change the nature of consumption," as his rapt, US $5,000-a-plate audience dined on "smoked trout salad, filet of beef in shashlik marinade, and a dessert of panna cotta with autumn fruit," was surely a high point of hypocrisy among the dine-for-hunger crowd. To manage this Brave New World, Gorbachev called for a vanguard of the proletariat in the shape of a global "Brain Trust."

Five years later, with the US still booming, he continues to claim that things are just getting worse and worse. Like the good Leninist he remains, however, he hasn't changed his tune, he's just modified his strategy. A new contingent has been brought on board in the shape of the non-governmental organizations (NGOs) of "civil society" – a term broad and meaningless enough to conceal a multitude of manoeuvrings. The "revolutionaries" of the Seattle and Washington demonstrations against international law and order have been eagerly embraced by the forum. But when Gorbachev talks about the need for democracy, he's talking about it in the Leninist sense, just as his fellow aspiring global puppetmaster Maurice Strong does. In line with these new strategies, this year's forum is titled, "Shaping Globalization: Convening the Community of Stakeholders."

At the forum's opening on Labour Day, Gorbachev claimed, yet again, that globalization needed to be "governed and guided." But now he is calling for a permanent "people's assembly," a "World Citizens Network for Security and Development." However, the same old Politburo – sorry, Brain Trust – will still be pulling the strings. The forum's website outlines its modest proposal "to guide humanity wisely." Its philosophy is "believing that humanity must be as committed to ecological sustainability as the generation of wealth; global governance as national sovereignty; and to a compassionate society as much as to the global flow of capital." What that really means is, the forum is against wealth generation, national sovereignty and free flows of capital.

The term "global governance" is a model of Orwellian obfuscation. The forum's president, Jim Garrison, declared that "The message is that we don't need global government but effective global governance." In a 1995 interview, Garrison told a San Francisco newspaper: "Over the next 20 to 30 years, we are going to end up with world government. It's inevitable...[W]e have to empower the United Nations...to govern and regulate human interaction."

Meanwhile, nobody appears emboldened to ask why, if Gorbachev is so keen to build a new civilization, he wouldn't start in the place that most needs it: the former Soviet Union. Just as Gorbachev sought to cover up the Chernobyl nuclear disaster, and refused Western help, so Russian President Vladimir Putin has repeated history in the case of the sinking of the nuclear submarine Kursk.

You can't teach an old Communist new tricks, but why anybody would want to learn from Gorbachev's repertoire remains a mystery, unless their aspirations align with those of the old Soviet Union.

Earth Council flees Costa Rica

12 May 2004

Global maestro of sustainable development Maurice Strong is in a pickle down in Costa Rica. The government in San José is chasing one of his most important global policy instruments, the Earth Council, for US $1.65 million, charging it with the wrongful sale of land that the government had granted it for a headquarters. As a result, the council has fled the country.

In the wake of the Rio Earth Summit in 1992, Strong – perennial United Nations player-referee and now a key advisor to Canadian Prime Minister Paul Martin – set up the Earth Council as a "watchdog" to keep up the pressure for Agenda 21, Rio's doorstop socialist wish list, as well as for global restrictions on carbon dioxide emissions (which brought us the horrors of Kyoto). The council was also to seed myriad new non-governmental organizations to spread the gospel of sustainable development, and push Strong's *Earth Charter*, which had been rejected at Rio.

As the location for this beacon of radical environmentalism, Strong chose Costa Rica, well known for its status as eco-tourist paradise and tax haven. In 1996, the Earth Council was granted land on which to build a new headquarters, with the provision that the land would have to be returned if the council shut down or moved on.

Intriguingly, the funds to build the new headquarters were to come from part of the proceeds of issuing Costa Rican Carbon Bonds, a trading instrument that entitled the bearer to emit carbon dioxide if they paid the government of Costa Rica not to cut down its rain forest.

Strong had long held land in Costa Rica, and had become embroiled in a tourist development for which he was harshly criticized by local native groups. In 1994, when he was head of Ontario Hydro, he again became steeped in controversy when he considered purchasing a swathe of Cost Rican rain forest, presumably to fund those bonds.

In anticipation of carbon-bond proceeds, the Earth Council

started spending its own money on development plans, eventually sinking $1.1 million into the centre. However, then a new Costa Rican government abandoned the carbon bond plan, and suggested the Earth Council share the facilities of the UN's University of Peace (UPEACE), which also happens to be in San José. No problem. Lots of "synergies" from two left-wing fronts on one campus, and guess who the president of the UPEACE council happens to be!

However, trouble arose in paradise when the Earth Council decided to reimburse itself for its expenditures by selling the land that Costa Rica had given it. The government cried foul, and the Earth Council upped and fled the country, citing the potential drain of a legal fight.

That Strong is miffed is obvious from a thinly veiled warning on his council's website. "This unfortunate experience of the Earth Council," it says, "will also affect the attitudes of other international organizations in deciding whether to locate in Costa Rica." The council, meanwhile, has moved its operations back to Toronto, which is now also threatened with the first offshore campus of UPEACE.

The world would be a much safer place without the Earth Council. Take, for example, its *Earth Charter*, the latest version of which was allegedly hatched under the auspices of Strong and his old buddy Mikhail Gorbachev (it's really all Strong). The charter is a typical mix of UN pablum and poison, declaring that "the dominant patterns of production and consumption are causing environmental devastation, the depletion of resources, and a massive extinction of species."

Beneath all the boilerplate about compassion and shared visions lies the fact that Strong wants nothing less than a destruction of the Western way of life. "Fundamental changes are needed in our values, institutions and ways of living," declares the charter.

Anybody seeking confirmation of the charter's target market might turn to unstinting praise from that widely-unread organ of the left, *Canadian Dimension*. The magazine's March issue describes the charter as a "shared positive vision...for anti-capitalism" that brings together the "Red–Green Alliance" and promises "a global coalition of progressive counter-hegemonic forces."

Put another way, it's a Green Communist Manifesto.

Strong's China Plan
9 August 2008

You've got to hand it to Maurice Strong. He is nothing if not consistent in his far-left beliefs. He also tends to show up where the political action is. I was thus wondering how this former puppetmaster of the United Nations and godfather of Kyoto might capitalize on the opening of the Olympics in Beijing. I found the answer in the pages of *Maclean's* magazine.

In this week's issue, Strong delivers an essay that combines stout support for the totalitarian Chinese regime with a truly fantastic conviction that China has to remake itself in his image.

Not for nothing is he nicknamed "Chairman Mo."

His take on history and economic reality is, as usual, *sui generis*. He suggests that "China has raised more people out of poverty than any nation has ever done." True, but primarily by abandoning the kinds of government ownership and/or control that Strong – as a life-long socialist – has always recommended. Also, when noting China's turbulent history in the past century, he significantly fails to mention the factor that has cost most in turmoil and lives: Communism.

Strong fantasizes that China "is embarking on a distinctive and unprecedented pathway to a new model of development based on utilizing the methods of capitalism to achieve the goals of socialism – a socialist market economy." He thus unashamedly projects the muddled principles on which he has tried to live his own convoluted life onto China, which he forbids from "following the example of the traditional industrialized countries." That wouldn't be "sustainable."

Strong ritually reviles the us, whose greenhouse gases, he claims, have caused "irreversible damage." This high-flying moralizer also castigates the "wasteful and indulgent appetites of the rich." Perhaps he should see how that line goes down with China's ever-proliferating group of billionaires.

Strong is certainly right in suggesting that attempts to shift the "onus for climate change" onto China and India is "neither fair nor workable," but then neither is it necessary. Whatever climate change the world is facing is best dealt with by local adaptation, not gigantic toxic policy stews such as Kyoto.

Strong inevitably calls for a "revitalized" United Nations, but this brings us to the thorny issue of why he is in Beijing in the first place. Interviewed for a recent profile in the *South China Morning Post*, he maintained that the oil-for-food scandal* had nothing to do with leaving his post as special UN envoy to North Korea, or his moving to the Chinese capital. His migration "was not a matter of going into hiding but of moving to a country he had long admired."

Strong claimed that the Volcker inquiry had exonerated him of wrongdoing when he took $1 million of laundered Saddamite money. According to the story, Strong said that "if anything, the report praised him." In a subsequent letter to the *South China Morning Post*, he again claimed that the Volcker report "made no adverse findings as to my relationship with the controversial Korean, Tongsun Park."

Not quite. What the report actually said was that Strong was "in a position to know or suspect the source of Park's funds." It also found that Strong received a "personal benefit," and noted that he "provided inconsistent accounts of his receipt of the money from Park." Perhaps the most intriguing aspect of this affair was why Strong was doing business with a figure like Park in the first place. Park – who also provided office space for Strong in New York – was ultimately convicted of money laundering and being an unauthorized agent for the government of Saddam Hussein.

Such messy business involvements aren't exceptions for Strong, they are the rule. Although he has never been found guilty of wrongdoing, these dealings – and numerous other business controversies – are significant not just for the questions they raise over his judg-

---

* The Oil-for-Food Programme was a plan to relieve Iraqis suffering under UN sanctions imposed in the wake of Saddam Hussein's invasion of Kuwait in 1990. The scheme, which permitted swapping Iraqi oil for food, medicine and other humanitarian aid, soon became a swamp of corruption and kick-backs. An investigation led by the former Federal Reserve chairman Paul Volcker implicated a raft of UN officials and their relatives, including the son of Secretary General Kofi Annan, previous Secretary General Boutros Boutros-Ghali and Benon Sevan, who had administered the program. The commission also found that Maurice Strong had been on the receiving end of a million dollar "investment" from Tongsun Park, an old associate of Strong who had been deputed by the Saddamite regime to buy influence at the UN. Strong claimed he wasn't aware of the source of the money.

ment, but for what they say about the radical disconnect between his personal experience as a businessman, and his megalomaniac plans for managing the world economy.

The recent *South China Morning Post* article suggested that attacks on Strong, a "genial old man," come from "the far right," but it is difficult to see how any reasonable person, presented with the bizarre facts of his business history and political ideology, could not be concerned about his malign influence.

Chairman Mo's little red website
13 November 2009

Why are people not more aware of the greatest threat to human freedom and prosperity since the collapse of Communism?

I refer not to the 2008 financial crisis, but to that eminent Canadian, Maurice Strong. He is, after all, more than any other person responsible for sending the nations of the world down the path to the "last chance" climate meeting at Copenhagen.

It seems that Strong too may be fed up with his lack of profile. He has set up a website, www.mauricestrong.net, where you will find the bald – but accurate – claim that "Maurice Strong is the world's leading environmentalist." From heading the first UN environment conference in Stockholm in 1972 to masterminding the 1992 Rio summit, "Maurice Strong," says Maurice Strong's website, "has played a unique and critical role in globalizing the environmental movement." Strong is now 80 years old and thus out of the running for the title of CEO of "Earth Inc.," but it is his environmental nightmares and dreams of global governance that will dominate Copenhagen.

Strong will join with the likes of Desmond Tutu and Sir Richard Branson to harass governments and cheer on NGOs through something called the Global Observatory, but whatever his reception in December, he has done a brilliant job of promoting climatism.

Strong reiterated his views on climate apocalypse and how to deal with it earlier this year in a piece titled "Facing down Armageddon." For evidence of the current "crisis," he cited a report by the Global Humanitarian Forum, an NGO run by former UN Secretary-General Kofi Annan (to whom Strong was a leading advisor), which suggested that man-made climate change was costing $125 billion and 300,000 lives a year.

This report had been eviscerated by Professor Roger Pielke Jr of the University of Colorado, who described it as a "methodological embarrassment and poster child for how to lie with statistics." One might also note the astonishing coincidence that $125 billion a year was exactly the amount that Strong said would be needed to compensate the poor for the West's environmental sins 17 years ago.

Now, Strong has just rounded it all up to a cool $1 trillion, which needs to be shipped from the West "over time" as a "climate security fund." Managed by the same folks who brought us oil-for-food. But what's a trillion? Strong points out that the US has spent more than that fighting in Iraq and Afghanistan. So apparently the route to global salvation lies in declaring economic civil war on ourselves.

Strong calls for a "new economic paradigm" that will set prices so as to reflect "real" values. It will be like taxing alcohol or tobacco. Strong admits that no nation could impose such taxes "without disadvantaging its own economy," but if everybody can be cajoled into suicidal behaviour, then apparently we shall all be the better for it.

Strong admits that governments are unlikely to welcome such schemes, so we have to give priority to "the organizations and the people participating in this dialogue." That is, to the Strong-sympathetic NGOs set up and/or funded through his unique skills in accessing taxpayers' and foundations' money.

Strong's transparent lifelong modus operandi has been to answer "calls to action" that he himself has instigated. Numerous examples appear in the *Armageddon* article. He praises the UN for "bringing climate change to the top of the global agenda," as if this had nothing to do with him. He claims that the 1972 Stockholm Conference cited the risks of climate change, but he's quoting himself. He supports the conclusions of the Brundtland Commission, of which he was a leading member. He dubs the *Earth Charter* a "citizen-based initiative which sets principles to guide the conduct of nations and people towards the Earth and each other," neglecting to mention that he, not "citizens," formulated those principles.

Strong quite blatantly promotes eco dictatorship. He declares that "Our concept of ballot-box democracy may need to be modified to produce strong governments capable of making difficult decisions, particularly in terms of safeguarding the global environment." He suggests that the world be run like a giant corporation: "[W]e must learn to manage our impact on the environment much as we manage our businesses – with amortization, maintenance, and depreciation accounts – to ensure continued sustainability."

This claim would be ridiculous even if Strong had not been the architect of so many private business foul-ups. Still, he realizes that if there is only one global "corporation" then its customers will have nowhere else to shop.

An icon with a very mixed record
30 November 2015

Maurice Strong has died at the age of 86. Multi-faceted does not begin to describe his life. More than any other individual, he was responsible for promoting the climate agenda with which negotiators are struggling this week at the UN meeting in Paris.

Strong also played a major role in Canadian affairs. When he celebrated his 85th birthday in Toronto last year, he was surrounded by Canada's left-liberal elite – from former Prime Minister Paul Martin to former Governor General Adrienne Clarkson and her husband John Ralston Saul. Martin had been an employee and protégé of Strong. Ralston Saul had been aide to Strong when Strong was the first chairman, president and CEO of state oil company Petro-Canada, just one of many executive positions in a remarkable career.

Ms. Clarkson claimed that Strong had "invented the environment." While that may have been somewhat exaggerated, he did play a critical role in promoting radical political responses to environmental concerns. As a lifelong socialist, he saw the potential of the environmental movement to fight capitalism and introduce a system of "global governance" that would coordinate and control all human activity.

Before the last great failed attempt to come up with a global climate agreement, at Copenhagen in 2009, which took place at a time of economic turmoil, Strong said: "The climate change issue and the economic issue come from the same roots. And that is the gross inequity and the inadequacy of our economic model. We now know that we have to change that model. We cannot do all of this in one stroke. But we have to design a process that would produce agreement at a much more radical level."

Strong was reputed to be a Buddhist, but when Pope Francis issued his climate encyclical earlier this year, he praised Strong's *Earth Charter* – a manifesto of green revolution co-signed by former Soviet president Mikhail Gorbachev – as a document that "asked us to leave behind a period of self destruction and make a new start."

Maurice Strong's own start was extremely modest. He was born in poverty during the Depression in Oak Lake, Manitoba, and escaped home as soon as he could. Pursuing a picaresque early career, he bounced from cabin boy to junior fur trader to United Nations functionary to oil analyst.

He started his own oil company and wound up running Montreal-based Power Corp. at an extraordinarily young age. While he would continue to dabble in business throughout his life, his first love, and prime objective, was acquiring power in pursuit of a "better world."

From Power Corp. he moved to Ottawa and set up in the Canada International Development Agency. His amazing networking abilities led him to be asked to organize the first great UN conference on the global environment, at Stockholm in 1972. After Stockholm he because the first head of the United Nations Environment Program, UNEP, one of the parents of the Intergovernmental Panel on Climate Change, the body set up to make the case for catastrophic man-made climate change. He was a key member of the Brundtland Commission, which promoted the notion of sustainable development, whose fundamental rationale was that (relatively) free markets were unsustainable. In 1992, on the 20th anniversary of Stockholm, he ran the giant UN conference in Rio de Janeiro on the environment and development, which was attended by more world leaders than any previous event. Out of Rio emerged the Kyoto Protocol, to which Paris is still seeking a successor agreement.

Strong had extraordinary influence in the business community, where he set up the World Business Council on Sustainable Development. He was also a significant promoter of the World Economic Forum, whose annual conference at Davos became an unprecedented example of elite networking. He was at one time chief adviser both to UN Secretary General Kofi Annan and to World Bank head Jim Wolfensohn, another of his protégés. Annan put him in charge of UN reform, where Strong cleverly turned what was meant to be a belt-tightening exercise into a program for expansion. He ran relief programs in Africa, and negotiated with North Korea.

One reason Strong was idolized within the UN system was his skill in conceiving agendas, initiatives, studies, meetings and new institutions. Paris, for example, is the twenty-first "Conference of the Parties" (COP21) to the UN Framework Convention on Climate Change, but it is just one of a much broader series of seemingly endless well-expensed international get-togethers.

While spinning off do-good schemes at an astonishing rate, Strong continued to be involved in both public and private business. Apart from Petrocan, he ran the giant utility Ontario Hydro. His private business affairs, like his public ones, were marked by controversy.

It was one such adventure, in 2005, when he became implicated in the Iraqi oil-for-food scandal, that finally dented his international reputation. He claimed that he was unaware that an investment in one of his companies had been laundered from the regime of Saddam Hussein, but a subsequent inquiry suggested that if he didn't know, he should have.

In the wake of the scandal he moved to Beijing, where he had long had connections. For a man with severe asthma problems, it seemed a strange choice, but Strong found China's political climate amenable.

One of the most remarkable things about Strong was how unremarkable he was in person. Somebody once said that you wouldn't pick him out of a crowd of two. Nevertheless, he was an avuncular and likable figure, even to those who disagreed strongly with his worldview, as I did. I interviewed him numerous times over a 20-year period, and found that he took scarcely-concealed delight in explaining his often Machiavellian political manoeuvrings. Meanwhile his perennially sunny demeanour contrasted starkly with his grim vision, not just of the present, but of the projected state of the world.

In his 2000 autobiography, *Where on Earth Are We Going?*, he projected the elimination of two-thirds of the world's population as "a glimmer of hope," thus betraying a distinctly ambivalent attitude toward the humanity he claimed to be so desperate to save.

Strong's green agenda now blankets the globe, from the UN through national governments to municipalities. Paradoxically, he freely admitted that governments were incompetent, cumbersome and resistant to change. He also acknowledged that the UN was marked by "petty politics and small-mindedness." And yet somehow such deeply flawed individuals were to manage "the entire system of issues."

Strong's passing was mourned on the weekend by key figures of the movement he did so much to create. Current UNEP chief Achim Steiner declared "Strong will forever be remembered for placing the environment on the international agenda and at the heart of development." Christiana Figueres, head of the UNFCCC, tweeted "we thank Maurice Strong for his visionary impetus to our understanding of sustainability. We will miss you."

Prime Minister Justin Trudeau, already in Paris for this week's climate meetings, declared that "Strong was an internationally recognized environmentalist and philanthropist who used his remarkable business acumen, organizational skills, and humanity to make the world a better place."

Many would argue with that glowing assessment, but there is no doubting Strong's extraordinary influence on the Trudeaus, father and son. Strong had an astonishing network among rulers, corporations, the "international community," and capitalist foundations, but perhaps the most important strategic element in his promotion of the environmental agenda was his sponsorship of radical environmental non-governmental organizations, whose government funding and entry into international meetings he promoted and facilitated.

Whether they appreciate it or not, the environmental groups that played a key role in demonizing the oilsands and killing the Keystone XL pipeline, and who continue to stand in the way of other Canadian pipelines, are Maurice's children. They will be present in large numbers in Paris in the next two weeks.

We should mourn the man, but continue to question his vision, which remains very much alive.

The nature of David Suzuki

Broomstick for Suzuki?

31 October 2007

It was depressingly predictable. Reuters recently dug up a nutrition and diabetes expert, Dr. Diane Finegood, to declare that "our society has prolonged the Halloween experience." She didn't mean by creating a state of permanent fear; she meant by eating too many candies. The story concluded that parents should look at "fun alternatives" for Halloween. It suggested small toys.

Small toys! You mean the kind that kids occasionally swallow?

We live in a world where well-funded special interests – above all radical environmentalists – draw power and prestige from peddling scary stories about capitalism via a willing media. Politicians without principle jump on the bandwagon. Big corporations without perspective tag along, beating their breasts. Little children are taught to believe that the web of life is in tatters, that species are disappearing wholesale, that long-distance travel (especially for fruits and vegetables) is a sin, and that using non-biodegradable plastic bags represents a thousand years of landfill anxiety. Dim bulbs have literally become a way of life. What is effectively a horror movie, *An Inconvenient Truth*, has now become a part of the core curriculum.

In Canada, the grand wizard of eco-fright is David Suzuki, who has been throwing around Halloween references himself recently.

In a profile in the latest issue of *Maclean's*, Suzuki cites the alleged significance of the Nobel Peace Prize going to his fellow frightmeister, Al Gore. "Despite what a few dinosaurs are saying," declared Suzuki, "it's the nail in the coffin of [climate change] skeptics. Now, the challenge is to get on with it."

I don't know about you, but this dinosaur finds it pretty goosebumpifying when the awarding of a non-science prize to a man convicted of multiple egregious scientific howlers is claimed to be conclusive proof that we no longer need to look at "the science."

What is even more terrifying is that two men who want to make us all poorer and less free are still regarded as "saints" or "saviours." One can only imagine what Halloween would look like on Planet

Gore or in Suzukiworld, with kiddies in recycled sackcloth costumes being handed slices of (local) turnip to chew on.

We might take relief, however, in the knowledge that support for Suzuki's anti-materialist campaign is both small and hypocritical. Materialism is here to stay. Demons will always be a ghoul's best friend.

Meanwhile, there is evidence that Suzuki's moralistic crusade is coming back to haunt him. His daughter, Severn, who starred at the 1992 Rio conference as a child too indoctrinated to go into the fresh air, reportedly recently told him: "Dad. You've got to stop flying." Perhaps he might try a broomstick.

Who's silencing whom?

23 March 2012

Radical environmentalists tend not to be famous for their objectivity or sense of irony. Canada's most famous eco-activist, David Suzuki, proved that this week by organizing a write-in campaign to protest a Senate inquiry into foreign funding of Canadian environmental activism.

Suzuki's form email ventriloquized that his acolytes were "disappointed by the recent attempts of some senators to silence and demonize those who don't share their positions." It suggested that the Conservative senators were trying to "stifle the voices of millions of Canadians." In fact, "Silence and demonize" could be the Suzuki Foundation's motto. On its website, right beside "Tell the Senate to stop silencing environmental groups" sits a piece by Suzuki that was recently published in *The Huffington Post* under the headline "Deny deniers their right to deny"!

There is no more objectionable term for legitimate skepticism than "denial," which equates honest questioning with barmy claims that the Holocaust never took place. The Puffington article is, however, fascinating because it implicitly acknowledges that the Kyoto policy juggernaut is coming off the rails, so Suzuki changes tack. What if the science isn't settled (ridiculous idea though that still is), asks Suzuki. How can we keep relying on "finite" fossil fuels and thus robbing the future? We need big plans!

Such Malthusian hooey confirms that Suzuki is blind to history and utterly clueless about how markets work. Meanwhile here's his idea of a scientific argument: his piece links to a news story about a study that suggests that denial is a function of being a conservative white male. Meanwhile, if you want to understand climate issues, according to Suzuki, don't even think of visiting the websites of dissenters such as Anthony Watts (creator of wattsupwiththat.com – well worth a visit). Watts, after all, is a mere "weatherman." (Watts reminds us that Suzuki is, or was, a mere fruit fly geneticist.) Suzuki suggests that instead you should get the straight goods from the likes of his close associate James Hoggan, a big-time corporate consultant who runs the skeptic-smearing website DeSmogBlog, or from Naomi Oreskes, a "historian of climate science" whose debunked studies were prominently quoted by Al Gore in *An Inconvenient Truth*. Ms. Oreskes wants to ban the phrase "climate debate." She is a leading proponent of linking skeptics to the tobacco industry. Some science.

Suzuki also links to a piece by environmental economist William Nordhaus. Insofar as Prof. Nordhaus addresses errors in interpretation of his own work, one can hardly disagree with him. However, Nordhaus also utterly misrepresents the position of skeptics, suggesting, among other canards, that they "deny" the small temperature increases of the past 100 years. He thus confirms that conventional warmists refuse even to hear what skeptics are skeptical about, which is catastrophic, projected, man-made global warming.

Suzuki goes on to claim a "stepping up" of denialism, but his two examples are in fact of skeptics coming under manufactured attack. He smears Tom Harris, who was recently assaulted for a climate course he taught at Carleton University. Don't bother to look at the science, suggests Suzuki (the course was in fact designed by eminent earth scientist Tim Patterson), just accept that Harris is a denier and a shill, and associated (without pay) with the skeptical us-based Heartland Institute.

When it comes to Heartland, Suzuki cites something called "denialgate," but fails to register that the only real scandal revolves around how a fellow eco-activist Peter Gleick obtained documents from Heartland under false pretenses then leaked forgeries to the media. Heartland's desire to teach some balanced climate science in schools had led to paroxysms of rage from other radicals such as Al Gore.

The Senate's inquiry into foreign activist funding and charitable tax deduction is entirely valid. The David Suzuki Foundation certainly receives major donations from the California-based Moore, Hewlett and Packard foundations, but Suzuki is also heftily supported by Canadian establishmentarians such as the Bronfman family, Power Corp., Jim Pattison, and Gerry Schwartz.

Do these prominent capitalists grasp that they are supporting an anti-development fanatic who believes that anybody who doesn't think like him on climate science is evil, mentally defective or a corporate shill? Do they agree with his 2008 suggestion that apostate politicians should be put in jail? Do they go along with his admiration for totalitarian Cuba? Do they support child-scaring propaganda such as his recent Christmas campaign based on "saving" Santa's North Pole workshop from Arctic melting? Do they fail to register that he demonizes "corporate profits and interests"?

The Suzuki Foundation's robo-email concludes that "A democracy functions best when all points of view are considered rationally and carefully." To be fair, Suzuki only wants to put those words in the mouths of others. He could never possibly say them himself. His pants would catch on fire.

Andean fantasy

16 January 2013

According to the 2013 Index of Economic Freedom, compiled and released last week by *The Wall Street Journal* and the Heritage Foundation, Canada ranks sixth out of 177 countries. Bolivia and Ecuador rank, respectively, 156th and 159th. The Fraser Institute, which publishes a similar index, last year produced a broader index of human freedom, which incorporates civil and other liberties. Out of 123 countries, Canada ranked fifth, Bolivia 64th and Ecuador 73rd. Canada's gross national income in 2011, according to the World Bank, was US $45,560 per capita, more than 10 times that of Ecuador and 20 times that of Bolivia.

It would surely seem – given these statistics – that Canada has far more to teach these South American basket cases than they have to teach Canada. Not, however, according to David Suzuki, Canada's anti-development guru and climate alarmist-in-chief.

Last week, on the CBC's *The Nature of Things*, in an interview on *The Current* and in an article in *The Globe and Mail*, Suzuki suggested that Ecuador and Bolivia have "new ideas" to teach those of us trapped in the "neo-liberal" paradigm.

The three big ideas for which Suzuki was shilling are extortion, economic autarchy, and giving "rights" to rivers and rocks. Two of these Brave New Ideas come from Ecuador. The most radical is that, under the Ecuadorean constitution, "Mother Nature" is protected. This idea is based on primitive anthropomorphism – that nature is a person – plus a misreading of humans' relationship with the natural world. Confusion is caused partly because we use "value" in two radically different senses: moral and commercial. The assumption of those such as Suzuki is that commercial values drive out the moral variety, including concern for the environment. This is the reverse of the truth. Nature has no value but that given it by humans, and the richer we are, the higher we tend to value it. Capitalist societies are the ones where nature is best protected. Poor, authoritarian societies are the ones where the environmental damage is greatest.

In the example that Suzuki gave in his documentary – a lawsuit in which two American immigrants to Ecuador sued the local government over dumping into a river adjacent to their property – the basic issue was in fact one of private property rights, which are the surest protector of the environment. Ecuador's Mother Nature constitutional clause was brought in on appeal when the basic system of private rights failed.

Those who claim to speak for Mother Nature inevitably want to use her as ventriloquist's dummy for their own often-warped values. She is also recruited as a puppet to justify eco-extortion, which was Suzuki's next "new idea."

The thuggish Ecuadorean government of Rafael Correa threatened three years ago that if the rest of the world did not cough up US $3.6 billion, it would proceed to drill for oil in the Yasuni reserve, a place of extraordinary biodiversity. The regime's chutzpah-fuelled rationale was that it could gain twice as much from oil development, so it was doing the world a great favour by doing nothing and thus not releasing carbon dioxide into the atmosphere.

In fact, the international community has overwhelmingly told Ecuador to take a hike. Suzuki claims the initiative has raised $300 million, but if you go to the trust fund's website, you will find that, after two years, only US $50 million has been committed, and just US $6.5 million has been deposited – a minuscule 0.2% of the ransom demand.

Suzuki's final big idea is Bolivia's desire to build its own battery industry in a remote location next door to its enormous lithium deposits. Inviting in foreign expertise and investment, perhaps via a joint venture, would appear to be a no-brainer, but since Bolivia has bought into the socialist canard that capitalist investors are pillagers, it insists on going it alone. Suzuki's authority for the wisdom of this notion was a local Bolivian salt shoveller. The project is years behind schedule. Things become even more bizarre when Suzuki suggests that Canadians – when compared with these committed Bolivian loco-upgraders – are mere "hewers of wood and drawers of water." He seems unaware that Canada has a vast manufacturing industry, a significant part of which is devoted to resource upgrading.

The degree of local upgrading of any resource depends on many factors, from market location through logistics to human capital, but it is best determined by private, profit-oriented, decisions subject to appropriate regulation. To imagine that all resources should be locally upgraded is a classic example of what British economist David Henderson has called "do-it-yourself economics," a set of false assumptions universally held by those without economic training but who are ever ready to castigate greed and materialism.

Innovation and wealth generation depend on those factors on which the Freedom Index is based: the rule of law, regulatory efficiency, limited government and open markets. These are the factors which Bolivia and Ecuador are sorely lacking. The more they indulge in klepto-socialism and centrally planned autarchy, and the more they are supported and encouraged by ignorant fantasists such as Suzuki, the poorer they will be.

The Carbonist Manifesto

10 October 2013

I am David Suzuki," said David Suzuki. "I stand here today as an elder, beyond the temptations of money, fame or power. I have no hidden agenda but to speak the truth."

The occasion was a photo opportunity on the steps of Toronto's University Avenue courthouse, where he would reveal his *Carbon Manifesto* and generate publicity for his upcoming "trial," an event due to take place at the Royal Ontario Museum, the ROM, on November 6.

His manifesto amounts to a plan to wreck the Canadian economy. Oil exploration has to stop at once. Seventy per cent of energy has to be generated from renewables within a generation. A carbon tax of $150 a tonne must be applied immediately.

Not that such views are off the wall for Suzuki, a man who glorifies impoverished dictatorships such as Cuba and Bhutan, wants to adopt the anti-economic policies of basket cases such as Bolivia and Ecuador, and suggests that rocks and water have equal rights with people. Usually, however, Suzuki expresses his wacky beliefs within the safe and scripted confines of the CBC.

The problem, however, was that the photo-op had already been hijacked by Suzuki's nemesis, Sun TV's Ezra Levant. Levant, whose persona might be described as somewhere between a steam roller and a pitbull, has been a relentless critic of Suzuki. He was there to make clear that the whole idea of a mock trial was a mockery.

Mock trials are indeed a key part of legal training, but they are not prejudged, which Levant suggested would be the case here. And another thing, demanded Levant. Why was Suzuki portraying himself as the victim when the person who most frequently suggested that people should be prosecuted or jailed for their beliefs – particularly about climate – was David Suzuki? And sure enough, Suzuki declared "I accuse Canadian politicians of intergenerational crimes."

During a recent trip to Australia, Suzuki not only accused the new Australian Prime Minister, Tony Abbott, of "criminal negligence" for scrapping the country's carbon tax, but repeated the claim that the government of Stephen Harper might be building prisons to lock up "eco terrorists," a claim Justice Minister Peter McKay dubbed – perhaps unnecessarily – as "absurd."

It also seemed strange that the mock trial's promoters were trying to claim that it represented a "public policy debate" when the policies had already been decided by Suzuki, who has resolutely refused to debate anybody on climate. One reason for the refusal became obvious when – during a televised interview on that Australian tour – Suzuki revealed that he didn't have a clue about the sources of the "official" global temperature statistics. He was also forced to back down on his outrageous claims against genetically modified foods.

Meanwhile nobody was claiming, as he suggested, that his recommendations were "treasonous." They are merely nonsensical, hatched in that impregnable echo chamber that is the home of the eco-moralist. Except that now somebody was banging a big Sun TV microphone on the eco-echo chamber. Suzuki fled, with the Sun TV mike hounding him all the way to his waiting Chevy Volt.

Next, Levant returned to quiz David Buckland, the British artist and founder of the organization Carbon 14, who was co-curating a ROM exhibit to coincide with the "trial." Buckland specializes in projecting words onto icebergs. He has achieved a measure of fame by taking groups of artists to "see" climate change in Northern Europe. A relatively gentle parody of one of those trips was featured in Ian McEwan's climate satire, *Solar* (one of McEwan's fictional artistic fellow-travellers had built a life-sized Monopoly set to emphasize "the unequal distribution of wealth," and as an indictment of "money-obsessed culture").

Buckland, even if he might be guilty of leading his fellow artists on a climatological fool's errand, seemed a thoroughly decent chap and stood his ground bravely. He even acknowledged that Levant had himself become part of the "theatre" that the exhibit was designed to promote. I decided it would be a silly question to ask Buckland if Levant would therefore be invited along as an expert witness.

Apparently, Suzuki's trial is to take a similar form to Ayn Rand's play *Night of January 16th*, in which the audience delivers a verdict. One can't imagine more ideologically polar opposites than Suzuki and Rand, but would it be paranoid to imagine that environmentalists have already snapped up most of the seats for the ROM's single performance?

I asked Laurie Brown, the veteran CBC-er whose brainchild the trial is, what would happen in the unlikely event that Suzuki were found guilty. Would there be a sentencing? Sure, she said with a laugh, they'd take him outside and hang him.

Maybe they should have had a gallows at the photo-op. I'm sure Suzuki would have had no trouble imagining Levant swinging from it.

Suzuki climate "trial" litigated in an echo chamber

8 November 2013

The *Trial of David Suzuki* at the Royal Ontario Museum on Wednesday night said far more about the mindset of Suzuki nation than the state of the planet.

The event was part of a *Climate is Culture* exhibit, which seeks to clarify global warming by bringing artists into the act. Imagine Jules Feiffer's classic flaky cartoon ballerina and her *Dance to Spring*. Only now imagine she's pirouetting against climate change.

The ROM event was a cross between a mock trial and a Soviet show trial. In show trials the victim had already been condemned. In the Suzuki version, the innocence of the self-accused environmental celebrity was never in doubt.

The court's stage set was a Kafkaesque vision in stark gunmetal grey, complete with an oil-barrel motif. Its most arresting feature was Suzuki's dock, which was high above the judge's bench, making clear who was in charge. The audience was treated before the show to sounds of chainsaws, and giant projections of open-pit oilsands mining and refineries. I think psychologists call that "priming."

The trial's conceit was that David Suzuki had been accused of "seditious libel" for promoting his *Carbon Manifesto*, a policy platform that would end the age of fossil fuels – at least in Canada – by immediately imposing a carbon tax of $150 per tonne.

In the real world, Suzuki is free to make all the suicidal policy recommendations he wants, and is protected by the Charter of Rights and Freedoms. However, he "waived" that defence so he could portray himself as being persecuted.

The trial began, somewhat unusually, with Suzuki spraying his own accusations left, right and centre. It was pretty obvious who was really on trial here: Stephen Harper, whose Conservative government was accused of "intergenerational crimes."

Presiding judge Todd Ducharme, who really is a judge (on the Ontario Superior Court of Justice), reminded the audience/jury of the presumption of innocence, a courtesy that Suzuki had singularly failed to extend in his opening statement.

The trial's most impressive performer was the prosecutor, Will McDowell, even though he knew he was bound to lose. The handpicked prosecution witness was academic and CBC commentator Michael Hlinka, who rightly projected economic doom if the manifesto – which would have zero effect on the climate – was enacted.

A naïve person might have found this promising, until defence lawyer Linda Rothstein had Hlinka agreeing with almost everything she said, including "Assume the science is correct."

The second part of the trial started with David Suzuki in the witness barrel and his defence lawyer leading him through the case for draconian action. Prosecutor McDowell got into unintended consequences, like the greater use of more-dangerous rail transportation as a result of blocking oil pipelines. He noted that Suzuki claimed that he stood up for the poor, but that his policies would hurt the poor.

Suzuki had an easy answer for that: equalization, fed by those huge revenues from the carbon tax. It wasn't explained how you could have ongoing hefty revenues from an industry you were closing down.

The loaded version of climate science from defence witness Gord Miller, the ultra earnest Ontario Environment Commissioner, was a snooze. When Prosecutor McDowell asked him about the likelihood of everybody being able to drive a $60,000 Volt, Miller responded that he had just bought one, and it was only $50,000. McDowell failed to follow up to ask if the difference was due to a subsidy cheque from the government.

The prosecutor did follow up by noting that official climate models had greatly overestimated actual temperature increases in the past couple of decades, but he could have produced a video of Suzuki smoking a crack pipe and it wouldn't have made the slightest difference.

McDowell's summary was witty and irreverent, but in the end he fell in line with the charade by suggesting that David Suzuki had to "bear the consequences of his illegal act." But what consequences? The point was that nobody had accused Suzuki of anything except being out to lunch on science and policy.

The defence closed by invoking projections of giant Asteroid-type Armageddon as a result of Canadians' culpable concern with their pocket books. Judge Ducharme then stepped in to instruct the jury/ audience that they were dealing – although he didn't put it quite that way – with postmodern justice: you could bend it any way you want.

Then came the vote. Would it be a nail biter? No, it was a Suzuki landslide from the audience, and an acquittal from the jury. There were whoops of victory over, er, nobody, except that tiny handful of brave masochists (such as yours truly) who had suffered through this charade then dared to put up their hands for "Guilty."

Since David Suzuki has resolutely refused to take part in a public debate on climate, and this entire event was under the control of Suzuki sympathizers, the fact that a real judge and real lawyers took part discredits the legal system. The lesson from this mock trial was what it said about the objectivity and openness of Suzuki nation. They reach consensus by having conversations in echo chambers. They try themselves, certain of acquittal. They claim persecution while suggesting their opponents should be silenced. It was, indeed, a mockery.

Suzukinomics

21 May 2014

One might ignore the rantings of David Suzuki were he not one of the most "trusted" and "admired" voices in Canada. That trust and admiration appear to arise from his scripted voiceovers on the CBC's *Nature of Things*, where he provides a kind of avuncular Mr. Roger's Neighbourhood approach to (most) science issues.

However, Suzuki's Dr. Jekyll changes rapidly to Mr. Hyde when the lefty activist takes over. Not only does he display bias and ignorance on scientific issues, he simply makes things up. Musing on the Fukushima nuclear disaster, he suggested that another such accident would mean "bye-bye Japan" and require the west coast of North

America to be evacuated. He subsequently expressed "regret" for his "off-the-cuff response;" that is, typically massive misrepresentation.

If Suzuki is cavalier when it comes to matters of science, on issues of economics he is totally out to lunch. His cluelessness was confirmed in a recent interview with the terminally left-liberal American TV personality Bill Moyers.

Following Moyers' ritual demonization of "big fossil fuel companies" and the "tsunami of money" with which they are allegedly destroying the environment and corrupting the political process, he asked Suzuki: "Is it practical to think we can change the paradigm when we're up against that wall of money?" Suzuki responded: "Well, I keep saying that the economic system is a human invention. The idea of capitalism, free enterprise, corporations, markets; these are not forces of nature for heavens' sake, but you talk to a neo-liberal and you say 'the market' and they say (here Suzuki raised his voice and made wild gestures, lifting his hands above his head and bowing down in a parody of an act of worship) 'Oh the market. Praise the market. Free the market' ...We invented the damn thing. What's going on? ...Why is it that we bow down before human-created ideas? We can change those things. We can't change our dependence on the biosphere for our wellbeing and survival. I don't get it. If it ain't working, change the darn thing."

First, one might note that we live at a time of unprecedented wealth and human wellbeing by every measure. However, if you are a hole-rather-than-doughnut kind of guy, all you can see is that "it ain't working." Also, I would be intrigued to know to which particular "neoliberals" Suzuki has been talking. My impression has always been that he lives in an echo-chamber.

Suzuki's lack of understanding, and moral condemnation, of markets starts with the fundamental but common error that they are a "human invention" and thus can be easily "changed." In fact, although markets emerge from commercial human interaction, they represent a much larger, and overwhelmingly beneficial, self-regulating system that transcends human intuitions. To begin to understand them requires the study of something called "economics."

Suzuki has called economics a form of "brain damage." When

people such as Suzuki admit that they are "not economists," they appear to regard this not as an admission of culpable ignorance but as a proud boast that their perspective transcends grubby self-interest. In fact, Suzuki's stance exposes not merely his ignorance but his hypocrisy. The fettered capitalist system seems to be working extraordinarily well for him. He is a member of the 1%, with numerous homes, and he certainly doesn't fly by magic carpet.

Just as Suzuki has no understanding of economics, he appears to have no interest in history. If he did, he might record that the most murderous regimes of the past hundred years – that is, Communism and fascism – have been based on the alleged shortcomings of free markets, and of freedom more generally.

Where ardent fans of free markets may err is in imagining that they might reason their opponents into agreement. People like Suzuki are as impervious to reason as they are blind to evidence.

It is depressing not merely that we fail to understand and appreciate the workings and results of relatively free markets, but that we are inclined to trust and admire those who would destroy them.

Naomi Klein: no logo, no logic

Maligning Milton, sugar-coating socialism
12 September 2007

Climate leadership in all the wrong directions
10 September 2008

Klein vs. Steyn
22 October 2014

Great Leap Backwards
16 September 2015

This Misrepresents Everything
18 February 2016

Maligning Milton, sugar-coating socialism
12 September 2007

In her new book, *The Shock Doctrine*, Naomi Klein literally links economic "shocks" with electroshock therapy, specifically the diabolical postwar experiments of a Montreal doctor named Ewen Cameron, who did contract work for the CIA. Ms. Klein invites us to connect the electrodes: CIA/torture/Iraq/George W. Bush/Dick Cheney/Halliburton. Isn't it obvious?

This paranoid concatenation leads to a very, very old thesis: that capitalism is the playground of greedy, repressive and exploitative corporations, whose dark purposes are served by wicked ideologues and compliant governments. Only now it's worse than ever: it's "Disaster Capitalism."

Ms. Klein's unlikely Father of Lies is her other alleged "Shock Doctor," Nobel-winning economist Milton Friedman, leader of the free-market, monetarist Chicago School. Professor Friedman is portrayed as the man indirectly responsible – among other crimes – for South America's "disappeared" dissidents, the Tiananmen Square massacre, the Iraq war, and climate change.

Ms. Klein's alleged smoking gun is Friedman's statement that "only a crisis – actual or perceived – produces real change." It seems this truism is OK when acted upon by Lenin, Fidel Castro or Al Gore, but only becomes really problematic when used to confront the sort of political and economic disasters conjured up by, well, Lenin, Castro and Gore. Ms. Klein claims that capitalism welcomes, thrives on, and indeed promotes crisis as an excuse to dismantle the welfare state, rob children of education and dispossess Third World fishermen living on prime post-tsunami coastal real estate.

Capitalism for Ms. Klein is a very flexible term. She blames this definitional looseness on the fact that her enemy is a "shape-shifter, forever changing its name and switching identities." Still, this means that she can fit almost anything into her capacious definitional dustbin, even wild inconsistencies. She can admit that Prof. Friedman was a staunch opponent of the International Monetary Fund, but still have them both as part of the same great conspiratorial ball of wax. Similarly, the Iraq war has always been staunchly opposed by much of the us "right," but let's just ignore that inconvenient detail. Again, every proponent of free markets acknowledges that economic structures must be based on the rule of law. Phooey, says Ms. Klein, it's all about "lawlessness," so let's not go there. South Africa's ongoing problems? The fault of Thatcherism! Chechnya? Milton did it! 9/11 and post-Katrina New Orleans? Both functions of 20 years of government downsizing!

When mendacity and sloppy analysis falters, there are always those stock epithets for the "C" word: "cutthroat," "barbarian," "unfettered," "savage," and now, "crisis" (a word to which we may soon have to add Ms. Klein's trademark).

A more selective history can hardly be imagined. There is no suggestion in *The Shock Doctrine* that the principles of privatization and deregulation might have been rooted in – and justified by – the obvious failures of state-run industries and over-regulated economies. Ms. Klein's economic hero is John Maynard Keynes, but Keynesianism collapsed not for want of kindness but because it led (as Friedman had forecast) to stagflation; and because it unleashed an orgy of government deficits.

For Ms. Klein, Communism was not always and inevitably a murderous system. The problem was only "authoritarian" communism. Meanwhile, her mixed-economy "third way" remains a magical, mythical land where smaller businesses are run by worker co-operatives, the commanding heights of nationalized industries are skillfully managed by bureaucrats, and "free" education and health care are all efficiently and effectively taken care of by selfless "public servants."

In calling for "democratic socialism," Ms. Klein does, however, highlight an important issue: the relationship between democracy and effective economic policy. Capitalism tends to promote democracy, but the reverse is not necessarily true. Democratic systems are always in danger of being led astray by attractive but counterproductive populist ideas. For example, there's nothing like "job security" policies for eliminating jobs. Similarly, the tyrannical majority can always vote themselves the earnings of the wealthy, but they'll paradoxically wind up the poorer for it.

Ms. Klein – like all good socialists – makes much of American interventions in South America, and in particular that alleged Mother of All Injustices, the overthrow by Augusto Pinochet of the democratically-elected Salvador Allende in Chile in 1973. Here the smoking gun, or rather smell of burning flesh, relates to the fact that Chile's subsequent economic policies were heavily influenced by the Chicago School. "The shock of the torture chamber," writes Ms. Klein, "terrorized anyone thinking of standing in the way of the economic shocks." Milton with a cattle prod? I don't think so. Torture is indeed repugnant, but Ms. Klein inevitably overlooks the unavoidable issue of messy transition from the types of failed economic experiments of which she is so enamoured (and which engaged in much more extensive torture). To blame capitalism for all the problems of the imploding alternatives is like blaming an alcoholic's withdrawal symptoms on sobriety.

Ms. Klein does see some light in current South America, where a new bunch of leftist leaders represent the hope for "markets existing alongside the nationalization of the banks and mines, with the income used to build comfortable neighbourhoods and decent schools – economic as well as political democracy." She suggests that "these ideas were never defeated in a great battle of ideas, nor were they voted down in elections."

True. But they were defeated in fact, by reality, wherever they were tried, and failed.

Climate leadership in all the wrong directions
10 September 2008

Naomi Klein, Margaret Atwood and Moses Znaimer are among the well-known climate experts and economists who have come together this week under the banner "Canadians for Climate Leadership" (CCL).

This is not just any old crowd of the terminally radical, terminally nationalist and/or terminally trendy. Also in the group – along with leaders of unions, students and Sikhs – are no less than four former Canadian Prime Ministers: Joe Clark, John Turner, Kim Campbell and Paul Martin.

I have an inconvenient question: if you are looking for policy credibility, why would you recruit a group of PMs who between them lasted less than four years in office, and who each, in his or her own way, presided over political disaster?

Admittedly, Turner and Campbell suffered from the unpopularity of their predecessors, but until Stephan Dion came along, when you looked up "hapless" in the dictionary, you found a picture of Joe Clark. Meanwhile having Paul Martin in this group surely amounts to parody. This is a man who was a key member, and then leader, of the Liberal government that led Canada into the Kyoto debacle and then proceeded, at huge expense, to renege – wisely if not conspicuously – on the commitment to decimate the economy.

According to Clark, when it comes to climate change policy "We are falling further behind other comparable nations." One wonders which other nations Clark has in mind. Could it be Britain, where it is estimated that a quarter of the population will be living next year in "fuel poverty"? Kim Campbell declared yesterday that there was a policy void on climate change. Her proposal was that we need to "work together" to make "strong laws and policies that will get the job done." Wow. That's telling 'em.

Today, the CCL is due to launch a "public campaign" in Toronto. Judging from the statement it released yesterday, *Time to Get Serious on Climate Change*, we shouldn't hold our collective breath. This muddled manifesto could easily have been penned by any average group of Suzukified grade eight students. The statement claims that there are two sets of risks, one from climate change, and one "from standing back and letting others lead." I don't know about you, but I'm prepared to stand well back when it comes to taking the lead in the lemming Olympics.

The alleged danger is that Canada might be forced into "ill-considered actions dictated by others." Ill-considered actions are apparently best dictated at home. Hence the signatories make a clarion call for "a new approach," except they don't quite specify what it is, apart from pricing carbon dioxide at a minimum of $30 a tonne through some combination of cap-and-trade and taxes. This glib suggestion is portrayed as a "market-based incentive," somewhat analogous to declaring that being gagged and bound is a "freedom-based state."

We can "no longer delay," but exactly what we can no longer delay is vague. All we know is that it will require "further planning, analysis and consultation." The resultant policies, even though we don't know what they are, will nevertheless be "affordable, or even bring economic advantages." More intrusive government will actually boost the economy.

Because we must.

One thing is clear. "We need to develop and deploy climate-safe technologies at a staggering rate." If we just rush about madly in all directions, it seems, our problems will be solved.

The signatories agree that they do not have a clue about the specific technologies required, but they know that government policy has to be out there in front. We must all be ready to "embrace uncertainty." We must also "harmonize" policy both within and without.

The ultimate organizers behind this pile of biomass are John Roy, a Nova Scotia businessman with hippy-dippy leanings, and Tzeporah Berman, a professional eco-activist who has been prominent in shaking down the forest industry and the oilsands. The last time we spotted Ms. Berman she was trying to lure Leonardo DiCaprio to the Athabasca region. All she got was NDP leader Jack Layton. Still, she has corralled four dim-bulb former Prime Ministers to her anti-development cause.

Ms. Berman is now the executive director of the NGO arm of the CCL, called PowerUp Canada. The CCL claims it is due to meet shortly with all political parties to discuss its lack of ideas. Mmm. I'd be interested to know when they have their date with Stephen Harper.

Klein vs. Steyn
22 October 2014

In the introduction to his new essay collection, *The (Un)docu-mented Mark Steyn*, the hilariously insightful Steyn notes the rapid changes in societies' attitudes toward issues such as gay marriage. The speed of such changes, he notes, has left "social conservatives" floundering. This is clear evidence that the liberal left is winning the culture war. However, social conservatism is one thing, fiscal conservatism quite another.

Moral values may change, but the iron laws of economics do not, even as hatred and moral condemnation of them, and of capitalism, continue unabated. But this raises another question: why does moral condemnation of capitalism persist in the face of its remarkable achievements? Given the intractability of conflicts throughout the Middle East, the rise of putative caliphates, and the spread of the poverty-rooted Ebola epidemic, it would seem an appropriate time to celebrate Western civilization, wealth, tolerance and empathy. And yet attacks, most recently in Naomi Klein's latest screed, *This Changes Everything: Capitalism vs. the Climate*, are relentless and impervious to reason.

Two hundred and fifty years after the start of the Industrial Revolution, and the unprecedented and stunning improvements in wealth and welfare that capitalism has brought, the system still stands indicted by an axis that stretches from ISIS without to Ms. Klein within.

This is partly due to a warped interpretation of history – inevitably peddled by Ms. Klein – that notes that early capitalism coexisted with slavery and colonialism. True, but the values of freedom that were promoted by – and flourished under – capitalism made slavery repugnant and colonialism unacceptable.

Ms. Klein is hardly alone in her rabid condemnation and facile policy remedies. Prominent business school professors and their media echo chambers tell us that the system is rigged, and that we need a new "model." Harvard philosophers rail against crass materialism. Meanwhile the world's great bureaucracies – the UN, the IMF, the World Bank, and the International Energy Agency, which are lavishly quoted by Ms. Klein – produce endless studies claiming that capitalism threatens the very existence of life on earth. The solution? More and bigger bureaucracy.

Although the liberal left has shifted its emphasis toward "social justice" in the wake of the egregious failure of state-owned enterprise, concentrating, as Steyn puts it, on "nationalization of the family," it certainly hasn't given up on control of the economy. Indeed, its ambitions have become even larger. They have also become even more unworkable and potentially damaging. This gets us back to that 64-trillion-dollar question: why haven't our moral sentiments evolved to appreciate capitalism as they have adapted to accept gay marriage?

One key reason is that, under capitalism, people can have their cake and condemn it too. We don't have to understand how markets work to thrive within them any more than we need to read and absorb a book on biology in order to stay alive. Although we are natural traders, we are born reflexively to believe in simplistic centrally planned solutions, and that local preference and self-sufficiency are "good." Similarly, many of the processes and results of capitalism are objectionable to moral sentiments that were formed in a very different environment from that in which we now live, an environment in which control of resources and oppressive power tended to go together.

The even more significant reason why the lessons of bad policy are not "learned" is that economic ignorance and outdated moral assumptions are effortlessly – indeed largely subconsciously – promoted and exploited by power seekers. Inequality demands redistribution. Corporate power requires "countervailing" power. Economies require "managing." The world needs saving.

The failures of top-down command-and-control policies – from Communism and the New Deal, through governments' role in promoting the 2008 financial crisis, to universal green energy policy fiascos – are furiously obfuscated, or shoved down the Memory Hole. Such obfuscation is part of the reason why the same bad anti-economic policies keep coming back time and again. They could not do so unless the general public had no fundamental grasp of Adam Smith's "Invisible Hand."

The whole world remains mired in delusions of top-down economic management which, far from rescuing us from the 2008 crisis, has merely perpetuated it. Only vibrant capitalist enterprise can save us, but it has to do so while standing perpetually morally condemned by those who don't understand it, those keen to exploit that lack of understanding, and those, like Ms. Klein, given literary awards for telling us we live in an economically rotten society (as opposed to a socially rotting one. Thank heavens for Mark Steyn!).

The ultimate problem for the liberal left – and the ultimate hope for conservatism and those who value freedom – is that the left perspective, in seeking control of economies as well as promoting an ever-expanding welfare state, has inevitably to crash against the realities of human nature, which may not understand markets but inevitably responds to excessive taxation and regulation by complaining more and creating less. Even then people may not grasp – or want to grasp – the root of the problem.

Sexual mores may change through cultural campaigning, but appreciation of markets requires comprehensive education. Even then, there are Nobel economists who despise capitalism. However, if condemnation of – and assaults on – free-enterprise pie-making go too far, the pie will shrink, or disappear altogether. No amount of moral outrage, wishful thinking, or occupying the financial district can change that fact.

Great Leap Backwards
16 September 2015

The *Leap Manifesto* issued on Tuesday by an asylum full of celebrity victims of Harper Derangement Syndrome – led by Naomi Klein and David Suzuki – is certainly a thought-provoking platform.

The main thoughts it provokes are: Does achieving celebrity cause a sharp drop in IQ and increase in hypocrisy? Does all-consuming artistic ego and/or power-hungry socialist inclination prevent all logical thought? Does becoming rich as an entertainer or writer under the capitalist system automatically make you blind to the wealth generated by that system – in particular your own – and lead you to take every opportunity to chomp on the Invisible Hand? Or does celebrity make you so desperate to be part of the in-crowd that you just sign on the dotted line for any alleged Good Cause that appears in front of you?

The *Manifesto*'s launch was a peripheral event at the *Toronto International Film Festival*, in which Klein has a movie based on her tedious book, *This Changes Everything: Capitalism vs. the Climate*. The book's thinking, or lack thereof, permeates the manifesto.

Its main points were also promoted in a piece in the *Globe and Mail* on Tuesday by Klein, Suzuki, and three other well-known policy experts: Leonard Cohen, Donald Sutherland and Ellen Page. Other credential-free supporters span all the way from Neil Young through Yann Martel and John Ralston Saul to the Canadian Union of Public Employees. The manifesto's "initiating organizations" include 350.org – the US billionaire-backed NGO started by Wild Bill McKibben – and other radical anti-development groups such as Greenpeace and ForestEthics.

You'd think that somebody among the Deep Thinkers might have reflected that "leaping" doesn't have the best of historical connotations. Specifically, it conjures up Chairman Mao's "Great Leap Forward," a lurch that led to tens of millions of deaths. Meanwhile isn't there that old saying about looking before you leap? Still, eco-alarmists perpetually claim that we should leap first and look later. No time to waste. That has been their theme for more than a quarter century, during which global economies and human welfare have as stubbornly risen as the global temperature has stubbornly failed to leap.

The majority of the *Manifesto* is taken up with peddling the fantasy of a total switch to alternative energy within a couple of decades, and demanding an end to fossil fuel activity. "Energy democracy" would involve a great leap backwards to a world of communes and co-ops engaged in endless and earnest debate. "We call," note *The Globe's* Gang of Five, "for town hall meetings across the country where residents can gather to democratically define what a genuine leap to the next economy means in their communities." Of course there will no discussion about whether the leap is necessary, wise or into the abyss. That decision has already been taken by the Green Vanguard. Not that the communes won't be connected and mobile. They will, via "high speed rail powered by renewables and affordable public transit." These will be "in place of more cars, pipelines and exploding trains that endanger and divide us." Funny that the list doesn't include air travel, but that's probably out of consideration for all the flights involved in travelling to meetings to save the world. And to film festivals.

Chairman Mao's Great Leap and its Stalinist equivalent in fact do crop up in a plan to collectivize and localize agriculture. This primitive emphasis on the local, which would inevitably exacerbate poverty, would be cemented by "an end to all trade deals."

Where would new jobs originate? From expanding "low-carbon" sectors such as "caregiving, teaching, social work, the arts and public interest media." And where would the money to fund *The Leap* originate? Easy. Soak corporations and the rich. End (non-existent) fossil fuel subsidies. Slap on transaction charges (thus punishing and reducing transactions). Raise resource royalties. Impose carbon taxes.

Klein is a great promoter of the notion that the dark forces of capitalism deliberately manufacture "crises" as an excuse for dictatorial control. She seems impervious to any suggestion that the "climate crisis" might come into the same category. It certainly does.

This misrepresents everything
18 February 2016

Apart from the stock shots of effluent pipes and belching smoke-stacks, Naomi Klein's idea of objectivity about the Alberta oil-sands is to find a worker in a Fort McMurray bar prepared to blow his nose on a banknote.

Scenes like this make Klein's documentary *This Changes Everything*, not just intellectually vacuous but downright objectionable.

The guy using the currency as nasal tissue might well now be out of a job, not just because of the oil price collapse, but because of the prominent role played by Klein and her ilk in killing the Keystone XL pipeline and thus draining billions from the Alberta economy.

Much of the movie, which is based on Klein's endless book of the same name, takes the form of a series of confrontations between local people and some form of development or effluent: the oilsands in Alberta; pipelines, coal and shale in Montana and Wyoming; a coal-fired electricity plant in India; a goldmine in Greece; killer smog in Beijing.

The propaganda sequence runs roughly as follows: offence against climate/social justice, riot, teargas (not required in Beijing), shots of people running and screaming, moral outrage, rinse and repeat.

This is not to suggest that consultation with local communities is not necessary. It is, but things are not quite as simple as presented. In Kleinworld, agitation is often organized by multinational environmental NGOs with an anti-development agenda and little or no concern for local people's welfare. Meanwhile it takes considerable chutzpah to suggest that Greece's problems might be due to capitalism.

The wobbly intellectual substructure under Klein's catalogue of capitalist crimes is the system's alleged belief that Mother Nature is there to be raped and pillaged, and that resources are infinite. The film never presents anyone who actually holds this view because, like most of Klein's claims, it is demotic nonsense. Klein's evil capitalist clincher is, of course, climate change, which is epitomized by Superstorm Sandy. But that storm can in no way, shape or form be laid at the door of man-made global warming.

It is ironic indeed that early on in the film Klein attends a meeting of the British Royal Society – home of Newton and Darwin – as the supposed epicentre of the scientific assault on spirituality. The meeting is to discuss geoengineering as a solution to climate change ("pollution to fight pollution"). But while there are indeed many questions about such schemes, the implication that the Royal Society is a bastion of objectivity, particularly when it comes to climate, is almost satirical. Indeed several recent presidents of the society have gone off the reservation when it comes to climate alarmism and had to be reined in by their own members.

The movie, which was directed by Klein's husband Avi Lewis, scion of one of Canada's most prominently canting socialist families, is outstanding only for its perspective-free hypocrisy.

Take the posturing of Crystal Lameman of the Beaver Lake Cree, a tribe living in the vicinity of the oilsands. Lameman, who will later appear delivering a speech to a mob in Washington, spouts fortune-cookie mysticism about the land owning the people, but the arresting point is that she is doing so while dressed and made up in very non-traditional fashion, against the backdrop of her modern kitchen, with its IKEA cabinetry, brushed-steel faucets and modern appliances. Then Crystal is seen driving her Kia to a Michael Moore-style confrontation at a spill site, which she knows she will not be allowed to enter. Meanwhile Crystal, like Naomi, presumably did not reach Washington by magic carpet. She also uses a cell phone, which definitely wasn't developed by "traditional knowledge."

At a Beaver Lake Cree band barbecue, no thought is obviously given to the system that produced the imported bottles of San Pellegrino or the watermelon that the child being conspicuously coddled by Klein is eating. The height of hypocrisy is reached when it is revealed that the Beaver Lake Cree are suing the government of Canada because oilsands development has "made traditional life impossible." Apparently it was already undesirable.

The film gets really intriguing when the credits begin to roll, and those who supported this pile of agitprop are identified. Chief among them is something called the Sustainable Markets Foundation, SMF. Since it's all the rage these days to bemoan *Dark Money*, the title of Jane Mayer's hatchet job on the Koch Brothers, it's worth noting that the SMF was highlighted in a report by a US Senate committee as an up-and-coming node of a progressive "Billionaires' Club" filled with capitalist foundations that despise capitalism.

"Can I be honest with you?" Klein asks at the beginning of this very dishonest film. "I've always kind of hated films about climate change…Is it really possible to be bored by the end of the world?" No, Naomi, but it is possible to be bored by people who prattle incessantly that the end of the world is imminent when it isn't, and who want to end the best world we've ever had.

Pope Francis: papal bull

My PLAN ENSURES THE POOR WILL ALWAYS BE WITH US

Habemus pap
3 January 2014

Is God green?
8 January 2015

The Pope's Eco-mmunist Manifesto
19 June 2015

Habemus pap
3 January 2014

At a recent dinner in New York, satirist Stephen Colbert said that if Pope Francis were present, attendees wouldn't know "because His Humbleness would be out washing the feet of the coat-check guy." Colbert, who describes himself as "America's most famous Catholic," also quipped "I believe the Pope is infallible. But he's also wrong about a lot of things."

It was certainly unusual for the new Pope – formerly Cardinal Jorge Mario Bergoglio of Buenos Aires – to be treated with less than Hosannas. *Time*'s *Person of the Year* has been fawned upon not just by the Catholic faithful but by the media as a promoter of peace, love and tolerance toward homosexuals – none of which exactly amounts to going out on a limb.

Colbert's mordant humour dared to expose the Pope's conspic-uous humility – he has abandoned the papal Mercedes for a Ford Focus (although one wonders why not a Prius) – but it also pointed to the serious issue of whether the Pope knows what he's talking about when it comes to his professed concern for the poor.

The appropriate approach to poverty is not to sanctify it but eradicate it. Whatever other issues may beset the new papacy – from child abuse cover-ups, through abortion, divorce and contraception, to the ordination of women priests – if Pope Francis really is con-cerned about relieving poverty, his reflexive anti-capitalist attitudes are pointing precisely in the wrong direction.

In the wake of the collapse of Communism, Pope John Paul II praised the free market as "the most efficient instrument for uti-lizing resources and effectively responding to needs." However, his successors – including the retired Benedict XVI – have returned to the Church's more traditional anti-capitalist stance, now larded with environmental concerns and support for UN-based "global govern-ance."

Pope Francis came out of the Vatican gate in March sounding like the theological wing of the Occupy movement. He condemned

greed and "easy gain." He berated the "tyranny" of the global financial system and the "cult of money." He ritually bemoaned "the gap"
between rich and poor. In a recent "exhortation" he assaulted straw-
man "trickle-down theories," and pointed to a "crude and naïve trust
in the goodness of those wielding economic power and in the sacralized workings of the prevailing economic system." In writing thus,
he exposed his own economic confusion, first in implying that social
benefits come only from charitable intention (vs. the mutual benefits
of the market), and second in peddling the canard that promotion
of markets represents some kind of quasi religious "sacralized" faith
rather than being the result of a willingness to study the counterin-
tuitive lessons of economic history. Significantly though, the Pope's
lack of economic training is not regarded as a disqualifier, but as a
virtue.

us right-wing commentator Rush Limbaugh suggested that Pope
Francis was a Marxist. This inevitably led not to analysis of Limbaugh's claim, but to demonization of Limbaugh. In fact, the Pope's
take does have much in common with the Marxist misrepresentation of capitalism. What is the Pope's suggestion that wealth deadens
concern for others but a regurgitation of Marx's "cash nexus?" But
then how does he explain Bill Gates' global salvationist inclinations?
Or billionaires' eagerness to sign up to the Giving Pledge? In fact,
the lesson of history is that capitalism does not supplant charity, but
facilitates it to an unprecedented degree.

Meanwhile, if the poor are truly his priority, then surely what is
important is not "the gap" but the massive reductions in levels of
absolute poverty in recent decades, and what has brought it about.

It has nothing to do with the kinds of statist policies implied by
the Pope. Indeed, one can't help asking whether the Pope is more
concerned with relieving the poor or bringing down the rich.

The Pope's musings have to be put in the context of his South
American origins. Although he reportedly did not originally sub-
scribe to the radicalism of "liberation theology," there is little doubt
his views were coloured by Argentina's default in 2001, and the clumsy
interventions of the International Monetary Fund, the imf. As with
most people who don't – or can't – follow too far along the trail of

economic causes and effects, former Cardinal Bergoglio appears to have fallen for the idea that what caused poverty and unemployment in his native land was not statism and feckless borrowing by a corrupt government, but "unrestrained capitalism."

True fans of capitalism have always seen the IMF not as the vanguard of "neoliberalism" but as a fount of moral hazard and a stoker of inevitable resentment. To the extent that the IMF's main purpose has been to bail out banks rather than help the poor, Cardinal Bergoglio does indeed have a point. But that's not capitalism, it's cronyism.

The other conundrum about the Pope's leftist leanings is that they are shared by many South American governments, whose people live in desperate conditions precisely because of their rulers' populist policies. Nicolas Maduro, the president of Venezuela, has appeared sporting a rosary bestowed upon him by Francis. Maduro remains firmly committed to the disastrous business-demonizing and inflation-boosting policies of his predecessor, Hugo Chavez. Does the Pope really believe that Venezuela is the model for an alternative to capitalism?

Is God green?

8 January 2015

A long time ago, the British satirical magazine *Private Eye* would occasionally append a humorous phonograph record. One such had a track that started something like "And now, The Pope speaks out on The Pill." There followed the voice of one of Dr. Who's Daleks declaring "I-am-the-Pope. You-will-obey."

A lot has happened to the Catholic Church since then, although not in its views towards contraception. In the wake of horrendous sexual scandals and a continued decline in membership, the Church has turned to an Argentinean "progressive," Pope Francis. He does not have very progressive views on contraception, abortion, or gender bias, but he is onside with homosexuality. More important, he will soon deliver an encyclical on the progressive issue of our age: projected catastrophic man-made climate change.

The timing of the encyclical is hardly random. It is obviously designed to call upon Catholics to pressure their governments to "take action" at the UN's 21st Conference of the Parties, COP 21, in Paris later this year. Obviously, the Pope will not be able to claim to speak *ex cathedra* – that is, with divine authority – on climate science, although most alarmists will regard that as a shame. Some have suggested that he is "pro-science" because he has come to terms with the Big Bang theory and evolution (sort of), but unfortunately Francis has also confirmed himself to be severely economically challenged, a defining characteristic of progressivism.

The contents of the encyclical were adumbrated in a recent joint statement from the Pontifical Academy of Sciences and the Pontifical Academy of Social Science. One had only to look at some of the signatories to know what its conclusions would be. They included Jeffrey Sachs, the UN development guru renowned for orchestrating development disasters; Naomi Oreskes, who is famous for a mendacious study denying the existence of scientifically-qualified climate skepticism; and Sir Martin Rees, a former president of the Royal Society who not only strongly supported the conclusions of the egregiously biased Stern Review, but also led a campaign against ExxonMobil.

The statement reads like any UN document, full of condemnation of the capitalist system, and pointing to a "better world" brought about by more global "cooperation" and "participatory democracy" (that is, democracy in which those who don't think the right way are not allowed to participate).

In practicality it ranks with hoping for another miracle of loaves and fishes. It aims not merely at stabilizing the climate but "giving energy access to all." It ritually conflates inequality with inequity. It calls for a vague but insidious "appropriate and sustainable organization of production and a fair distribution of its fruits." It castigates market forces as "bereft of ethics." It ritually criticizes the shortcomings of Gross Domestic Product. It speaks as if those poor people made sick by indoor fires are the result of globalization rather than of its absence. It wails about food insecurity without mentioning the role of subsidized biofuels – a key climate policy – in creating it. It calls for "universal access to public services" (a policy that should be of some interest to those who will be forced to pay for such access), and for "ethical finance reform," and throws in opposition to forced labour and sexual exploitation, as if anybody supports them.

"We need, above all," it concludes, "to change our convictions and attitudes, and combat the globalization of indifference with its culture of waste and idolatry of money." The New Socialist Man will become the New Vatican Man.

Some see this initiative as an "interfaith issue" that will bring all religions together. The CBC's *The Current* earlier this week had a segment that sounded like the introduction to a joke. It featured a Catholic ecological theologian, a green Muslim, a desperately-keen-to-be-with-it evangelical, and a clip from a rabbi. Host Anna Maria Tremonti noted that the Dalai Lama had signed onto 350 parts per million (of carbon dioxide in the atmosphere) in 2008. The theologian declared, astonishingly, that climate had not been a moral issue to date. In fact, it has been nothing but. The green Muslim seemed to look to climate to turn Muslims away from the lures of wicked materialism.

One might forgive the Pope his good intentions if his approach to solving possibly non-existent problems didn't threaten – indeed guarantee – to create some very real ones. What the poor need is more capitalist investment and fossil-fuelled growth, not more moral posturing and destructive aid, especially of the green variety. Meanwhile the Pope's involvement in such a flagrantly political issue is likely – particularly given the inevitable failure awaiting COP 21 in Paris – to further roil and divide an already tottering institution, not make it seem more "relevant."

Obedience to the Pope on contraception remains a controversial moral issue. Obedience on his climate agenda would be outright immoral.

The Pope's Eco-mmunist Manifesto
19 June 2015

Apart from the religious references, Pope Francis's climate encyclical, *Laudato Si' (Praise Be)*, could have come from any branch of the UN, any environmental NGO, or the World Economic Forum. This is hardly surprising since they all promote Global Salvationism, which is based on projections of doom to be countered by morally-charged, UN-centric, globally-governed sustainable development and corporate social responsibility. The one non-religious reference that receives laudations is the *Earth Charter*, a bogus consultative document dreamed up by Canadian eco-meister Maurice Strong and former Soviet supremo Mikhail Gorbachev. According to the encyclical, "the *Earth Charter* asked us to leave behind a period of self-destruction and make a new start, but we have not as yet developed a universal awareness needed to achieve this."

We might note that the universal awareness of Strong and Gorbachev has left a trail of policy disaster in its wake.

The Pope appears to be blinded by a moral vision that he shares not just with Strong and Gorbachev but with Naomi Klein, Al Gore and David Suzuki: capitalism is evil, is destroying the earth, and involves oppression of the poor and a zero-sum struggle for resources that promotes war.

Laudato Si' not only allies the Church to UN master plans, it wallows in Gaian mysticism, and promotes policies that would damage the very people whom Francis claims are his priority: the poor.

Apart from a general condemnation of free markets, property rights and fossil-fuelled growth, Francis suggests that unreliable and expensive renewable energy be forced on the wretched of the earth, albeit with the guilty rich footing the bill. Does he want to keep the poor "always with us" because they are his main constituency? He seems far more concerned with afflicting the comfortable than comforting the afflicted.

Ultimately, it seems, Pope Francis doesn't want to save the poor from bad weather; he wants to save them from Walmart. His most bizarre example of a runaway technology driven by market madness is…air conditioning.

Meanwhile, unsupervised corporate social responsibility does not fare so well. "If in a given region, the state does not carry out its responsibilities," declares *Laudato Si'*, "some business groups can come forward in the guise of benefactors, wield real power, and consider themselves exempt from certain rules, to the point of tolerating different forms of organized crime, human trafficking, the drug trade and violence, all of which become very difficult to eradicate."

That's some pretty bad business. No examples are cited.

The Encyclical demonizes wicked, heartless and short-sighted straw men. This unnamed "they" are proponents of "throwaway culture" and "compulsive consumerism," of "rampant individualism" and the "self-centred culture of instant gratification." They claim "an unlimited right to trample his creation underfoot." They regard "other living beings as mere objects subjected to arbitrary human domination." They view nature "solely as a source of profit and gain." They believe that "maximizing profits is enough."

So, as Lenin asked, what is to be done? The setting up of a Green Comintern ruled by positive adjectives. "What is needed," declares the Encyclical, "is a politics which is far-sighted and capable of a new, integral and interdisciplinary approach to handling the different aspects of the crisis."

That is, a politics of panoptic wisdom and virtue that has never, ever been seen anywhere on the face of the earth. This new and unprecedented political power will somehow be devoid of the career interests that pervade lesser power structures, such as, say, the Vatican. Still, a more totalitarian global approach is necessary because silly old public opinion resists measures that restrict consumption, while national governments don't want to discourage foreign investment. So, "Society, through non-governmental organizations and intermediate groups, must put pressure on governments to develop more rigorous regulations, procedures and controls." NGOs must also control corporations via product boycotts.

Agreeing with his retired predecessor, Benedict XVI, Francis concludes that "there is urgent need of a true world political authority."

But doesn't it seem rather bizarre to be castigating the "technocratic paradigm" when that is the UN's guiding principle? Also, condemning the "cult of unlimited human power" sits a little uneasily with supporting Strongian plans to control everything, including the global climate.

One thing is for sure: the higher eco-morality needs teeth. "Because the stakes are so high, we need institutions empowered to impose penalties for damage inflicted on the environment." Those so empowered will apparently avoid the pitfalls of "earthly power" because of their qualities of "self control."

The actual shape of this Brave New Papal World is – as ever – a bit vague. The specific example of self-sufficient renewable local energy co-operatives offers thin policy gruel (although St. Naomi would approve), as does the promotion of locavorism against evil agribusiness. The eco-fiscal crowd will be disappointed if they were looking for specific backing for their emission-control plans. The Pope rejects cap-and-trade out of hand as speculation, putting Quebec and Ontario in the sin bin. He makes no mention of carbon taxes. It may be that the Ecofiscaliens' plans are not draconian enough for the Pope, who wants nothing less than a root and branch makeover of human nature. Echoing every doomster doorstop since *The Limits to Growth*, the encyclical declares a radical change in lifestyles essential.

The encyclical was immediately greeted with Hallelujahs by the global bureaucrats whose kingdom it heralds. According to UN climate high priestess Christiana Figueres, "This clarion call should guide the world towards a strong and durable universal climate agreement in Paris at the end of this year. Coupled with the economic imperative, the moral imperative leaves no doubt that we must act on climate change now."

World Bank president Jim Yong Kim – who runs an institution charged with preventing fossil-fuelled development for the poor – claimed "today's release...should serve as a stark reminder to all of us on the intrinsic link between climate change and poverty."

Or should that be the intrinsic link between climate change and the relentless search to justify and enhance bureaucratic power, both religious and secular?

Stern warning

Attack of the kiwifruit moralists
1 November 2006

Stern warning!
16 February 2007

The Dark Lord
2 May 2009

Attack of the kiwifruit moralists

1 November 2006

Who would have thought that eating kiwifruit would become a moral issue? This week, the UK's review of the alleged economic consequences of climate change, chaired by Sir Nicholas Stern, suggested that new taxes be introduced to discourage the long-haul import of exotic fruits. Public Enemy *Numero Uno* was identified as the New Zealand kiwifruit. Former British Cabinet minister Stephen Byers claimed that every kilogram of kiwifruit flown into Britain was responsible for adding five kilograms of carbon to the atmosphere (presumably the same equation applies to every kilo of UN bureaucrat, the only difference being that people willingly pay for kiwifruit).

New Zealand politicians pointed out that most fruit moves by boat. Still, moving fruit halfway round the world may seem like a crazy idea, except, that is, if you are actually concerned with serving consumers and economizing on energy and resources. Such a perspective is morally unacceptable to radical environmentalists. Economic calculations are now to be thrown out of the window because of the alleged giant "market failure" represented by global warming. The risk is so great that assured government failure is a preferable alternative.

Leading edge alarmists have been pointing the finger at long-distance fruit for some while. In his hysterical but influential book, *The Ecology of Commerce*, Paul Hawken wrote, "[W]e should be prepared to bid farewell to energy- and resource-consumptive luxuries such as Chilean strawberries and nectarines flown in daily during New York winters."

There was a certain irony in the fact that less than 48 hours before the release of the Stern Review, New Zealand Prime Minister Helen Clark had been bloviating that her country might become the world's first "sustainable economy." She soon found herself defending long-distance fruit exports instead.

Meanwhile, it also happened that British Trade Minister Ian McCartney was in New Zealand this week. This was how he allayed the fears of New Zealand fruit growers: "This is not about people in Britain not eating kiwifruit, this is about working…to prevent Pacific nations disappearing and the total devastation and dislocation of society."

Which I guess does make it about kiwifruit, and every other commodity and product on Earth. If it has to be extracted, or manufactured, or grown, or picked, or processed, or transported, it's a moral problem. What does the consumer society matter in the face of Pacific islands sinking amid the prospect of "total devastation and dislocation?"

Stern warning

16 February 2007

If a student of mine were to hand in this report as a master's thesis, perhaps if I were in a good mood I would give him a 'D' for diligence; but more likely I would give him an 'F' for fail."

This from Prof. Richard Tol of Carnegie Mellon University, one of the world's leading environmental economists. He is referring to the Stern Review, the report produced last October by British government economist Sir Nicholas Stern.

Prof. Tol's words might be borne in mind by any members of the media who turn up this coming Monday for a "briefing" with Sir Nicholas in Toronto. That is, if they fail to spot the implications for Sir Nicholas's objectivity of the fact that he will be sharing a platform with radical environmentalist David Suzuki.

The Suzuki Foundation has been an enthusiastic promoter of Sir Nicholas and his review. Dale Marshall, a Suzuki "policy analyst," has praised Sir Nicholas as "one of the world's most respected economists." Marshall went on to claim "Global warming has nothing to do with ideology or political affiliation. This is economics."

In fact, according to many critics, including Prof. Tol, the Stern Review is terrible economics, and blatantly skewed for ideological

purposes. That starts with the fact that it was commissioned by the
uk's Chancellor of the Exchequer, Gordon Brown, in response to a
scathing review of uk climate policy by the House of Lords.

The review – whose main text runs to 550 pages – was accompanied by a government press release that cut straight to its overcooked
conclusions: "[T]he review calculates that the dangers of unabated
climate change would be the equivalent of at least 5% of [global] GDP
each year." However, the dangers "could be equivalent to 20% of GDP
or more." The costs of avoiding the worst impacts, according to the
press release, could be "limited to around 1% of global GDP each year."

Spend 1% of global output to save between 5% and 20% of global
output? Surely a no brainer, especially if you wanted to address,
according to Sir Nicholas, "the greatest market failure the world has
seen." How big a failure? Greater than the two world wars and the
Great Depression put together.

Few among credulous reporters thought to ask whether a return
on climate-change investment of somewhere between 500% and
2,000% annually didn't look like a suspiciously good deal. Instead,
Sir Nicholas was treated by much of the mainstream media with reverence. A lighter-than-air editorial in *The Globe and Mail* declared
that Sir Nicholas "is not one of those outspoken academics who have
political axes to grind or who love tilting at windmills...[He] is a
long-time public servant who was once asked by his bosses whether
a controversial tax proposal made political sense. He is said to have
replied that it was not his responsibility to deal with politics, but only
with economics."

Yes Minister.

In fact, as economists who looked at the review soon pointed out,
it was thoroughly political. Its most flagrant skewing was to use an
artificially low discount rate that brought the cost of vague horrors
from more than a century hence right to our present-day front door.
It also used a "social cost" of carbon dioxide emissions of US $85 a
ton. This compared with the figure of US $2.50 calculated by Yale's
Richard Nordhaus, perhaps the best-regarded climate economist
in the world (whom Sir Nicholas claimed as a kindred spirit). The
review also assumed that the world would be pumping out carbon

dioxide from fossil fuels well into the 22nd century, and thus implied that there would be no major technological breakthroughs.

The most comprehensive critique of the Stern review appeared in an article by a group of climate scientists and economists in the journal *World Economics*. The authors included MIT Professor of Climate Sciences Richard Lindzen, Ian Castles, a former head of the Australian Bureau of Statistics, David Henderson, former chief economist at the OECD, and the University of Guelph's Ross McKitrick, co-debunker of the IPCC's "hockey stick" graph. Their analysis found the Stern review "doubly deficient." The scientific section of the critique concluded that "the review's analysis of the prospective impacts of possible global warming was consistently biased and selective – and heavily tilted towards unwarranted alarm." Apart from the critical issue of using a low discount rate, it noted that the review failed to take account of obvious precautions or adaptations. Bjorn Lomborg, author of *The Skeptical Environmentalist,* pointed out that the review assumed that people would simply let rising waters slowly lap around their ankles without doing anything about it.

Harvard Professor of Economics Martin Wietzman, in a review for the *Journal of Economic Literature*, concluded, again, that the Stern review was "a political document" that was more about "gut instincts" and "uncertain rare disasters" than about economic analysis. While Prof. Weitzman acknowledged that the review might be attempting to address a real but politically unpalatable problem, he too concluded that Stern "predetermines the outcomes in favour of strong immediate action."

An investigative report by BBC Radio concluded, yet again, that the review overestimated the risks of severe climate change and underestimated the cost of action. Prof. Tol, the man who gave Stern an "F," was quoted as saying that the report contained "a whole range of basic economics mistakes…Stern consistently picks the most pessimistic for every choice that one can make. He overestimates through cherry picking, he double-counts particularly the risks and he underestimates what development and adaptation will do to impacts."

Yale economist Robert Mendelsohn pointed out that the review's estimated costs of mitigation of 1% of GDP annually were way too low. "We will," he said, "have to sacrifice a great deal to cut emissions dramatically."

Significantly, the *World Economics* analysis criticized Stern for relying almost exclusively "on a small number of people and organizations that have a long history of unbalanced alarmism on the global-warming issue." That would explain why he is due to appear this Monday on a platform with David Suzuki.

The Dark Lord

2 May 2009

It was once said of Maurice Strong – the Canadian envirocrat at the root of the current climate change policy mess – that you wouldn't pick him out of a crowd of two. If the other person were Nicholas Stern, Chairman Mo might have a shot.

Lord Stern, who was at the Economic Club of Toronto yesterday peddling his new book, *The Global Deal*, has other things in common with Strong besides bureaucratic blandness. These include apocalyptic environmental visions, a professed burning desire to help developing countries, preferably by bashing the rich ones, a belief that those with alternative views should be silenced, and a quasi-religious faith in big – and I mean really big – government.

Stern came to international prominence in 2006 after writing a blatantly biased review for the British government on the economics of climate change. For his political services he was elevated to the House of Lords. His new tome is based on the review.

The Global Deal he has in mind, and which he hopes will be forthcoming at the grand climate conference in Copenhagen in December, is as simple as it is implausible. Rich countries must agree to slash their greenhouse gas emissions by 80% below 1990 levels by 2050 (Canada is currently around 27% above the 1990 level). How? Simple: by switching to a bureaucratically engineered "low-carbon economy."

The diminutive Lord Stern spent many years as chief economist at the World Bank, an organization that has devoted six decades to retarding Third World development. His burning egalitarianism slipped its leash only once yesterday, when he asked by what right anybody could dare to emit more than her personal global "share" of two tons of carbon dioxide come 2050 (present developed countries' emissions range between 10 and 20 tons per capita).

What Lord Stern essentially presages therefore is the end of wealth and freedom, although he suggested yesterday that there would be no "powerful carbon policemen." Don't bet on it. There will certainly be a lot of powerful carbon bureaucrats.

His lordship believes that those who question the Al Gore school of climate science are like those who denied the association between HIV and AIDS, or smoking and cancer. Anthropogenic global warming, he asserts, is not a theory but a fact, and represents "the greatest market failure the world has ever seen," even though we haven't actually seen it.

Lord Stern's most contentious "truth" is that we can control the weather "at modest cost." He asserts in his book that "The arguments offered by those who would deny the case for strong and timely action are a tissue of confusions about both the science and the economics." Thus there is no need to respond, or even listen, to them, which is a convenient policy position indeed.

The Stern review was eviscerated by numerous well-credentialed critics. How does Lord Stern deal with such criticism? By ignoring it and writing off critics as morally defective and/or politically motivated. "[M]ost of them," he writes in his new book, "back away from, suppress or trivialize the basic ethical issues."

Lord Stern has been treated with kid gloves by the media, although even the terminally leftist *Guardian* is now having doubts, noting that his lordship's claims to outspokenness seem to stop at the hypocritical policies of the British government.

When he last came to Canada, *The Globe and Mail* grovelled that Stern was "not one of those outspoken academics who have political axes to grind or who love tilting at windmills." In fact, Stern worships windmills, and regards those who don't as infidels.

Macro Mark Carney

Mr Carney channels Mr Micawber
19 December 2008

Zamboni driver
15 December 2010

Carney passes the buck
14 December 2011

Mark Carney's fundamentalist regulation
6 June 2014

Mark Carney's threat of 'sustainable finance'
16 April 2019

Mark Carney channels Mr. Micawber

19 December 2008

This has been a week for Dickensian revisionism. Doctors writing in the *British Medical Journal* have concluded that – contrary to the fictional diet put forth in *Oliver Twist* – Victorian orphans were relatively well fed. Of greater potential significance, Mark Carney, Governor of the Bank of Canada, is attempting to rehabilitate *David Copperfield's* Mr. Micawber as a model not of financial fecklessness but of "macroprudence." Mr. Micawber, you see, would never have been caught falling into the trap of the Keynesian "paradox of thrift," threatening the economy by the pernicious habit of putting aside money for the proverbial rainy day.

Although Carney didn't actually mention Mr. Micawber (who was based on Dickens' father), his warning against the paradox of thrift this week pointed to a further straw in dangerous policy winds.

Speaking on Wednesday in Toronto, Carney suggested a more prominent advocacy role for the bank; that is, himself. What he appears to be advocating is a brand of populist Keynesianism that suggests that banks are "hoarding" money, combined with the much less saleable notion that individuals are doing damage by being similarly prudent.

Carney acknowledged the abject failure of central banks, ministries of finance and international financial institutions in predicting current problems, but claimed that valuable lessons had been learned. We have, he said, to avoid regulating for past rather than future problems. We must not build a regulatory "Maginot line," that famously-useless ribbon of defensive concrete around which the Germans waltzed into France in the Second World War. Still, we might remember that the structure was the very model of Keynesian infrastructure "stimulus."

"Rather," said Carney, "we must develop early-warning systems with precision and with teeth."

So much better than imprecise gummy gnawing.

"Internationally," declared Carney, "both the Financial Stability Forum (FSF) and the International Monetary Fund (IMF) must become more effective." How? By being more macroprudent. Which means? "Put simply," said Carney, "a macroprudential approach focuses on the forest, not the trees."

Certainly, the FSF and the IMF conspicuously failed to see the current financial Birnam Wood creeping up on them. But could it be that the forest-not-the-trees approach is actually a big part of the problem? Could the very Keynesian conceit that policy wonks can work with stratospheric "aggregates" and soar above those messy individuals and companies who actually create wealth be a dangerous delusion? Certainly economic history suggests so.

Keynes was brilliant at coming up with easily-grasped concepts that appeared to demonstrate that markets were prone to fail, and proposing that what was needed was a policy "toolbox" to stimulate "aggregate demand," avoid the "liquidity trap" and juice the "multiplier." In fact, this toolbox turned out to be an improvised explosive device that went off in the 1970s. Although government expenditure is necessary for defence, justice and certain infrastructure, it can never be a substitute for private activity, not least because it is guided by politicians whose concern is perpetually short-term and vote-oriented.

Carney uses the "paradox of thrift" as an example of the kind of allegedly short-sighted action against which the macroprudent have to be perpetually on guard. Under this view, as noted, Mr. Micawber was a model, and the grasshopper was more prudent than the ant. Carney has "successful" policy instruments in hand. We know they are successful because that's what he calls them. It is apparently "well-known" that the paradox of thrift can be addressed by "timely and properly calibrated monetary and fiscal policy." Sure. But what about the untimely and improperly calibrated versions?

Carney, typically, wants "more tools." Monetary policy, he admits, is a "blunt instrument," presumably because it has been unsuccessful in promoting imprudent lending and borrowing. So his new tool is…"advocacy!" Carney plans to talk sense into fellow bureaucrats and politicians, and tell the private sector where it's going wrong. The Bank wants to identify stresses so it can change "behaviours, conventions and even regulations."

Its latest is a Financial Stress Indicator, which "is now showing record levels of stress."

We would never have guessed.

Carney wants to have not just a real-time indicator, but a forecasting tool, a bit like those wooden balls that identified future murderers in the Tom Cruise movie *Minority Report*. This will presumably spot upcoming "thriftcrime."

Zamboni driver

15 December 2010

On Monday, Bank of Canada Governor Mark Carney issued another "stern warning" about record levels of household debt, thus completely reversing his position of two years ago, when he was complaining about culpable prudence.

But is it not the Bank's artificially low rates that are behind both the extent of the borrowing and the continued elevation of house prices, which in turn have encouraged cranking up home equity lines of credit?

Canada's average household debt levels relative to disposable income in the third quarter, at 148.1%, surpassed those of the US. This is not a problem *per se*. The problem is the possibility of a further economic downturn that takes jobs and house prices with it, and leaves debt levels unsustainable when interest rates rise, as Carney is furiously signalling they will.

"Cheap money is not a long-term growth strategy," warned Carney during a speech in Toronto on Monday. But where did this cheap money originate? From what I can remember of Economics 101, cheapness is a signal to purchasers to buy, and that includes buying money.

Carney did a nice job on Monday of trying to slough off the blame. "The responsibility," he said, "obviously starts with the individual, it extends to the financial institutions, and then we as policymakers need to ensure that a suite of policies are appropriate to ensure sustainable growth."

That has it totally upside down. What actually happens is that government policy interferes with markets and imposes regulations that control the behaviour of the financial institutions, which in turn influence the conditions under which borrowers act.

Adam Smith famously pointed out that governments never need concern themselves with private borrowing. It is public debt that is always the danger. Meanwhile, with all due respect to Carney, while he likes to talk as if he is an aspiring coach of Economic Team Canada, his actual job equates neither to coaching nor managing, much less dashing down the ice scoring goals. Although the economy is not a game of hockey, if it were, Carney would be the Zamboni driver. His official job of checking inflation equates to keeping the ice flat so the real economic "players" can do their productive thing.

Carney passes the buck
14 December 2011

Bank of Canada Governor Mark Carney, fresh from his elevation to the command of the G20's Financial Stability Board, delivered an address on Monday that superficially suggested that he had come somewhat closer to earth from Cloudmacroland. Cloudmacroland, for the uninitiated, is a region just high enough in the policy sky that one can see forests from it, but not trees. Its denizens' wonky perspective is that to grow a forest involves not primarily the planting of seeds but the creation of a Boreal Stability Board.

On Monday, Carney suggested that it was time to give forestry companies – indeed the entire private sector – a chance at promoting growth. But this was perhaps less a reluctant recognition of where jobs actually come from than an example of passing the buck. Sorry, I mean "baton."

The speech, delivered to a joint meeting of the Empire Club of Toronto and the Canadian Club of Toronto, was entitled *Growth in the Age of Deleveraging*, which is to say keeping your business expanding when your customers – especially governments and the private households that government policies have encouraged to load up with debt – are trying to pay down their burdens.

Carney gave a masterful summary of the current global crisis on Monday, although one couldn't help feeling he was being a little harsh on markets and a little too forgiving of the culpability of government policies. He suggested that households got into trouble in the us and uk not because of borrowing against government-promoted housing bubbles, but because they were on some mystical consumptionist treadmill.

He did not try to apply any lipstick to the eurozone pig, but claimed that the us policy response to the subprime crisis had been a "success," at least by the standards of the Great Depression. However, that assumes that the us policy response hasn't set in train another Great Depression somewhere down the line. He didn't even countenance how a less regulated, less bailout-friendly, less debt-heavy stimulative policy might have been more successful, certainly in the long run.

Three years ago, just after the us banking crisis hit (and when all those snooty European socialists were condemning Anglo-Saxon capitalist "greed"), Carney, as a good Keynesian, was warning against the "paradox of thrift," the notion that saving was potentially dangerous and that spending was good. Canadian consumers didn't so much take his advice as rationally pursue the signals that he delivered via artificially low interest rates, which were in turn dictated by the artificial rates of our southern neighbour.

Unlike the us, however, those low interest rates have not only kept Canadian real estate bubbling, they have also inclined homeowners to continue to take advantage of their home equity lines of credit. Canadian household borrowing, noted Carney, has actually gone up and is now higher than in either the us or the uk.

Carney has for some time been signalling – with his words rather than his policies – that this is a very bad idea. He was signalling a bit less vigorously on Monday, although he still implied that if individuals were overborrowing, it wasn't his fault. Nevertheless, the overborrowing has to stop. He really means it.

Unfortunately, bringing down household debt and government deficits will leave a demand "gap" that has to be filled, mixed metaphorically, by the passing of that baton. According to Carney, the "most palatable strategy to reduce debt is to increase growth." So it's over to you, Canadian Businessperson, for a bit of "rebalancing," which is yet another euphemism for passing the buck.

Carney claimed that Canadian businesses "panicked" after the initial meltdown at the end of 2008, exercising culpable prudence and forgetting the paradox of thrift. Now, according to the Governor, they are letting Canada down again. They need to be more aggressive in investing to increase productivity, and stop being "underexposed to fast-growing emerging markets."

"What we really do want to avoid is having another sudden stop on investment in this country because it's 'all too difficult,'" Carney declared at a press conference after his speech. "Well, it's actually not that difficult; we're not as productive, we're not as exposed to bigger markets."

See? Business looks easy when you inhabit the policy clouds. Carney's logic is certainly impregnable, even tautological: "A virtuous circle of increased investment and increased productivity would increase the debt-carrying capacity of all, through higher wages, greater profits and higher government revenues."

If only businesses thought in such magnificently facile macro terms. Sadly, they tend to concentrate – in their grubby micro-blinkerdom – on such mundane realities as actually making and marketing specific products and services to actual customers, managing supply chains, meeting wage and tax bills, and staying solvent.

I scanned Carney's speech for an example of a particular piece of productivity-enhancing equipment that a named manufacturer might be guilty of having failed to purchase, or a specific example of a business opportunity in a particular emerging nation, but could find none. I assume that Carney neglected to give such examples because he did not want to embarrass any dimwitted manager or entrepreneur, or start any investment stampede to a surefire winner somewhere in Africa.

I suppose it's also possible that he didn't provide examples because he didn't have any, but then up there in Cloudmacroland you don't have to sweat the small stuff.

Mark Carney's fundamentalist regulation
6 June 2014

Following last week's assault on "fundamentalist capitalism" by Canadian "rock star" Governor of the Bank of England Mark Carney, I thought I might get a quote from the Institute of Fundamentalist Capitalism, but guess what: there isn't one.

Carney was hypocritically flailing away at a straw man. Still, his claims about capitalist True Believers running amok fits nicely into his own aspirations as a Solomon-like purveyor of panoptic macroprudence who can regulate "the system" back to virtue.

Carney wittered on last week about how fundamentalist capitalism was increasing inequality and hurting the poor, but it is fundamentalist regulation, in particular regarding the greatest bureaucratic pretension ever – controlling the weather – that is really hitting the poorest throughout the world.

Carney's attack is nothing less than outrageous when set against the broader collapse of green industrial strategies, massive government debt, the inevitable failure of Keynesian "stimulus" (a major contributor to the debt), and the unsustainability of welfare entitlements.

It is pretty much a rule that anybody who attaches a qualifier to the word "capitalism" is seeking to undermine it, either because they do not understand it, or because they realize that free markets are fatal to their own pretensions to power and influence. No surprise, then, that Carney's comments came during a convocation of the left-liberal elite at a London meeting titled "Inclusive Capitalism."

Carney may be among the most overrated men in recent history. It's not that he lacks raw intelligence. It's that the feats attributed to him – primarily, as Governor of the Bank of Canada, to have "steered" the Canadian economy through the post-2008 recession – are within the capacity of no man. He is a classic example of Adam Smith's "Man of System," who regards economic actors as so many chess pieces, only in his case not just to be moved against their will, but lectured.

Carney's input involved lowering rates and keeping them low, a policy which has arguably contributed to an asset bubble, particularly in Canadian housing. His name has been indelibly attached to "forward guidance," which declares essentially that, as a Central Bank Governor, you will lash yourself to the mast and dictate a firm course. This looks great until you suddenly need to change course.

Carney's halo was always bound to slip, and it has done so over his past year at the Bank of England. He lashed himself to the commitment that he wouldn't raise interest rates until unemployment fell to 7%, but had to be cut loose when that target was reached much sooner than anticipated. He's still wrestling with the pretence that he's "forward guiding" the market, but the booming UK economy is inevitably confirming that the economic ship likes to set its own course.

Carney's speech last week amounts to hubris on stilts, the typical rationalizations of a global bureaucratic class that appears entirely incapable of grasping the flaws in its self-serving perspective.

An explanation for this dangerous state of mind is contained in a must-read paper – *Are Regulators Rational?* – by academic Slavisa Tasic. Tasic concludes that bureaucrats suffer from "illusions of competence" and are entirely blind to the power and subtlety of markets. Then again, while potentially disastrous for economies and people, their delusions tend to be highly personally rewarding.

Mark Carney's threat of 'sustainable finance'
16 April 2019

"Sustainable" is a weasel word that sounds good but threatens both freedom and prosperity. It has recently cropped up in the promotion by UN-centric cabals of "sustainable finance."

Never heard of the concept? Well consider the following:

It is 2028. We have come a long way since "the dark years preceding the grand transition," when the global financial system had been pushing the world towards the climate precipice by investing in fossil fuels. The Fundamental Principles of Sustainable Finance were finally adopted at the UN Summit on Global Financial Governance in 2025. Despite "some last resistance from a few jurisdictions," financial regulators and standard setters now acknowledge that "the purpose of the finance system is to serve the needs of sustainable development."

A worldwide "clean air" campaign has led to the mass deployment of electric vehicles financed by "blockchain-assured green bonds." Unspecified climate problems have led to the downgrade of an unnamed sovereign bond, in the wake of which governments, investors and credit rating agencies have introduced a trillion dollar programme "that invested upfront in real resilience." Carbon-intensive companies have been sued into submission by a "seemingly endless series of legal cases." Stocks and bonds that don't meet UN standards have been dismissed from stock indices, although this reportedly led to a "transition tantrum." Meanwhile "rapid dietary change" has resulted in the stranding of fishing and agriculture assets. There are now Nobel Prizes in sustainable economics. Green infrastructure is being go-fund-me'd. Sustainable finance rules.

The above Orwellian scenario comes from a 2017 report, *Making Waves*, by the United Nations Environment Program. Normal people might be inclined – even if they were aware of it – to write it off as the autocratic musings of far-left global governors, but sustainable finance has been embraced by many countries, and is being promoted by a powerful group of regulators, billionaires, capitalist foundations and environmental non-governmental organizations, ENGOS. Its point man is Mark Carney, Governor of the Bank of England, head of the Financial Stability Board, and former Governor of the Bank of Canada. Its most prominent billionaire supporter is media mogul Michael Bloomberg.

Sustainable finance is a key weapon in the supposedly essential and inevitable "transition to a low-carbon economy." As such, it represents a particular threat to Canada, where demonization of "dirty" oil has already resulted in pipeline delays and capital flight. Its suite of tactics include "voluntary" corporate disclosure to ENGO overseers, along with show-trial like confessions of what worst-case weather scenarios might look like. This is linked to ENGO-masterminded campaigns of pressure on investors to divest fossil fuel assets. Then come ENGO-initiated climate lawsuits, along with the bullying or co-opting of regulators.

However, the inconvenient truth for the shock troops of climate finance is that if climate risks were quantifiable, and likely to have a material impact any time in the foreseeable future, they would already be incorporated into financial reporting. Also, if there were profits to be made in renewable energy and climate-resilient infrastructure, investors would not need to be "crowded in" by scare tactics.

Sustainable finance, like all parts of the UN global governance agenda, has spawned a plethora of institutions, processes, studies, initiatives and funding mechanisms, most of which tend to operate out of the public view. However, shortly before the Paris climate meeting in 2015, Carney gave a major speech at the insurance market Lloyd's of London. Entitled "The tragedy of the horizon," its theme was that the financial sector was woefully short-sighted when it came to climate threats. Carney chose the insurance industry for his address both because it appears most at risk from grisly projections of natural disaster, and because insurers are also major investors. He attempted to scare them by projecting that fossil fuel reserves might have to be "stranded" to save the world. The relevant legislation might not yet exist, but investors should get out while the going was good.

Carney produced a raft of scary and misleading statistics, including those for rising insurance claims from extreme weather events.

No less a financial authority than Warren Buffett has rejected such claims, pointing out that rising losses are due not primarily to worse weather, but to more valuable property being built in areas prone to natural disasters.

Nevertheless, claimed Carney, much worse was to come, so why wasn't enough being done? The answer was short-sighted greed, creating a situation analogous to the "tragedy of the commons," where un-priced collectively consumed resources are depleted to the point of exhaustion. Climate disaster was not only beyond the time horizon of conventional financial calculation, it was beyond the horizon of democratic political concern, and even the official mandates of those charged with applying macroprudential regulatory wisdom, such as Carney himself.

However, bloviated Carney, "Forward-looking regulators consider not just the here and now, but emerging vulnerabilities and their impact on business models." Thus he called for global management of the world's "carbon budget." He even threatened the insurers with nationalization.

Carney declared that "the risks will only increase as the science and evidence of climate change hardens." But how could he possibly know that? What if the science and evidence weakens (as it in fact has been doing)?

Carney's bottom line was that "green" finance "could not conceivably remain a niche interest." The threat of potential destabilization was too great. The role of the far-seeing regulatory elite was to develop "the frameworks that help the market adjust efficiently." More had to be done "to develop consistent, comparable, reliable and clear disclosure around the carbon intensity of different assets," on the basis that "that which can be measured can be managed."

Carney's perspective was facile, tendentious and dangerous. While carbon emissions might be meticulously calculated, nobody could specify what the impacts of vague "climate change" might be on particular companies, beyond Biblical laundry lists of floods, droughts, forest fires and hurricanes.

The very real immediate financial threat is not from climate change but from climate change policy. If anything threatens uncertainty, instability and wealth destruction, it is the very regulatory arm-twisting that Carney is proposing.

Carney confirmed that the carbon disclosure shakedown was already well underway. He cited the Carbon Disclosure Project, the NGO which took carbon confession from 5000 companies and "made it available" to "investment managers responsible for over $90 trillion of assets." In fact, he noted, there were almost 400 such disclosure "initiatives" with no common standards. Thus Carney suggested a task force "to design and deliver a voluntary standard for disclosure by those companies that produce or emit carbon."

Myriad ENGOs had softened up the corporate sector. Now it was time to formalize global arrangements. Not only would companies have to confess to carbon crime, but also reveal detailed plans of their "transition to the net-zero world of the future." There would even be carbon "stress tests." Carney's regulatory pretension almost leapt through the roof when he suggested that such stress testing could act as a "time machine, shining a light not just on today's risks, but on those that may otherwise lurk in the darkness for years to come."

Two months later, Carney announced the Task Force on Climate-Related Financial Disclosures, TCFD, chaired by Michael Bloomberg. Bloomberg is part of what the *Wall Street Journal* has dubbed a "Climate Mafia." He had been mayor of New York during Superstorm Sandy in 2012, and had subsequently joined radical hedge-fund billionaire Tom Steyer and former Treasury Secretary Hank Paulson – the man who had deluged Wall Street with cash in the wake of the 2008 crisis – in the "Risky Business Project," which had produced a typically alarmist report. His Bloomberg Philanthropies are involved in "multiple climate efforts," including partnering with the Sierra Club in its Beyond Coal Campaign, and "supporting state efforts to transition to renewable energy sources." Bloomberg was also the UN Secretary-General's Special Envoy for Cities and Climate Change. As such, he played a key role in establishing networks of mayors who were committed to meeting "ambitious climate-related goals." The fruit of such initiatives in Canada might be seen in Vancouver's stout opposition to the TransMountain Pipeline, and in Montreal's rejection of the Energy East project.

The 31 members of the task force were hand-picked by Carney's Financial Stability Board; that is, by Carney, and were all involved in green initiatives and investments. They included Al Gore's radical business partner, David Blood.

The TCFD delivered its report to the G20 Summit in Hamburg in July, 2017. Behind all the neat recommendations on climate governance, impacts and targets lay the monumental uncertainties of climate science and policy, but the report was sure of one thing: large investors should pressure the companies in which they invest to get with the program.

The Bloomberg report inevitably spawned scores of similar inquiries – including in Canada. In the next month or so, a Canadian federally-appointed "Expert Panel on Sustainable Finance" is due to deliver a final report. Set up by Ottawa early in 2018, last fall the panel delivered an interim report that received virtually zero media coverage. The chairman of the panel is Tiff Macklem, Dean of the University of Toronto's Rotman School of Management and former number two to Carney at the Bank of Canada. Its other members are Andy Chisholm, a board member of the Royal Bank of Canada; Kim Thomassin of the Caisse de Dépôt et Placement du Québec; and Barbara Zvan, from the Ontario Teachers' Pension Plan.

When the panel was announced in April of 2018, it was sold as helping Canada tap into a "trillion-dollar opportunity from clean growth and climate action," and creating "good jobs for Canada's middle class." Nothing was said about killing the fossil fuel industry.

According to the government's press release, the Expert Panel would build on the insights of Bloomberg's task force, which was "recognized worldwide for its ground-breaking work to develop voluntary recommendations on climate-related information that companies can disclose to help investors, lenders, and others make sound financial decisions."

It might more accurately have been described as part of a plan to pressure companies and investors to make unsound decisions in support of a subversive global political agenda.

While Justin Trudeau's Liberals were keen to jump on the Carney/Bloomberg bandwagon, one complicating factor was that financial disclosure in Canada is a provincial responsibility. In fact, the Canadian Securities Administrators (CSA) – the council of the securities regulators of Canada's provinces and territories – had already held public consultations on carbon disclosure and published a report. That report pointed to carbon disclosure's key problem: assessing "materiality," which is generally "the determining factor in considering whether information must be disclosed to investors."

But how does one assess the materiality of a heavily politicized – and scientifically corrupted – theory that in fact doesn't forecast catastrophe for many decades, and even then does so in the most vague – if alarming – of terms? The CSA noted that some respondents had stated that disclosure was "driven by considerations other than investment." You bet.

On October 25, 2018, the Expert Panel delivered its interim report. Perhaps its most stunning admission was that sustainable finance – which had been pushed by the UN for a quarter century – still lacked a definition. Moreover, the panel admitted that it found little enthusiasm for moving towards a "Paris-aligned future." One alleged reason was that investments such as Index-based funds merely entrenched the dreaded status quo. Another was that perceptions of materiality were "outdated." Thus Canada was "lagging." The panel pointed to the necessity of the "support ecosystem" of lawyers, accountants, auditors, and ratings agencies becoming appropriately "knowledgeable" about projected climate catastrophe. Perhaps mandatory training might be the answer. Perhaps the "voluntary" recommendations of the Bloomberg TCFD should be compulsory.

The report's implications were alarming. Currently it would be contrary to fiduciary responsibility to invest in dubious low-carbon transition schemes to serve political purposes, but what if fiduciaries were subject to prosecution for investing in fossil fuels?

In terms of new and exciting sustainable financial products, the report suggested that building retrofits might be securitized. Remember Collateralized Debt Obligations, CDOs, those murky instruments that were at the heart of the 2008 sub-prime crisis? The panel seemed to be suggesting Collateralized Sustainable Development Obligations – CSDOS! What could possibly go wrong?

As for sustainable infrastructure, there was already a Canadian Infrastructure Bank, but why stop there? More bureaucratic institutions needed to be set up. Private capital needed to be "crowded in." Meanwhile "Cleantech" was a "massive cross-cutting opportunity." Just forget Germany's disastrous *Energiewende*, or Ontario's Green Energy Act, or a thousand other climate-policy snafus. What was needed were more green banks, more green bonds, and more green procurement.

Then came the touchy bit: oil and gas. The panel noted that the industry faced "pressure from many fronts." These included access to capital (the cutting off of which was the main thrust of sustainable finance), "market access" (that is, not being able to build pipelines because of lawsuits and illegal action by ENGOs and their puppets), and divestment campaigns (which were again part of The Agenda).

In February of this year, the Canadian Association of Petroleum Producers (CAPP) responded to the interim report. It stressed all the sustainable and responsible things it was doing in the vain hope of fighting off its enemies. It noted that oil and gas were going to remain dominant as global energy sources, and that responsibly managed Canadian exports could replace more carbon-intensive coal. Material financial risks already had to be reported, while big companies already disclosed their emissions. CAPP stressed that its members were engaged in multiple reporting initiatives. The industry didn't need even more duplicative reporting. CAPP concluded that the Canadian financial sector was doing just fine, and would continue to serve its customers "without [more] government in the marketplace."

The good news from the Expert Panel's interim report was that investors, insurers and banks are refusing to be rushed into action on the basis of pressure from the UN/regulatory/billionaire/ENGO axis. Its final report is bound to suggest a raft of new institutions and initiatives, but the fundamental issue is whether Canadian companies and financial institutions should be aligning themselves with Mark Carney's sustainable finance agenda instead of exposing it as the subversive threat to wealth, jobs, and freedom – and indeed even the environment – that it is.

4

Justin Trudeau's Flying Liberal Circus

Justin Trudeau succeeded Stephen Harper as Prime Minister of Canada in 2015. Harper, a Conservative who had held office since 2006, was the focus of extraordinary vitriol. This was particularly inspired by his perceived apostasy on climate. By contrast, Trudeau was the very model of virtue-signalling climate obsession.

Crouching Tiger, Hidden Harper
23 November 2012

Justin's China syndrome
15 November 2013

Pierre's slush foundation
25 November 2014

The left's enemies list
19 August 2015

"Harperman"
2 September 2015

Justin Trudeau's Flying Paris Circus
21 October 2015

It's all in the delivery
10 February 2016

Shut up and dialogue
13 September 2017

Climate Barbie?
8 November 2017

Obama mocks Canada. And Canada laughs
8 March 2019

Crouching Tiger, Hidden Harper

23 November 2012

Let's start with something positive about *Life of Pi*, the new Ang Lee movie based on the book by Yann Martel, self-designated literary guide to Prime Minister Stephen Harper. I would definitely prefer to watch *Pi* before certain other bits of Lee's *oeuvre*. I am thinking here – and I wish I wasn't – about that scene in the tent in *Brokeback Mountain*.

Apart from that, and despite all the computer graphics that money can buy – in particular the tiger that shares a long, long trip in a lifeboat with the eponymous hero – this is a turgid movie. Based on Martel's Man Booker Prize tome, its most interesting plot twist (spoiler alert) comes too late to save it. It is that the shipwreck story that the mature Pi is telling in flashback is in fact an allegory based on the psychological suppression of a very nasty experience in the lifeboat.

The theme of delusion as a response to psychological trauma is particularly relevant to Martel. Indeed, far more fascinating than anything in the movie – and worthy of a satirical screenplay (have your studio call my agent) – is the four-year monologue of unrequited hate that Martel waged against Stephen Harper. This followed the Prime Minister's failure to acknowledge Martel's literary genius at an Ottawa event in 2007 to mark the 50th anniversary of the Canada Council for the Arts. Of course, it wasn't about the alleged snub to Martel's massive ego. No, no. It was about the Conservatives' lack of cartwheel enthusiasm for arts funding (even though they were in the process of increasing it at the time). Martel's concern was educating the ignoramus who had – as Martel would never tire of telling interviewers – once said that his favourite reading was *The Guinness Book of World Records*. Martel's hypersensitive powers of literary observation had perhaps missed the tongue in Harper's cheek while concentrating on the horns on the Prime Minister's head.

Martel's battle – sorry, I mean education – plan was to lob a book at the Prime Minister every two weeks, along with a pompous didactic covering letter. Martel wanted people who had "power" over him to read, "because their limited, impoverished dreams may become my nightmares."

As it happened, however, Martel's David and Goliath scenario got flipped upside down worse than Pi and the tiger during the movie's spectacular storm scenes. Martel did soon bring to mind a Biblical David, but it was the one portrayed by Richard Gere in the universally panned 1985 bomb *King David*, in which an enthused Gere *Hava Nagilas* through Jerusalem in his underwear (it's on YouTube).

Martel soon wound up looking like a giant literary bully in a diaper, but once he started dancing, he just couldn't stop. The result was 101 unrequested packages being checked for explosives as they landed at the Prime Minister's office.

Apart from demonstrating mindboggling narcissism, Martel's first open letter to the Prime Minister revealed his own purblind lack of appreciation for the system that had made him a multi-millionaire. He worked himself up into a hissy fit about how philistine Harperism would lead to "frustrated serfdom at the service of the feudal lords of profit."

Although *Animal Farm* was on Martel's list, *Nineteen Eighty-Four* wasn't, perhaps because its theme was totalitarian insistence on prescribed reading. Then again, the list did contain *A Clockwork Orange*, where forcing people to read the "right" books is ridiculed as counterproductive. Martel's idea of balance was to include *Anthem*, by Ayn Rand, although he suggested that her books appealed to "American capitalists bent on making and keeping too much money."

Mmm. Perhaps Martel could tell us at what point he found the royalties from *Life of Pi* excessive, and started sending them back.

Worse than ignoring him, meanwhile, the Prime Minister's office sent a number of polite letters of thanks, as if Martel was some... some ordinary Canadian!

Martel had claimed that he would continue his campaign as long as Harper remained in government, but early in 2011, a couple of months before the electorate rewarded Harper's illiteracy with a majority, Martel gave up. He was, he claimed, living with two pregnancies: that of his second child and of a new novel. "It will be called

The High Mountains of Portugal and it shimmers in my mind," he wrote, still trying to shimmy his way out of the hole he had dug for himself.

Martel claimed he had tried to keep his submissions to Harper short, presumably so as to prevent excessive Prime Ministerial lip bruising, but he had one last ultra-pretentious bunker-buster down his dancin' diaper, a 101st book that would perhaps crush the Prime Minister literally as well as literarily: Proust's *Remembrance of Things Past*. Again ironic, since Proust has so many characters who make fools of themselves because of their obsessive self-unawareness.

Justin's China syndrome

15 November 2013

Justin Trudeau's mind may be a bit like a teenager's bedroom, but the Liberal leader's recent praise for Chinese dictatorship was surely more a case of careless wording than careless thought. He used "dictatorship" when he should have said something like "well-designed sustainable governance."

Trudeau was asked at a Ladies' Night function which nation's administration he admired most outside of Canada. His response was "You know, there's a level of admiration I actually have for China because their basic dictatorship is allowing them to actually turn their economy around on a dime and say 'we need to go green fastest …we need to start investing in solar.'"

The contention that China is some sort of green model is flat out ridiculous. This week's 2013 IEA *World Economic Outlook* confirmed that the smog-bound Middle Kingdom is destined to be the world's largest and fastest-growing consumer of fossil fuels – in particular coal – for at least the next decade.

Criticism arose not over that gaffe, but over Trudeau's praise for dictatorship, but was he really saying anything outrageous? Dictatorship – that is, comprehensive control of people's lives and thought –

has always been a motivating force of leftist ideology.

Praise for dictatorship as a more efficient and more moral system has a long history. Trudeau's father Pierre declared "We have a great deal to learn from the Soviet Union." As Liberal Prime Minister, Pierre was an unabashed fan of both the Castro and Mao regimes. In the wake of the 1989 Tiananmen Square massacre, he took Justin and his brothers to China, where he was treated as a hero.

Support for dictatorship tends to be based on power lust and/or economic ignorance (even on the part of Nobel economists) hiding under a blanket of moralism. It went through a bit of a rough spot in the wake of the Soviet collapse, but had already been building a new head of steam in the environmental movement.

The enormously influential 1972 book *Limits to Growth* called for a "totally new form of society," with much greater restrictions on human freedom. In 2012, one of *Limits'* authors, Jorgen Randers, produced another book, *2052* (launched at the annual meeting of the World Wildlife Fund) in which he specifically praised the Chinese model, and expressed concern at the danger of "counterrevolution."

Maurice Strong, the man who organized much of the United Nations' political manoeuvering behind the climate fandango, has always been a sinophile. Following his implication in the Iraqi oil-for-food scandal, he moved to Beijing.

In 2006, Peter Tertzakian, a prominent Calgary-based energy economist, wrote a book, entitled *A Thousand Barrels a Second,* in which he claimed that China was lucky because it had "a golden opportunity to engineer a society that does not fully experience the level of oil addiction that we have known in the West."

The New York Times' Thomas Friedman, another thought-leader of the liberal left, has written that a single-party state such as China "can just impose the politically difficult but critically important policies needed to move a society forward in the 21st century."

In fact, China's economic success is largely due to the fact that its government has, over several decades, loosened its chokehold on private initiative.

If Justin Trudeau had merely said that he admired China's resolution to deal with its environmental problems and promote alternative energy, there would have been much less controversy. He would merely have been parroting Al Gore, who has always praised China's "leadership" on – that is, its hypocritical manipulation of – climate policy.

One line of damage control instigated by Trudeau's political supporters (such as the CBC) was to suggest that Stephen Harper, too, had turned into a toady for China, since he had praised the country's economic advance. But that is very different from praising its government. Harper has also been criticized for pointing to the flaws in democracy, particularly in the case of India, as if that is somehow tantamount to supporting dictatorship. This points to critics' confusion. What China needs, like India, is not more democracy, it is more freedom. The two are by no means synonymous.

Pierre's slush foundation

25 November 2014

The Pierre Elliott Trudeau Foundation last week held a conference entitled "Weathering Change: Pathways to Sustainability in Canada." It confirmed that the road to green serfdom now makes its way through the thickets of climate hysteria, past social-mediated mobs, and via smokeless backrooms filled with radical NGOs.

The foundation is essentially a sleeper cell to promote the kind of big government favoured by its eponymous hero, who died in 2000, and now by his son, Justin. It was endowed in 2002, by a Liberal government, with $125 million of taxpayers' money. According to the foundation, the cash was gifted "with the unanimous support of the House of Commons." In fact, the announcement was sprung on the Canadian Alliance – predecessor of today's Conservatives – moments before it was made. Jason Kenney subsequently identified it as a slush fund for the Liberal agenda. An editorial in the *National Post* dubbed it a "partisan raid on the public treasury." The Chrétien government's weak justification was that it was part of Canada's

"Innovation Strategy," and that the foundation's scholarships would rank with those named for Cecil Rhodes. Critics pointed out that to the extent that Trudeau-the-elder had any economic ideas, they were innovation retardants. Also, Rhodes scholarships were funded with Rhodes' own money and certainly weren't restricted to pursuing the interests of their founder.

Last week's conference confirmed that taxpayers' money was spent on a very partisan "non-partisan" organization. Although The Agenda has shifted since the days of Trudeau *pere*, some aspects of the left-liberal mentality never change. They may often be wrong, but they are never in doubt. Typically, there was endless talk of "joining the conversation," but only if you agreed with its conclusions.

The recent China/US non-deal on climate was talked up as a great policy breakthrough. Painless government guidance to bright new technologies-of-the-future remained an unshakeable conviction, despite all evidence to the contrary. John McCall MacBain, the foundation's chairman, is closely associated with the European Climate Foundation, which launders big US foundation money to radical European NGOS. He called for a "more progressive orientation" in the face of prospective climate apocalypse. Foundation president and CEO Morris Rosenberg made the arresting claim that the Syrian civil war was rooted not in religious sectarianism and tyranny, but drought.

One big strategic difference since the days of Pierre Trudeau is that much of the bogus conversation has been hijacked by radical environmental groups masquerading as "civil society." One of the movement's stars, Tzeporah Berman, was a conference favourite. Ms. Berman also confirmed her status as a world-class name dropper.

"I met (former Clinton Cabinet member and lefty academic) Robert Reich last night," she confided. "And he said 'What's Canada doing?' He said 'it's crazy…the oilsands will be a stranded asset.'"

She also reported an exchange with the Prime Minister of Denmark. She had asked him how he had imposed draconian policies (although she didn't call them that), "And he looked at me like I was crazy," she said. "He said 'Civil Society demanded it. I didn't have a choice.'"

She suggested however that it was a mistake to lump all environmental NGOs together. "Some will be partners, some will be watchdogs." Then again, if you didn't do what your NGO partners demand, you'd find those watchdogs biting at your rump.

Ms. Berman predicted that President Obama would veto Keystone XL, and concluded: "We should be having a conversation about capping, cleaning up and getting out [of the oilsands]. There is no responsible way to build new fossil fuel infrastructure."

End of conversation.

She, like others, presented the Canadian Boreal Forest Agreement, CBFA, as a great achievement of industry/NGO "collaboration," when in fact it was rooted in naked intimidation.

Avrim Lazar, who, as head of the Forest Products Association of Canada, had led the forest industry into the CBFA, was another Trudeau Foundation "mentor" and conference star. His closing keynote speech cleaved to another foundational conceit of left liberals: that they, and the Trudeau Foundation, aren't "ideological" but merely concerned with getting out "the facts" and doing "the right thing" (the 15-plus year "hiatus" in global temperatures was one fact that didn't make it into the conversation).

Climate change, he said, forces us to "look in the mirror." What we would see would be a species lacking sufficient collectivist sentiment and political will. Those who refused to get with the program were foolish, callous and just plain unevolved, willing to "send waves to drown small islands."

According to Lazar, most humans simply aren't wired with the caring, panoptic perspective of the liberal left. They are selfish and thus subject to a "denial mechanism."

The former bureaucrat and Canadian negotiator of the suicidal Kyoto Accord noted that Thomas Malthus's notion of limits to growth had been overcome by two centuries of technical "fixes," but this time it was different.

How, he asked, could we move from the egocentric to the "ecocentric?" His "fantasy," he said, was an "Environmental Spring…We will rise up through the net and say 'Save our commons.' Our leaders will not be able to resist…"

Foundation president Rosenberg closed the conference by suggesting that the public needed educating through the use of "compelling language." Preston Manning's recommendation that a carbon tax shouldn't be called a tax was cited as a useful model of Orwellian linguistic perversion for the public good.

"If this conference helped you connect," concluded Rosenberg, "I'd like you to consider making a donation to the Trudeau Foundation." Thus making sure that the echo chamber continues to reverberate until another Trudeau – more sympathetic to an Environmental Spring – makes it to Sussex Drive.

The Left's enemies list

19 August 2015

Almost 20 years ago, American humorist P.J. O'Rourke produced *The Enemies List: A Vigilant Journalist's Plea for New Red Scare.* It sought to revive "the best traditions of McCarthyism" by fingering people with silly and/or dangerous ideas, from Yoko Ono to the "entire country of Sweden." Most targets were on the left, although O'Rourke included Donald Trump because he didn't like him. As he wrote, "if McCarthyism isn't good for settling grudges, what is it good for?"

O'Rourke's brilliant concept came to mind when perusing a new book of essays: *Canada After Harper: His ideology-fuelled attack on Canadian society and values, and how we can resist and create the country we want.* The book confirms that the left's treatment of its enemies tends to be humourless to the point of derangement.

Its contributors – ranging from David Suzuki to Maude Barlow to Linda McQuaig – would form a reasonable basis for a Canadian enemies list. Indeed, the book's introduction is even written by one of O'Rourke's chief targets, Ralph "Unsound on any Topic" Nader.

For O'Rourke, the distinguishing feature of his "cluster of dunces" was silliness rather than political subversion. However, *Canada*

After Harper presents not just examples of comprehensive Harper Derangement Syndrome but a forewarning of what we might expect should Justin Trudeau or the even farther left New Democratic Party wind up in Sussex Drive.

The book was concocted by an old lefty warhorse named Ed Finn, who portrays Canada as a land of inequality, poverty, excessive corporate power, environmental crisis, sexual assault etc. etc. He admits that his inspiration was a lecture by Nader, a version of which forms the introduction to the book.

Nader sees the Canadian dream fraying beneath "greed and narcissism" as the country adopts the "US model." But surely the US model under President Obama is that of social democratic Europe. Canada and the US have rarely been farther apart politically.

Stephen Harper, as the Prince of Darkness, agitates some contributors so much that they can't even spell his name. Still, that pretty much reflects the factual accuracy of the book, which presents Harper's Canada as a cross between Putin's Russia and Assad's Syria. Only meaner.

The essays are a compendium of how the left tends to see the world through a stained-glass window. They are St. George; Stephen Harper is the dragon. It's always fascinating to see the left attribute even the slightest appreciation of markets to pseudo-religious "fundamentalism." Harper reportedly answers to many masters, from Canada's super-rich through international corporate behemoths to a "theo-con"-spiracy. Indeed, according to one contributor, Joyce Nelson, Harper's purported lack of concern for the environment may be rooted in his belief in the imminence of "end times."

Inevitably, Harper's alleged "gutting" of environmental legislation due to the gigantic power of Big Business is condemned, but if corporations are so powerful, why are pipeline and other fossil fuel development projects on hold from sea to shining sea?

Chief hysteric David Suzuki presents a world of environmental horrors in the "Anthropocene Epoch," where man tramples the earth and pollutes the atmosphere willy nilly. Inconveniently, however, measures of air and water quality have been improving in Canada for decades.

Suzuki's contribution is sprinkled with straw men, such as an unnamed forestry CEO who tells him that trees only have value when they are cut down.

Harking back to the book's title, it is a peculiarity of the liberal left to regard "ideology" as only for their enemies. They use the term in the Marxist sense of bogus rationalization for the political status quo. Their own take, by contrast, is rooted in nothing but objectivity and the most selfless concern for the country and its people. Their administrations would be incorruptible.

That view is justified by two sacred stained-glass visions that are impervious to analysis. The first is that inequality is unalloyed evil, and is always increasing. The second is that corporate size is synonymous with political power, and that "the rich" and corporations will always game the system at the expense of the greater good, without any restraint by the competitive system or legislation.

Hardly coincidentally, both these articles of faith require real coercive power to put things straight. Inequality requires the power of "redistribution;" corporate power requires "countervailing power" to bring the economic royalists to heel. It is also essential to believe – or at least claim – that "the rich" cannot possibly have become that way through their own efforts. "More often," writes Linda McQuaig, "today's super-rich are receiving gigantic rewards because of luck, ruthlessness, speculation, cheating, or simply being well-connected or positioned to take advantage of lucrative possibilities." Such a view might be taken as just another example of loopy lefty demonization were McQuaig not a potential NDP cabinet minister.

"Harperman"

2 September 2015

Second quarter GDP figures emerged on Tuesday, followed by predictable cries that Canada was in recession; Finance Minister Joe Oliver tweeted that there had in fact been an increase in GDP, albeit a modest $4 billion, which most normal people would interpret as growth.

Good point. Seems strange to be talking about entering recession when we're actually moving out of one, but only if you don't understand the real subtext of recession talk, which is that: STEPHEN HARPER IS A WICKED, INCOMPETENT, EVIL LIAR AND IT'S TIME FOR HIM TO GO.

I hope that wasn't too technical for you. Can you believe that Kim Jung Harper? Not only has he personally tanked the economy, but now he's trying to muzzle folk singers! Specifically, an Ottawa folk-singer named Tony Turner, who happens to be a government environmental scientist. Turner has been suspended from his job (with pay) for nothing more than writing a hate song – *Harperman* – putting it on YouTube, and blowing up the code that says that bureaucrats should not appear partisan.

If the nauseating self-righteousness of folk singer Pete Seeger made you gag, *Harperman* may be dangerous to your health, not least because the backup group is a Unitarian church choir filled with Sixties retreads. The song is destined to be the anthem of Harper Derangement Syndrome, HDS. It poses rhetorical questions such as: Who controls parliament? Who squashes all dissent? Who has no respect for the environment? Who's the king of secrecy? Who won't buy into climate change, until it's sold on the stock exchange? Whose smarmy smile is a thin veneer? Who preaches the politics of fear?

The catalogue goes on through ignoring aboriginals, bombing Iraq, rigging elections, calling "troubled people" terrorists, suppressing press freedom, and on and on. For obvious reasons, it doesn't mention Harperman's religious "fundamentalism," although Unitarians don't appear to believe in much except recycling.

The song gets outright loopy when it asks "Who reveres Uncle Sam?" Have these wrinkled remnants of Kumbaya looked at Stephen Harper's relationship with Washington lately?

Meanwhile Turner's protest was hardly an act of principled bravery since he is about to retire, no doubt with a hefty indexed pension.

Attitudes towards Stephen Harper have to be categorized under psychopathology. In Canada, he has become, for the Canadian left, the modern equivalent of *Nineteen Eighty-Four*'s Emanuel Goldstein, object of a compulsory daily "Two Minutes' Hate." *Harperman* amounts to a five-minute and forty-seven-second hate, but it's only one of an increasing pile of bizarre examples of HDS.

Last week, Oakville mayor Rob Burton, the man who contributed to Ontario's reasoned debate over energy by stating that "gas plants explode and kill people," suggested that Harper's hiring of veterans to provide election security made them analogous to Hitler's Brownshirts. Burton was roundly criticized, but not for comparing Harper to Hitler. That's just obvious. Although let's be fair, there are some small differences. Hitler liked dogs. Harper likes cats. Hitler killed six million Jews. Harper supports Israel.

Last week, the *Globe's* Lawrence Martin penned a flailing hatchet job that featured an illustration of Harper as Joseph Stalin. Again, pretty obvious apart from a few minor details. Stalin liquidated millions of kulaks. Harper wants to reintroduce the home renovation tax credit.

It's not that HDS is exactly new. Before he came to power, the mainstream media was eagerly quoting Marxist Canada Research Chairs who claimed that Genghis Harper was controlled by the dark forces of the "Calgary School," such as Tom Flanagan. These dark masters in turn worshipped at the altar of an obscure academic named Leo Strauss, who was said to be an inspiration for US bomb-dropping neo-cons. Once Harper reached power, despite parting ways with Flanagan (who had indeed been a political advisor), there were relentless claims of a neo-con "secret agenda." Nine years later, it's still secret.

Certainly Harper has been a disappointment to many on the right, even driving some to HDS, but "uniting the right" involved a Big Tent that had to contain both social conservatives and libertarians. Also, reaching, and staying in, power inevitably involves compromise. We should remember that compromise for free marketers involves kowtowing to populism while controlling the damage. Compromise for the left involves ignoring economic reality until it bites them in the rear. See Greece.

Check out *Harperman*, and listen all the way through to the intifada-style ululation at the end. And remember, when Adolph Harper accompanied himself on the piano while singing a Beatles classic at the National Arts Centre six years ago, what he really wanted to sing was "With a Little Help from My Storm Troopers."

Justin Trudeau's Flying Paris Circus
21 October 2015

Pierre Trudeau's infamous 1980 National Energy Program was an economic disaster, but the Liberal urge to regulate, redistribute and centrally plan has not disappeared, despite the intervening collapse of the Berlin Wall. Indeed, the urge has swelled to global proportions on the back of projected catastrophic man-made climate change. Pierre never seemed to take that much interest in the NEP or economic nationalism, which bubbled up out of Liberal backrooms and from the popularity of Petrocan among a naïve electorate. By the time the ultimate backroom man, Maurice Strong, had become the first head of Petrocan in 1976, he had already established himself as a key figure in the international environmental movement. Although his own influence has obviously waned with his advancing years, his Agenda lives on.

There are significant similarities between the NEP and climate-policy obsessions. Newly elected Prime Minister Justin Trudeau, son of Pierre, is also manipulated by backroom advisors, and the local fight boils down, yet again, to Ottawa vs. Alberta, although it has also now drawn in other provinces.

The NEP inevitably soured relations with the US. Relations are pretty sour now too, but the polarity flipped under Harper and Obama. President Obama, apart from being himself subject to the left-liberal do-good power-lust syndrome, is also in thrall to Maurice's children, the environmental NGOs that Strong helped to infiltrate the UN and Davos, and who have been gaining in power at the national and local level ever since. However, for anybody who imagines that Justin will now simply join Obama on the seashore, commanding the oceans to roll back, things are about to get a little complicated. Similarly, anybody who imagines that Justin's handsome profile will persuade radical environmentalists to come up with "social licence" for pipeline development is dreaming. Indeed, Obama's election gift to Trudeau may be to nix Keystone XL, the only pipeline that Trudeau supported during the election campaign.

Stephen Harper was in fact skilful in "ragging the puck" (an ice hockey term meaning controlling the puck so it doesn't wind up in your own net) on the climate issue, mirroring US regulatory policies and commitments while ditching the irresponsible commitment to Kyoto made by the Chrétien Liberals. Even then, Harper made commitments that he knew the country was unable to meet (short of economic collapse). In doing so he was being no more hypocritical than most governments.

Trudeau may not be so adept on the climate-policy ice. One of his many problems, as he will rapidly learn, is the different energy profiles of the two countries. Canadian electricity is already significantly fuelled by "clean" hydro sources, while the US is still significantly dependent on coal, and can lower emissions via switching to booming natural gas.

Trudeau cannot possibly make commitments more draconian than the Conservatives'. The question is how he plans to achieve the ones they made. That's where we get into relations with the provinces who, at a meeting last July, wittered on about a national energy strategy that would effectively deal with emissions. Harper was condemned by some provinces for not playing ball, but if this is a ball game it is like that pre-Columbian version where the losing team captain gets decapitated.

The provinces have a crazy quilt of climate policies whose coordination makes herding cats look relatively easy. Trudeau has apparently promised to take all the provinces with him to Paris. Thus John Cleese's tweet of welcome is appropriate: Paris will become Justin Trudeau's Circus.

Justin does Davos

20 January 2016

Justin Trudeau arrives at the World Economic Forum, WEF, in Davos this week as a global celebrity, ripe for high-altitude schmoozing and selfies with Leonardo DiCaprio.

He will be welcomed not merely as the winner of a surprise election majority, but as a leader – unlike his predecessor, whose name we can't recall – who is amenable to the WEF's Global Salvationist agenda. Under that agenda, governments, business, "civil society," and – above all – those who run the WEF sit down to solve the problems of the world from a panoptic perspective.

Trudeau's problems are admittedly more immediate and mundane. Word from the Liberal backrooms is that Justin will be on a rebranding mission, just in case anybody had failed to notice that the last guy's "Energy Superpower" brand hadn't been moving off the shelves.

Every year, Davos' cast of thousands addresses some impossibly huge issue. This year it's the Fourth Industrial Revolution, which WEF supremo Klaus Schwab describes as "a fusion of technologies that is blurring the lines between the physical, digital, and biological spheres."

Certainly, if the WEF is about anything it's about blurring lines, mainly the ones between reality and pretentious flapdoodle. Which is where we get back to Canada's Prime Minister, who is due to give a keynote speech on Wednesday, then participate in a gender parity session with Melinda Gates. Since Trudeau's cabinet is 50% female, he'll clearly shine on that panel. The problem is the speech, whose authors didn't dig too far into the thesaurus of clichés for a title: "A New Chapter for Canada."

Trudeau, while a proponent of Sunny Ways and solar power, is not known for having any well-thought-out ideological convictions, but he is manipulated by several who do. His principal secretary and ventriloquist, Gerald Butts, is a former head of the Canadian cell of the World Wildlife Fund, WWF, perhaps the preeminent environmental NGO. We may be sure that Butts will meet many old WWF friends in the Swiss Mountains.

Trudeau is to be squired around at Davos by two leading decriers of that great fiction "fundamentalist capitalism:" Canadian Bank of England governor Mark Carney and McKinsey super-consultant Dominic Barton. Carney will have to grin and bear it through the conviction that he should have Trudeau's job. Barton makes huge fees from peddling the entirely false notion that corporations are over-committed to the bottom line.

In some ways Trudeau's "middle class agenda" comes straight from the WEF playbook. When bloviating about "Industry 4.0," Schwab starts off almost celebrating the ever-multiplying wonders brought by increases in computer power – from driverless cars to 3-D printing – but he inevitably winds up searching for the cloud in front of the silver lining. The computer revolution, he claims, "helps explain why middle classes around the world are increasingly experiencing a pervasive sense of dissatisfaction and unfairness. A winner-takes-all economy that offers only limited access to the middle class is a recipe for democratic malaise and dereliction."

So better call everybody in to pay hefty fees to talk about it.

Perhaps Trudeau's main usefulness to the WEF comes from his government's firm – and possibly even naïvely genuine – commitment to "fighting" climate change, which remains the central plank of the WEF's global governance/soft dictatorship agenda.

In terms of Canada's real global standing, its non-invitation to the Defence Minister's conference in Paris this week is far more practically significant than the intellectual flatulence of Davos. ISIS doesn't worry too much about its carbon footprint. Still, if Canada is looking for some rebranding, especially since peacekeeping has lost its lustre: what about Climate Keepers? We can ride it all the way to increasingly-indebted economic oblivion.

It's all in the delivery
10 February 2016

When I first read that the federal Liberals were to install a "delivery unit" – inspired by British government guru Sir Michael Barber – my thoughts immediately turned to an area in which the British are almost unparalleled: satire.

The delivery unit is intended to make sure that policies are pushed through, and that aspirations become outcomes. Who could argue? What could go wrong?

Try watching *Yes Minister*, which was one of Prime Minister Margaret Thatcher's favourite TV programs. Its overarching theme was how brilliantly and deviously the bureaucracy manipulates its political masters. Specifically, it dealt with how a naïve and vain minister, Jim Hacker, was tied in knots by his permanent secretary at the Department of Administrative Affairs, Sir Humphrey Appleby.

Sir Michael Barber, who was once described by *The Economist* as a "monkish former teacher," sounds more like Hacker than Sir Humphrey. Author of the modestly titled *How to Run a Government*, Barber created a delivery unit for former British prime minister Tony Blair, which was subsequently ditched by David Cameron in favour of "Implementation Taskforces."

The term "delivery" also brought a more recent and even more relevant BBC Britcom to mind: *Twenty Twelve*. Set in the run-up to the 2012 London Olympics, it takes the form of a mockumentary about a fictional entity known as the Olympic Deliverance Commission, which is headed by Ian Fletcher (played by Hugh Bonneville, best known as the lord of *Downton Abbey*).

The series is not so much about the infighting between bureaucrats and politicians as about the politically correct flapdoodle in which all forms of modern administration are marinated.

Bonneville's Fletcher not only has to negotiate the turgid currents of "sustainability," "legacy" and "inclusivity," he has to deal with the commission's branding consultant, a ditzy marketer both prone to malapropisms and possessing an extraordinary ability not to listen.

The new Liberal government is nothing if not sustainable, inclusive and brand-conscious, which brings us back to Justin Trudeau.

Yes Minister was followed by *Yes Prime Minister*, which starts with Hacker being negotiated into the top job because the bureaucracy finds him "malleable."

While Canada's bureaucrats were conspicuously delighted with the election of Trudeau *fils* (breaking into joyous applause in his presence on one occasion), they didn't exactly put him in power, except perhaps by thwarting his predecessor, Stephen Harper, whose small(er) government inclinations made him a natural enemy.

One big difference between the job of the fictional Ian Fletcher and the very real former Ontario bureaucrat, Matthew Mendelsohn, who has been appointed Trudeau's "deliveryman," is that Fletcher had a specific target to deliver: the Olympics. Mendelsohn's job is infinitely more complex. Can you imagine keeping an eye on all the 94 recommendations of the aboriginal Truth and Reconciliation Commission, on each of which Trudeau has promised to deliver?

Barber's theories of delivery have been big in Queen's Park for the past decade, which should set off Big Ben-sized alarm bells. Mendelsohn, who it goes without saying is academically brilliant, was originally recruited to the Ontario government as deputy minister for the Democratic Renewal Secretariat, a title itself overflowing with satirical potential.

The notion that politicians should be held to account for the execution of their policies is the most obvious common sense, but there's many a slip between policy and delivery. Also, it should never be forgotten what policies are ultimately designed to deliver: votes.

It makes all sorts of sense to measure progress on priorities such as reducing hospital wait times or increasing educational test scores, which are (relatively) easy to measure, but how might Ontario's commitment to delivery square with the devastating criticisms of the recent report from the provincial auditor general?

Whatever Ontario's Green Energy Act was designed to deliver – apart from conspicuous commitment to sustainability – what it actually delivered was infuriatingly high electricity bills.

As the old Soviet Union and *Yes Minister* remind us, bureaucracies display their greatest flexibility in evading targets, or reaching them in easy but perverse ways. Set the state-run button factory an output target by weight and you'll get one gigantic button. There actually was a case in Britain where a hospital dealt with the wait-time problem by not allowing patients through the doors.

Meanwhile, there are far bigger problems with delivering on issues such as climate policy. In any sane world, such a policy would be measured against its impact on the climate, but no Canadian policy could have more than a micro-marginal effect on global temperatures. So what's the desired deliverable? Accolades from global bureaucracies? Less protesting from radical ENGOs? Keeping the public in the dark about the pointless costs?

In his latest book, Barber claims that "The effectiveness of government is one of the big moral issues of our time." True, up to a point (Minister), but being effective at delivering bad policies is hardly a step in the right direction. Unless, that is, you are a bureaucrat. Or a satirist.

Shut up and dialogue

13 September 2017

While waiting at Tim Hortons the other morning for my breakfast sandwich, after perusing the government-mandated health warning about its calorie content, I noted an invitation to "carry on the conversation on Twitter, at #myTimHortons."

I'm old enough to remember when "conversation" meant actually talking to someone. Now, however, invitations to "join the conversation" are either a cover for marketing or – much worse – for bogus political consultation.

Tim Hortons' coffee conversation is a fairly innocent marketing campaign, but if you go to the Ontario government website to find out about those calorie figures – which became mandatory for chain restaurants to display at the beginning of this year – you are led into a much-less innocent conversation. "We want your ideas about making health information easier to access," it reads. "Take our survey." The more fundamental question of how far governments should be in the health-information business is not up for discussion.

Joining the conversation has become the siren call of the loquacious left-liberal looter. How can you complain if you get policies you don't like? You had your chance to put in your two-cents' worth. The problem is that the policy swamp is so deep and wide that most ordinary people have neither the time nor interest in joining endless political conversations, even if those conversations might have a significant impact on their lives.

The great British conservative intellectual Arthur Seldon noted that the object of politics shouldn't be to try to involve as many people as possible but as few as necessary, "so that we can get on with the business of improving life instead of perpetually contending about who shall control it."

Joining the conversation all too often means an invitation to step into a social-media echo chamber. The concept is most enthusiastically promoted by professional left-liberal conversationalists, who are only looking for input on how better to promote their agenda. Not "Should we do this?" but "How should we do this?" Not "Should we have a calorie policy, or a climate policy, or an innovation policy?" but "What sort of calorie, climate or innovation policies should we have?"

What sort of Big Government do we want?

Meanwhile if politicians don't like the way the conversation is going – say over something like the Ontario gas-plant scandal – then they seek to "change the conversation." Justin Trudeau even declared that there can be no conversation on issues such as pipelines in the Great Bear Rainforest.

On the bright side, the citizenry does sometimes seek to blow up the one-way conversation, as in the cases of Brexit and the election of Donald Trump, but this tends to make the conversationalists very angry. They start condemning xenophobes and deplorables, people with whom you just can't have a conversation.

I came across a prime example of bogus political conversation the other day in something called "The Citizen Dialogues on Canada's Energy Future." Convened by Simon Fraser University's (SFU's) Centre for Dialogue and Forum Research, it involves selecting 150 citizens to "sit down to hear about one another's values and how they relate to energy." It all starts with "laying all the information on the table," because too much of what we read is "cherry picked."

SFU has provided the random-yet-representative 150 with a "discussion guide" that "surfaces multiple perspectives without censorship." For example, "[Greenhouse gas] emissions mean that the energy sector is a major contributor to climate change." But surely that is a moot point even if the science is "settled," not least since the guide also admits that the Canadian economy produces only 2% of global emissions. I also wonder if the facilitators will be eager to discuss the uncertainty of climate science "without censorship."

According to SFU's Robin Prest, "There's too much at stake and Canada's people, diverse regions and industries are too interdependent for us to continue to shout at one another indefinitely."

But who is shouting, apart from those who want to close down the oilsands, fracking and pipelines? Social media is great for assembling mobs, but mobs usually aren't too interested in having a respectful chat. Meanwhile those in the business community who have been seeking "social licence" through dialogue have merely legitimized their opponents' intransigence.

The SFU exercise is funded by the federal Department of Natural Resources. To the extent that the 150 selectees reflect what the government thinks already, their views will be sombrely regurgitated. To the extent that they don't, they are talking into the wind turbine.

The Citizen Dialogues are a part of the government's *Generation Energy* project. Its typically trite motto is "Moving Canada Forward." Any suggestion that federal policy might be moving Canada backwards is not up for discussion. After all, there is a world to save. The transition to a low-carbon economy is a job creator. You think otherwise? Shut up.

Climate Barbie?

8 November 2017

Canadian Liberal Environment and Climate Minister Catherine McKenna chose a particularly inopportune moment last Friday to complain about climate name-calling. That's because earlier in the week Governor General (and former astronaut) Julie Payette had attacked climate skepticism with a combination of misrepresentation and association with unrelated and/or "unenlightened" beliefs, especially that old standby, creationism.

McKenna, in a testy exchange at a press conference with Rebel Media reporter Christopher Wilson, complained about *The Rebel* referring to her as "Climate Barbie."

Perhaps the main problem with alleged "sexist slurs" is that they detract from the much more serious issue of the non-debate over climate science and policy.

McKenna sought a commitment that *The Rebel* wouldn't call her names, talk about the colour of her hair or make fun of her. What? A politician demanding that the media not make fun of her, no matter how perverse or ludicrous her policies?

She continued "The reason I'm asking you not to do this is because I have two daughters. There are lots of girls that want to get into politics, and it is completely unacceptable that you do this."

With respect, I have a daughter too, and I believe that she should follow any career she chooses, but if she wanted to become a politician – heaven forbid – the first thing I would suggest is that she gird herself against insults. I certainly wouldn't attempt to ease her chosen path by demanding media self-censorship. Rona Ambrose's hair was also a target of NGO climate activists when she was Environment

Minister in the Harper government. That attack, too, was rightly castigated as sexist, but nobody – least of all McKenna – would dare suggest that NGOs be "silenced."

At the press conference, *The Rebel*'s Wilson shot back that he found it unacceptable that climate skeptics were cast as "deniers." There, he had a point. Last year, McKenna even fingered "gender climate deniers," who refused to acknowledge that climate change is worse for women. In fact, women in poor countries are being further impoverished by climate policies that prevent access to cheap, reliable fossil fuels.

McKenna, who is a lawyer, seems to believe that all you need to know about climate science can be contained in a Barbie-style ringpull tweet, specifically: "Science is science. And climate change is real and man-made." That statement is facile and misleading, whatever the gender of the person making it (Barack Obama tweeted almost exactly the same message).

In a speech to a science policy conference, Governor General Payette went further; she equated climate skepticism not only with creationism, but with astrology and quack medical treatments. She subsequently received sharp criticism for her attack on religious belief, but her attack on skeptics was equally outrageous. Payette asked, incredulously, "Can you believe that still today in learned society, in houses of government, unfortunately, we're still debating and still questioning whether humans have a role in the Earth warming up or whether even the Earth is warming up, period?"

But no sensible skeptic denies that the earth has been warming for the past century, or that human activity has had some impact. The crucial questions are: How much impact, and what if anything should be done about it? (I sent a note last week to the Governor General's office asking for the identity of these benighted souls who deny global warming or some human impact upon it. I'm not holding my breath waiting for a reply.)

Certainly, nobody could deny that the models on which catastrophic projections are based have overestimated the warming of recent decades, but then the Climate Industrial Complex doesn't deny that "fact," it simply ignores it. Similarly, it ignores the malign economic impact and ineffectiveness of its climate policies.

The Orwellian framing of skeptics as "deniers" has played a key role in shutting down debate. Skeptics have also been compared to dolts who believe that the earth is flat, or that there is no link between smoking and cancer, or who would have opposed ending slavery or giving women the vote. But it's worth noting the vitriol poured on women who have dared to go against the conventional climate wisdom and dig into its perverted science, secret funding, and counterproductive policies – brave women such as Professor Judith Curry in the US, or Donna Laframboise and Vivian Krause in Canada. Laframboise has noted the insults heaped upon her by people who "try to link my climate views to racists, Holocaust deniers, child murderers, mental illness, and the tobacco industry."

Payette's position received a revealing defence in the *Post* on Tuesday from Professor Barbara Messamore. She agreed that the Governor General "should not express views about what is suitable for discussion in legislative chamber," but suggested that it was "absolutely" appropriate that she be "an advocate for awareness of climate change." Messamore suggested that there could hardly be "a more important cause and one better suited to Payette's background," but it is precisely the importance of the cause that needs debating. Meanwhile if distance travelled from the earth's surface was any gauge of scientific validity or policy insight, then Payette should surely defer to skeptical American astronauts Harrison Schmidt and Buzz Aldrin, both of whom have been to the moon.

Payette concluded that we must be vigilant so that we can deconstruct misinformation and don't wind up in an echo chamber. Great advice. She and McKenna should try following it.

Obama mocks Canada. And Canada laughs
8 March 2019

One can understand how former President Obama would be greeted enthusiastically in left-leaning, green-crazy Vancouver, but what brand of amnesiac sado-masochism would lead Albertans to give him "a rock star's welcome"? Perhaps the analogy would be appropriate if the rock star were, say, Neil Young, who was recruited by the us-funded Tar Sands Campaign to suggest that Fort McMurray was "like Hiroshima." But would Neil Young get a rock star's welcome in Calgary? There would surely be a few placards outside the venue.

The most salient reason for doubting the mental grasp of those in Calgary cheering the former us president, who was in town Tuesday for a live "conversation" at the Saddledome, is that he is significantly responsible for the desperate state of the Canadian oil industry, specifically through his nixing of the Keystone xl pipeline. That rancid decision, which was without any coherent rationale but to burnish Obama's "legacy," has cost tens of thousands of jobs and tens of billions of dollars to the Albertan and Canadian economies. It is worth noting that Prime Minister Justin Trudeau shares similar legacy aspirations.

Obama's Calgary "conversation" was the middle of three such engagements this week, starting in Winnipeg and ending on the left coast. Local media in all three places drooled over him, despite the fact that he delivered nothing but a pastiche of family bromides, bogus integrity, fake facts, policy revisionism, gross political partisanship, and climate porn. He even took swipes at the beleaguered Trudeau. According to a barf-worthy news report in the *Calgary Herald*: "With divisive politics and changing economies stoking fear and anxiety on both sides of the border, former us president Barack Obama brought messages of hope and optimism to Calgary on Tuesday, paving the way to a kinder, gentler and cleaner planet."

An equally star-struck *Herald* columnist took the opportunity to dump ritually on the current incumbent of the White House, highlighting the contrast between "grace and vulgarity, integrity and corruption, kindness and cruelty." But while President Donald Trump may have reality-TV-sized personal shortcomings, any suggestion that his narcissism approaches that of Obama is a stretch. After all, as a presidential candidate in 2008, Obama declared that his accession to power would be the point at which the earth would begin to heal and the seas cease to rise. King Canute without the irony.

Apparently nobody threw anything or stormed the Calgary Saddledome dais when Obama patronized the locals by saying that they ought to be proud of their oil and gas because it had "powered the world...and is still the cheapest means for us to power everything that we do."

This is the guy who declared oil a "dirty and dwindling 19th-century resource" shortly before presiding over a spectacular US petroleum boom due to advances in fracking technology, for which he subsequently tried to take credit.

Although Obama admitted that you couldn't link any particular weather event to climate change, he inevitably got into floods and droughts and hurricanes, and projected that "with the current pace we are on, the scale of tragedy that will consume humanity is something we have not seen in perhaps recorded history." The bubonic plague? World wars? Communist and fascist genocides? Mere blips. He suggested moose might become extinct.

"I am an old-fashioned guy," he said boldly in Vancouver. "I believe in the facts, and the facts are that the planet is getting warmer."

But nobody denies that fact. The pertinent question is: how much of that (mild) warming is attributable to man? Obama's idea of science was established years ago when he tweeted the bogus claim that 97% of scientists believe that climate change is "real, man-made and dangerous."

Obama was declared to be above grubby partisan politics in Calgary, but appearing at a similar event in Vancouver later that day, he claimed that mainstream Republicans had "lost control" of the party when Sarah Palin was appointed as John McCain's running mate in 2008. No mention of mainstream Democrats having more recently lost control of their party with the arrival of Alexandria Ocasio-

Cortez and her flat-out barmy Green New Deal. But then how could Obama oppose the idea that such extreme measures are needed to save the world from neoliberalism? Sorry, I mean from climate catastrophe.

Obama ridiculed Justin Trudeau for being concerned about softwood lumber. "I was, like, 'Dude. I've got Syria, the Paris Accords. Is that how we want to spend our time? On a timber agreement?'" He had used the same line in Winnipeg, but there – to his infinite credit – interviewer Michael Burns noted "You just insulted us and we all laughed."

Obama gave his wingtips one final wipe on the Maple Leaf flag by suggesting that Canada was merely paying "lip service" to its commitments to the Paris climate accord (from which his own country is now opting out entirely). He didn't note – or probably didn't know – that this mere lip service has thrown interprovincial relations into turmoil. And this from the guy who included in the Paris accord a desperate "agreement" with China under which the us would commit to hard reductions, while China would commit to nothing.

And still nobody booed.

5

Pre-teen traumatic stress disorder

In 2019 a Swedish schoolgirl, Greta Thunberg, became the face and voice of climate alarmism. Thunberg is on the autistic spectrum and prone to deep anxiety. Her use by environmental activists amounts to a form of abuse. The use of children as human shields and unwitting mouthpieces for political agendas is hardly new, but it has been a key feature of radical environmental strategy for several decades.

Save the children from green education
2 July 1999

Breath-taking manipulation
10 December 2002

Halloween society
1 November 2003

Al Gore requires parental guidance
7 February 2007

Little Miss Apocalypse
28 February 2007

Morgan Stanley's boys and girls
6 June 2007

Warning: May contain ecoporn
8 May 2015

Save the children from green education
2 July 1999

The environmental movement, like the Jesuits, understands the importance of moulding young minds early. "Environmental education" attempts to freight young minds with concerns about complex issues they cannot understand. Johnny might not be able to read, but he can be persuaded that he might "save the planet" if he marches on McDonald's demanding an end to Styrofoam containers.

Agenda 21, the voluminous socialist blueprint that emerged from Maurice Strong's 1992 Rio Earth Summit, declared: "Students should be taught about the environment and sustainable development throughout their schooling." Here is what *Agenda 21* wished to teach them: "The world is confronted with worsening poverty, hunger, ill health, illiteracy, and the continuing deterioration of ecosystems on which we depend for our wellbeing." That is, a bunch of hysterical lies.

Environmental education has amounted to a transparent attempt to further rig the political debate by worrying children to death in school, and then have them regurgitate what has been forced into their heads. Implanted worries are then put forward as evidence of the reality of environmental concerns.

According to *Agenda 21*: "Governments should consult with and let youth participate in decisions that affect the environment. Youth should also be represented at international meetings, and participate in decision-making at the United Nations." The sort of youthful input the Rio crowd had in mind came from David Suzuki's 12-year-old daughter, Severn, who ascended the Earth Summit podium and told a rapt audience of world leaders: "I'm afraid to go out in the sun now because of the holes in the ozone. I am afraid to breathe the air because I don't know what chemicals are in it." Afterwards, Al Gore rushed up to congratulate her. Nobody thought of calling Children's Aid.

Similarly, the World Wildlife Fund has used children for fund-raising. Some years ago, an 11-year-old was quoted in WWF literature, declaring: "...I am a member of a five-billion-person family. We live on the third planet from the sun and our home is falling apart. I'm in a grade six class...but we aren't just any grade sixers, we're special. We're trying to save our home..."

A child indoctrinated to think this way is a victim, a conduit for hatred against Western civilization, a pawn in a power game.

The extent of environmental miseducation was made clear in a recent US book, *Facts, Not Fear*, by Michael Sanera and Jane Shaw, a Canadian version of which was published earlier this year by the Fraser Institute. Dr. Patrick Moore, co-founder and former president of Greenpeace (but who parted from them because of their warped view of "science"), wrote in the book's introduction: "The environmental movement has given a whole new meaning to the idea of teaching our children about the birds and the bees. Not only has the subject matter expanded to include everything under the sun, we are now faced with the challenge of helping our children separate fact from fiction in a highly charged political debate.

"As a father and an environmentalist, I am often discouraged by the amount of misinformation conveyed to our young children through the school system and the media."

Breath-taking manipulation
10 December 2002

Among the more transparently nauseating plans to "celebrate" today's forced Commons vote in favour of Kyoto is a ceremony at which asthmatic Ottawa pre-school children will "thank" Prime Minister Chrétien. Manipulated by their teachers and by the Canadian Union of Public Employees, they will hand over a big card and, bizarrely, their puffers.

Not merely is the cynically-manufactured organization "Kids for Kyoto" disgraceful, but air quality and global warming are two significantly separate issues. In particular, carbon dioxide, the main target of Kyoto, is not a pollutant. And are kids taught that air quality in Ontario has been improving for decades?

Halloween society

1 November 2003

The mood at my house last night was more somber than ghoulish as I prepared the celery sticks and cucumber slices. Normally, I would have been dispensing more flavourful treats, but then I read this week's series in *The Globe and Mail* about how eating Doritos, Goldfish, popcorn and even Granola bars was pretty much a death sentence due to these foods' trans fats.

Meanwhile, I wasn't chopping those vegetables too vigorously. I had seen in the *Post* on Wednesday that, since I have borderline high blood pressure, I am a "walking cardiac time bomb." I shuddered as I thought that I had once eaten a Tim Hortons' muffin, which, according to the *Globe* series, could already have lopped years off my life. I also felt a little hemmed in from two recent studies about aspirin. My doctor told me some while ago that popping aspirins reduced the risk of heart disease, but a new report said the drug caused cancer. Then another report said that coming off aspirins could send you to the morgue.

Still, I tried to get into the spirit of the evening. My daughter looked resplendent as a black-caped skeleton with scythe. However, as I surveyed her with deep parental affection, I suddenly felt a twinge of guilt when I remembered taking her to McDonald's. Yet another study this week had indicated that a group of Boy Scouts and Girl Guides were already showing signs of heart disease.

Not that Lulu doesn't have plenty to worry about already. She is currently working on an "autobiography" as a school project. This project came with a set of suggestions for the chapters. One of the titles is "If I could change the world I'd..." The guidelines then ask

(I'm not making this up) "What types of things in our world bother you the most?" before offering a list of helpful suggestions: "acid rain, pollution, poverty, hunger, war, famines, loneliness, death, disease, illness, discrimination, destruction of the environment, etc."

My daughter is eight years old.

Having done my shift at dispensing the vegetables – at least I got to see genuine horror on children's faces! – we took off to trick-or-treat and view the neighbourhood's front-yard tombs, figures hanging from trees, severed limbs, cackling witches and looming zombies. It was all so wonderfully mock-horrific, so different from real life.

The problem is that we live in a Halloween society, in which we are bombarded every day with new alleged threats to our health, welfare and environment. This growing stream of horror comes from a number of swampish sources, both institutional and psychological. One is environmental special interests, who take a totally unbalanced view of the benefits of economic development. Many of these have a political agenda. They are the old anti-capitalist crowd spreading alarm from behind pictures of pandas and red wolves, and manipulating idealistic and naïve young people who are told that unless they start worrying – and worrying others – then the planet is doomed. The other source of concern is, surprisingly, the very medical advances and studies that make our lives longer and healthier. Here, media sensationalism plays a key part, but researchers also know that the surest way to extend their grants is to grab headlines.

When it comes to health, the larger problem is that bandage-swathed figure that lurches ever-larger, threatening to engulf us: not The Mummy, but socialized medicine. Socialized medicine leads to a real invasion of the body snatchers. If the state has to pay for, and administer, your medical care, then it is obviously concerned about your "lifestyle." Your personal choices become a public matter.

Most of our diet problems relate to the fact that we still have hunter-gatherer bodies and hunter-gatherer cravings. Lead those cravings to a sugar- and fat-abundant all-you-can-eat buffet and you are inviting trouble, at least for those with poor parental guidance, or problems with self-control. We also have easily spooked hunter-gatherer minds, which are prone to mysticism and bad at understanding science and statistics. Those minds all too easily fall victim to those who are either peddling a political agenda or – indulging the licence of Halloween on a permanent basis – just enjoy frightening people.

Al Gore requires parental guidance
7 February 2007

My daughter announced the other day that her Grade 6 class had been shown a film about a man named Al Gore. This movie, *An Inconvenient Truth*, comes with a PG (parental guidance) rating, but I don't think any permission slips were sent out. I asked her what she remembered about the film. She said that Gore had come up with a funny line: "I used to be the next President of the United States."

If she remembers any of the rest of the film's claims, I want to make sure that she runs them past me. After all, I'm one of the "P"s in the PG, and if kids need guidance on anything it is about the bizarre notion that they should be saving the earth before they've come to terms with feeding the hamster.

One has to be careful when trying to inoculate one's children against possible miseducation. You don't want them questioning the rules of grammar or the definitions of mathematical averages. You want them to learn some things by rote, like the multiplication tables, even if they possess calculators. But you also want them to be able to think for themselves, to know the difference between fact and opinion, and, much more so, between fact and hysteria.

At least Gore's movie hasn't been made a part of the school curriculum in Canada, as it has in the United Kingdom. Tony Blair's government is sending a copy to every secondary school in the country. UK Environment Minister, David Miliband, said "I was struck by the visual evidence the film provides, making clear that the changing climate is already having an impact on our world today, from Mount Kilimanjaro to the Himalayan mountains."

Evidence? Kilimanjaro? According to scientists with the Intergovernmental Panel on Climate Change, if Kilimanjaro's snows are disappearing, the main driver is solar radiation, not suvs. This is just one area where Gore bends the truth to support his claim that man-made climate change is already rendering the globe like a "hike through the Book of Revelation." The Biblical reference is appropriate. Gore is at heart an Old Testament prophet, telling us the end is nigh, except that his solution is very secular: that we must follow some unspecified "Marshall Plan" to save the planet.

UK Education Secretary Alan Johnson claimed that he hoped Gore's film would "cause young people to press for lifestyle changes that will lead to lower emissions." Shades of Orwell's young "Spies" in *Nineteen Eighty-Four*.

The environmental movement has long had a clear role for children in its campaign to end industrial civilization. Children are to be indoctrinated, and in turn badger their parents. They are to be frightened to death so that environmentalists may say "Listen to the babes. They are wise. And scared."

It is disgraceful to use children for environmental agitprop, but it starts by filling their heads with stories they are ill-equipped to evaluate, particularly when they come masquerading as the straight goods from an authority figure in a "documentary."

If Al Gore's movie was presented along with the long list of his inaccuracies, it might form the basis of an interesting classroom discussion, but I suspect that Gore is too frequently presented by teachers as Gospel. Since religious education isn't on my daughter's curriculum, I don't think that Al Gore should be on it, either.

Little Miss Apocalypse
28 February 2007

Little Miss Sunshine's Abigail Breslin isn't the only cute little girl to have made a media splash lately.† Canada has seven-year-old Gillian Wiley, another adorable moppet, who is being promoted by eco-warrior David Suzuki as the star of his "If I Were Prime Minister" campaign.

Suzuki has just finished a cross-country propaganda bus tour, under the guise of seeking policy ideas. Needless to say, cutting taxes or removing trade barriers aren't the kind of recommendations that Suzuki was looking for.

As part of the campaign, he utilized YouTube to invite aspirational postings. "Tell me in 20 seconds or less what you would do," says Suzuki. "Would you make polluters pay? Give real protection to endangered species? Or show how Canada can help fight global warming? I want to hear your concerns and your solutions…I'll make sure the politicians listen. Elect yourself at David Suzuki dot org."

Suzuki's favourite candidate so far is little Gillian. She delivers the message that if she were living on Sussex Drive, she would make some big changes "so that we don't destroy the planet with fossil fuels and carbon dioxide." She castigates suvs, wants to stop the tar sands, and tells the camera that "Kyoto is not enough." This Littlest Pigovian wants to "institute a carbon tax right away."

Gillian is very obviously reading from a cue card. Only the final words of her message might possibly be her own: "If I were Prime Minister," she laughs, as if wanting to shake off all this forced earnestness, "I'd have blue hair."

Her performance was featured on Global News. Explaining why she did it, she pointed out, with admirable candour, that it was because her father had told her that afterward they could work on her cardboard castle. Her dad, Keith, confessed the obvious: that he

---

†   *Little Miss Sunshine* was a 2006 comedy about a severely dysfunctional family from Albuquerque taking a road trip to California so their seven-year-old (played by Abigail Breslin) can participate in a beauty pageant.

wrote her script, but he said that he did it for her, and we should not doubt his good intentions.

Abigail was asked by the television reporter if she really did want to be Prime Minister when she grew up. "No," she said firmly. Asked about her hopes for the earth's future, she said "A planet with no poisons, and," she concluded, with a slight hesitation – as if she was really smart enough to understand that she didn't know what she was talking about – "carbon dioxide."

I have an 11-year-old daughter, and I naturally attempt to guide and influence the way she thinks. I have deliberately tried to inject some skepticism into her when it comes to the environmental "education" to which she is subjected at school. I am also concerned that she should not be loaded with the sins of the world just yet, particularly when so much of what she is being taught is politically motivated alarmism.

Educators are not dealing with "objective science" when it comes to climate change. Not only is the science of human contribution not "settled," despite the angry assertions of Suzuki and Co, but the crucial features of this great debate are quite beyond the understanding of the vast majority of adults, let alone youngsters. It is all about ideological agendas that attempt to juice the science, cook the economics and ignore the politics. Most pernicious is the deliberate attempt to induce anxiety in the young.

According to one press report, when Al Gore came to town last week, a mother who had been unable to get tickets called up the University of Toronto and said that her daughter hadn't been able to sleep since seeing *An Inconvenient Truth*. She claimed that seeing Gore in person might make her daughter feel better: that another dose of Gore-y detail would take away the terror that he had inspired in the first place.

Education experts have coined a term, "ecophobia," for the dread and helplessness children feel when confronted with apocalyptic forecasts. According to a recent British survey, half of the children between the ages of seven and eleven are anxious about the effects of global warming and often lose sleep over it. And that, remember, is without any identifiable effects, since no particular weather occurrence can be linked to anthropogenic climate change.

The urge to nurture and protect children is universal. This explains why they are so often used by those with an ideological – or sometimes merely hypocritical – purpose. Keith Wylie obviously loves his daughter, but his decision to make her the mouthpiece for his own anxieties is questionable. Much more reprehensible is David Suzuki's presentation of these ideas as if they were the thoughts of a seven-year-old.

Let's hope little Gillian regarded her YouTube performance as just the price of getting her cardboard palace built, and that she won't lose too much sleep over the words she was reading.

Morgan Stanley's boys and girls
6 June 2007

Would Morgan Stanley put kids on its audit or strategic planning committees? Presumably not. Children have neither the knowledge nor the experience for such tasks. Strange then that the Morgan Stanley International Foundation, a British charitable institution funded by the investment giant, is one of the promoters (the other being UNICEF) of an organization called J8, or Junior 8. J8 sends 13-to 17-year-old "representatives" from G8 countries to lecture their elders on problems that make dealing with the convoluted provisions of Sarbanes-Oxley look easy. These include HIV/AIDS in Africa, climate change, and underdevelopment. The J8-ers will be delivering a "communique" to leaders of the G8 in Germany tomorrow.

The premise behind the J8 is the question: "If you had the opportunity to tell world leaders what they should do to solve global problems, what would you say?"

The team that will represent Canada comes from *École Secondaire de Rochebelle* in Quebec City. According to their submission: "The world has reached a limit. In a society where corporations own animals' genetics and treatments to disastrous sickness for their own

benefits, where we are risking nature and the humanity itself to businesses' profit, we must see the limit which is now so close. We haven't
reached the breaking point, yet it is still time to change for children's
sake."

This portrayal of greedy Frankenstein corporations holding back
drugs from the poor as they trample on nature is the winner of a
national Canadian competition, judged by a group vetted by Morgan
Stanley and UNICEF.

The facile views expressed could come straight from that anti-
corporate snuff flick *The Corporation*. In fact, they did. The school
team's very first reference is the documentary. Among the team's
modest proposals is a "World Charter of Corporate Rights and
Responsibilities."

The notion that we should "listen to the children" is fondly cultivated by organizations such as the UN because children are naïve and
easily manipulated. They make wonderful mouthpieces for noble-
sounding but dangerous collectivist ideas.

Where do they get such ideas? Well, try the J8 website, which provides all kinds of "fact sheets" and "lesson plans" to help make "global
citizenship accessible to the classroom."

The climate-change fact sheet is filled with scary factoids about
floods, droughts and melting glaciers, and claims that climate change
already kills 150,000 people a year. J8 inevitably promotes *Agenda 21*,
the voluminous busybody wish list from the 1992 UN conference in
Rio.

The website's claim that things are getting globally worse is hotly
debated, but you will find no links to Bjorn Lomborg, the Fraser
Institute, the Cato Institute, the American Enterprise Institute or the
Institute of Economic Affairs on the J8 website. You will, however,
find links to the UN Environment Program and Greenpeace.

"Lesson plans" include pressuring local businesses on their commitment to corporate social responsibility. Then there are "games"
that examine such fun topics as the "uneven distribution" of proceeds
from the coffee trade, deforestation, flagging fish stocks, hunger,
AIDS, water shortages, ecological footprints, carbon calculators and
climate change modelling (with Play-Doh?).

The political manipulation of children is age-old, and disgraceful. It has become particularly egregious during the modern age of environmental hysteria.

In 2005, Ontario Premier Dalton McGuinty used a bunch of seven-year-olds as a political backdrop, asking them what he should do with the Lakeview coal-fired generating station.

"Close it," they parroted.

Can you spell "blackout?"

The G8 is a meeting of the leaders of more or less democratic countries, each of whom has been elected. By whatever route these J8 kids were chosen to "represent" their nations, they have no political legitimacy. They also don't have a clue beyond what their activist indoctrinators tell them. Morgan Stanley should be ashamed.

Warning: May contain ecoporn

8 May 2015

The state has long attempted to impose its values by indoctrinating children. The "Junior Spies" of Orwell's *Nineteen Eighty-Four* were taught to monitor their parents for "thoughtcrime."

The thoughtcrime of the moment for Ontario parents, which many are daring to express, is lack of enlightenment about gay or trans sex education. But while knowledge, tolerance and age-appropriate understanding are one thing, in-your-face indoctrination is another. Or, as one grumpy character in a recent *New Yorker* cartoon put it: "I'm still not interested in Bruce Jenner."

Enforced learning about non-traditional sex seems to have much in common with environmental propaganda, especially in provoking anxiety. A classic example was David Suzuki's campaign, a few years ago, to worry children that Santa's workshop might be disappearing through melting Arctic ice.

Another recent example is a radio ad for Earth Rangers, "the Kids' Conservation Organization," that asks if listeners know that "the future of animals everywhere is at risk?" It goes on to claim that "In the last forty years, over half of the world's animal populations have disappeared. Biodiversity is in crisis."

I approached Earth Rangers and asked where their figures came from. They directed me to the WWF, where a similar inquiry sits waiting for a response.

Earth Rangers did send me the results of an Ipsos Reid survey of 8–11 year olds. It claimed that "Protecting animals from extinction is the #1 environmental concern for Canadian kids." But declining animal populations is in no way synonymous with extinction, an issue that has been grossly exaggerated. Causing little children to fret over disappearing animals is reprehensible.

Another of the survey's conclusions is that "84% of all kids report having influenced the environmental behaviours of their parents."

Music is another conduit for promoting eco-anxiety. Recently, a monologue entitled "Sorry," by a US rapper named Prince Ea, has leaped to the top of the alarmist pops, at least if you believe sources such as the *Huffington Post*. The Prince, whose real name is Richard Williams, is a black millennial version of Al Gore. His video takes the form of an apology to "Future Generations" (Generation F?) for wrecking the earth and cutting down all the trees (Didn't Joni Mitchell sing about that 45 years ago in "Big Yellow Taxi"?). The Prince, addressing those of the future who are familiar only with the "Amazon desert," peddles the mendacious meme that 50% of the earth's forests have already been destroyed. He boldly challenges Fox News: if they don't believe climate change is real, they should interview homeless people in Bangladesh.

Now there's some scientific method for you.

"Sorry," he intones, "we paid so much attention to ISIS, and how little to how fast the ice is melting in the Arctic."

Get it? "Ice is."

The Prince's *oeuvre* may not be yet part of the Ontario school curriculum, but don't discount that possibility. He warns us not to trust "politicians run by corporations," but I'm sure he doesn't mean the wind, solar and biofuel corporations favoured by legislatures and politicians around the world.

His video was sponsored by something called standfortrees.org, which is an instrument of USAID and the UN's anti-deforestation programme, which monetizes alarmism by peddling carbon credit certificates.

The millennial fruits of eco-indoctrination appeared recently in *Corporate Knights* magazine's list of "30 under 30," a bunch of naggy "social entrepreneurs" who regard the main current thoughtcrime as not being obsessed by sustainability. They are all committed to fossil fuel divestment and exhibit a "raw awareness" that explains why more of them "demand action on climate change than the average voter." But are they typical? Here's the good news: apparently they are less and less so. According to the Harvard Opinion Project, there is a large and growing minority of young people who – gasp – are skeptical about man-made climate doom, and even more skeptical about government policies to address it. An abysmal 55% of 18–29 year olds agreed with the statement, "Global warming is a proven fact and is mostly caused by emissions from cars and industrial facilities such as power plants." The percentage of 18–20 year olds in agreement was even smaller.

Even more worrying to eco-manipulators, less than a third of young Americans agreed that "Government should do more to curb climate change, even at the expense of economic growth."

The *Harvard Political Review* treated these figures with horror. According to one of its commentators, "the scientific community still has a lot to do to convince young Americans to be real skeptics, not cynics." In other words, skepticism about science is great, but you can't be a skeptic about climate science. That would make you a cynic.

Ipsos Reid's survey of Canadian kiddies too found that although they are concerned – i.e. have successfully been alarmed – about air and water pollution and "energy waste," climate change comes at the bottom of their concerns, as it does for their parents.

Kids are not being taught to love nature, much less to understand the scientific method. They are being taught to obsess over every aspect of their lives, and to distrust and despise the wealthy societies into which they were born. The good news seems to be that by their late teens, at least in the US, fewer are buying it.

Sixties hippies were told not to trust anybody over thirty. Now teenagers seem to be less inclined to buy the censorious message of the "30 under 30." Or their rap artists.

6
Bioperversity

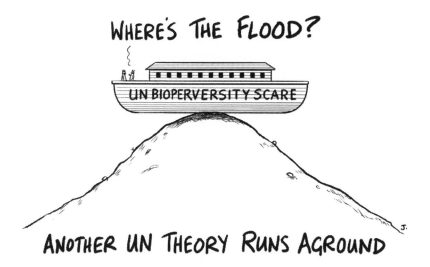

Wildly exaggerated claims about the loss of biodiversity, like climate alarmism, were boosted by the huge UN conference in Rio in 1992. However, those concerns had first been hyped by two scientists who became darlings of the radical environmental movement: E.O. Wilson and Norman Myers. Their assumptions were less bogus than flat out ridiculous, but they were eagerly regurgitated to stoke fears about a new geological era – the "Anthropocene" – where mankind's impact on earth is equated to that of the killer asteroid that wiped out the dinosaurs.

What biotic holocaust?
13–14 September 2007

Norman Myers' sinking ark
15 June 2011

The Keystone XL beetle boondoggle
12 June 2013

Man as killer asteroid
20 March 2014

Breaking fake eco news
26 July 2017

What biotic holocaust?
13–14 September 2007

Last month, when I was with my daughter at the famous Field Museum of Natural History in Chicago, we came across an arresting exhibit. Its message: humans are destroying life on earth at an apocalyptic rate.

According to the display, which was for some reason illustrated by a dead swan (a life form which as far as I know is in no danger of extinction): "[F]or the first time in Earth's history, a single species is the primary cause of a mass extinction. Early on, extreme climate and environment change may have led to species loss. But today, human activity is destroying habitats, causing species to go extinct at a rapid rate...What has died? Almost too much to count. Scientists estimate we've lost 30,000 species in the last year. But because the earth is home to far more species than we've identified, there are surely many species going extinct unnoticed."

To bring home this terrifying message, there was a clock indicating the "Number of species that have gone extinct since 8:00 this morning." The culprits were identified as garbage, population, transportation, industry and logging. In a word, humanity. We should, presumably, feel both ashamed and horrified.

This grim picture seemed to be confirmed by the release yesterday of the World Conservation Union's (IUCN) annual "Red List of Threatened Species." "Extinction crisis escalates," declared the press release. "Red List shows apes, corals, cultures, dolphins all in danger." It then proceeded to claim that "Life on Earth is disappearing fast and will continue to do so unless urgent action is taken."

According to Julia Marton-Lefevre, director-general of the IUCN, the "invaluable" efforts made so far "are not enough...We need to act now to stave off this global extinction crisis. This can be done, but only with a concerted effort by all levels of society." Presumably those levels would stretch from frightened schoolchildren through anti-development NGOs and huge self-serving international bureaucracies to national government environmental agencies.

How could I be so cynical? Well, step this way and I'll show you.

There can be no denying that the astonishing proliferation of the human race, and its stunning technology, have had an environmental impact. It could hardly be otherwise. What makes us unique, however, is that we care. Even capitalists.

Although there are many symbiotic relationships in nature, humans are unique in seeking to preserve fauna and flora. Among the characteristics that make humans different from other animals are empathy and sympathy – the fact that we can put ourselves in the position of others and "feel" both with and for them – and anthropomorphic projection, the fact that we attribute human characteristics to animals and even inanimate objects. The second may be a "cognitive error," but it fuels concern, and makes for wonderful flights of imagination. A purely "rational" species of intelligent beings would look with incomprehension at the work of A.A. Milne, Beatrix Potter or Walt Disney. Human concern for nature is seen in the rapid growth of well-funded environmental organizations in recent decades, and in the enormous array of policy instruments – from national parks and wildlife reserves to endangered species laws.

But there are less attractive aspects of human nature, and one of them is the tendency to exploit humanity's finer instincts in pursuit of power, pelf and status. Hence "biodiversity" has been turned into a political issue, which has been taken up by the United Nations and used as an excuse for bureaucratic empire building, cheered on by well-funded professional activists.

There is always one clear sign of those seeking to exploit any problem for political purposes: gross exaggeration. This is frequently portrayed as morally justifiable. After all, action needs to be taken. So what's wrong with amping up the facts?

Plenty. An alleged ongoing "biotic holocaust" has become a central, unquestionable, tenet of radical environmentalism. But is it true? For a start, let's take a look at one glaring "fact:" the enormous discrepancy in the extinction numbers between the Field Museum and the IUCN. According to the IUCN, and despite its apocalyptic language, the total number of species that has gone extinct since 1500 is about 1.5 per year. How can that figure possibly fit with the Field

Museum's claims that the earth is losing 30,000 annually?

Oscar Wilde's Lady Bracknell famously declared that: "To lose one parent...may be regarded as a misfortune; to lose both looks like carelessness." We might similarly reflect that to lose one and a half species a year may be a cause for sorrow; to claim that there are another 29,998.5 that went extinct without us knowing their names is, well, suspicious.

I contacted the Field's PR department and was originally told that the 30,000 figure was taken from the work of Edward O. Wilson, a "world-renowned scientist." True. But E.O. Wilson isn't just any old Pulitzer Prize-winning Harvard boffin. He has an intriguing background in scientific controversy.

In the 1970s, Prof. Wilson was at the centre of an academic slugfest over the implications of Darwinism for human nature and human society. In his book *Sociobiology*, Prof. Wilson claimed that to understand society, we had to understand man's evolved biological nature. For this quite obvious suggestion he was pilloried by Marxist academics as a determinist, genocidal racist, and promoter of the capitalist "status quo." These slurs were particularly painful to Wilson, since he considered himself, like most academics, particularly at Harvard, "of the left."

According to the brilliant book *Defenders of the Truth*, by Ullica Segerstrale, the attacks on Prof. Wilson led to a remarkable personal transformation. By the end of the 1980s, he had "reinvented" himself, she wrote, "from Wilson I, the politically incorrect sociobiologist, to Wilson II, the politically correct environmentalist...Here Wilson – supported by a general neo-catastrophist trend with tales of dinosaur deaths, asteroids, and the like – was able to make a convincing case for the importance of the preservation of biodiversity."

Since the catastrophic loss of biodiversity was yet another alleged adverse side-effect of "untrammelled" capitalism, Prof. Wilson was now once more on-side with his old buddies on the left. Significantly, he is a member of the board of the David Suzuki Foundation. According to the Suzuki website, Professor Wilson believes that "The David Suzuki Foundation embodies the principles of scientific environmentalism."

In fact, the Foundation is as wildly alarmist as extinction figures are hyped. The calculations work like this: you assume that the "background" rate of extinction is, say, one species per million species per year. Then you assume that there are 30 million species on earth (versus the 1.9 million so far classified). Then you assume that the present rate of extinction is, what the hell, say a thousand times the "background level." Hence you arrive at a figure of 30,000 by assuming vast numbers of species that have never been identified, and plucking a wildly alarmist extinction rate out of a hat.

This means that another egregious error at the Field Museum exhibit is the claim that "because the Earth is home to far more species than we've identified, there are surely many species going extinct unnoticed." But *all* the claimed 30,000 extinctions are "unnoticed." The Field cannot name any of them.

This is obviously not considered a problem by the most radical proponents of global action to prevent the ravages of capitalism. Gro Harlem Brundtland, whose 1987 UN report on sustainable development is central to socialism's highly successful environmental counterthrust, has put it this way: "The library of life is burning, and we don't even know the titles of the books."

Prof. Wilson's figures have come under attack, but only by the very brave. Dr. Patrick Moore, an apostate founding member of Greenpeace, suggested that the only place you could find the alleged plethora of lost species was in Prof. Wilson's computer: "They're actually electrons on a hard drive."

Similarly, Bjorn Lomborg, in his much reviled but little refuted book, *The Skeptical Environmentalist*, noted that actual observations of habitat loss in no way backed up apocalyptic extinction estimates.

You might imagine that the slight matter of a factor difference of 20,000 (30,000 vs. 1.5) in extinction figures would lead to some disagreement between the IUCN and the Field Museum, but no. Just as the old revolutionary slogan is "No enemies on the left," so the present variant is "No environmental exaggeration too great." Indeed, the IUCN appears clearly frustrated that it is bound by actual observed science in doing its tendentious environmental work. Its assumptions of invisible species loss is right up there with that of the Field. Nevertheless, its "hard" figures, despite the hysterical spin put on them, suggest that the "biotic holocaust" is a myth. In a good cause, of course. Donate today.

Further requests for information from the Field eventually produced a reply from the scientist in charge of the extinction exhibit. He concluded, after appropriate citations from "the literature," that "the overwhelming consensus of scientists studying biodiversity around the world is that Earth is currently involved in a period of incredible species loss."

Incredible indeed.

Norman Myers' sinking ark

15 June 2011

Alarmist projections fall apart as they fail to materialize. Junk theories eventually get junked. A case of the former is the failure of 50 million "climate refugees" to appear on schedule. An example of the latter is a recent study that suggests that forecasts of species loss have been significantly exaggerated.

What links these two cases is the man who both made the 50 million projection and who is also, perhaps more than any other individual, responsible for hyping the extinction scare: Oxford environmentalist Norman Myers. Intriguingly but not untypically, the more Prof. Myers is proved wrong, the more he goes on the attack, while his supporters castigate critics for just not "caring" about refugees and extinction.

Prof. Myers' projections of 50 million climate refugees by 2010 came from research funded by the United Nations Environment Program, UNEP. They were widely regurgitated by other UN agencies and governments, and cited in the alarmist UK Stern review. In 2005, UNEP put up a website map featuring the alarmist forecast. When blogger Gavin Atkins pointed out earlier this year that the areas that were meant to witness a refugee exodus had in fact shown healthy population growth, UNEP quietly removed the map. Stephen Castles of the International Migration Institute at Oxford meanwhile declared that Prof. Myers' methodology was crude and his projections "absolute nonsense." When Prof. Myers was interviewed by the BBC, instead of defending his methodology, he proceeded to point out how many countries and refugee camps he had visited – as if science were based on accumulating frequent flier points. He suggested that the lack of evidence was analogous to the fact that "You can't prove that smoking causes cancer." He told the magazine *New Scientist*: "It may be very difficult to demonstrate that there are 50 million climate refugees, but it is even harder to demonstrate that there are not."

This is not the first time that Prof. Myers has been linked to wild exaggerations in the cause of promoting "an entirely new mode of Earthling existence." In his 1979 book, *The Sinking Ark*, while acknowledging that the current recorded rate of species loss was around one a year, he "supposed" that one million species might be lost by the end of the 20th century, i.e. 50,000 a year. The millennium has come and gone, but there is no evidence that even a handful of species have disappeared, let alone a million.

The fact that Prof. Myers' species-loss claim was unscientific was pointed out by economist Julian Simon 20 years ago – when extinction was being played up to coincide with the 1992 UN Rio conference. Ten years later, Bjorn Lomborg – who was prompted to environmental research by what he believed was Professor Simon's excessive optimism – agreed. In *The Skeptical Environmentalist*, Lomborg established that species loss had been enormously exaggerated. He pointed out that insofar as species-loss projections had a scientific basis, it was in supposed correlation with loss of habitat. However, he noted that the models did not fit with real-world experience.

Confirmation that projections are exaggerated came recently from a study in the journal *Nature* by biologists Stephen Hubbell and Fangliang He. They suggested that assumptions of species loss had been exaggerated by as much as 160%. In fact, while this appears to expose yet another example of going with the alarmism and not checking the science, it still leaves the alarmism largely in place. Indeed, Prof. Hubbell claims that the world still faces an "extinction crisis" and could lose 20–50% of species over the next 100 years, even though he admits that those projections might be based on the science he has refuted, and also depend on catastrophic climate projections coming to pass. He conspicuously does not criticize Norman Myers.

Stephen Castles, the Oxford don who said that Prof. Myers' refugee projections were "absolute nonsense," nevertheless also claimed that scaring people in order to take action on climate change was "a very laudable motive." Oli Brown of UNEP suggested that Norman Myers deserved praise for sticking his "head above the parapet." The metaphor is telling; it caters to environmentalists' self-image of being under siege by wicked forces that would fecklessly destroy the world. Such a Manichean perspective tends not to make for good science.

Perhaps the biggest question is this: Given the non-appearance of those 50 million refugees, why has nobody made a bigger deal of the non-extinct million species? One projection seems certain: as the ark of his dubious science sinks below the non-rising waters of reality, you won't receive any apologies from Norman Myers.

The Keystone XL beetle boondoggle
12 June 2013

When government-promoted biodiversity crawls under the door, cost-benefit analysis – not to mention common sense – seems to fly out the window. One startling recent example is a beetle capture-and-relocation program being forced on the proposed Keystone XL pipeline at a cost of close to $100,000 a beetle. Biodiversity is one of those concepts that seems unarguably "good," but, like its co-conspirators, sustainability and corporate social responsibility, its very breadth and vagueness makes it a happy anti-hunting ground for those who oppose development, seek to bring corporations to heel, enjoy scaring children, and/or want to rule the world.

Keystone XL, which proposes to take 830,000 barrels per day of diluted bitumen from the Alberta oilsands to the refineries of the US

Gulf Coast, has been subjected to numerous comprehensive reviews. Its route has already been moved once in order to minimize ecosystem risks to the Sand Hills area of Nebraska. Now, as part of its own mammoth environmental analysis, the US Fish and Wildlife Service, FWS, has insisted that the project's sponsor, TransCanada Corp., relocate American burying beetles (ABBs) from a Nebraska section of the proposed pipeline.

The burying beetle is indeed custom-made for time-lapse nature TV. It recycles dead birds and small animals by burrowing underneath their bodies, covering them up, then rearing its young on the subterranean carcasses. TransCanada has been given elaborate instructions on how to trap the black and orange spotted insect using thawed-out pre-frozen laboratory rats. The trapping process involves building little ramps to buried plastic drums, from which the dead rats are raising a stink. From there the beetles are to be moved, after being marked, to a safe location, kind of like a witness protection program. TransCanada is also required to remove animal carcasses from the construction site, lest some beetles get homesick and wander back into the killing fields.

All pipeline workers in areas of ABB habitat will have to be educated about the beetle, and refrain from bringing dogs and cats onsite (do pipelayers really bring cats to work?). The company must produce "a full-color endangered species card with a picture of the ABB" along with comprehensive information. Other provisions include the shielding of artificial pipeline-related lighting. All beetle injuries or deaths must be reported.

The company estimates that it will successfully relocate 119 beetles. The total cost of the program is around $10 million. That works out to the aforementioned jaw-dropping $100,000 a pop.

The ABB is already subject to several well-financed and meticulously monitored recovery programs, and is now present in eight states, so while its numbers are in secular decline due to such factors as habitat loss, it is not close to extinction. Ironically, one of the reasons for loss of habitat is the conversion of land to make ethanol to fight climate change, from which the beetle is also inevitably declared to be under threat.

It has been calculated that ethanol production in fact leads to increased emissions of carbon dioxide, as well as raising grain prices for poor people. Now we can add another victim; one with six legs. Ethanol is, however, great for farm votes.

One can't help wondering if the relocation funds might not have been better used elsewhere. Aren't there quite a few poor people in America who could benefit from a $100,000 relocation? Significantly, the FWS has, in recent years, diluted its cost-benefit calculations to ignore inconveniences such as private property, or, apparently, any trace of balance.

The FWS – which is part of the Department of the Interior – has demonstrated a clear bias towards radical environmentalism via a manoeuvre known as "sue and settle." NGOs that are cozy with the administration are encouraged to bring suit, thus "forcing" it to make a deal that it wanted anyway. Significantly, the biggest such deal was with a group including the Center for Biological Diversity, under which the FWS claimed it had to take legal action on some 750 species. The immediate result was to restrict development on millions of acres of private property, thus threatening to shut down oil and gas activity and grazing operations. The Center for Biological Diversity had dubbed Keystone XL "an environmental disaster in the making."

The burying beetle will not be the end of Keystone XL's regulatory travails, which are primarily based on junk claims about its impact on the climate. The junkiest was that of ex-NASA scientist and global warming maven James Hansen, who said that the line's construction would mean "game over" for the planet.

Man as killer asteroid

20 March 2014

There were climate talks last week in Bonn. Who knew? A recent Gallup poll confirmed that climate change ranks in the basement of public concerns. It thus seems doubtful that the now-ritual "leak"

of the most alarming bits of the next report from the Intergovernmental Panel on Climate Change, the IPCC, suggesting more – ho
hum – cataclysm, chaos and hay fever, will have much policy impact.
Nor will the ritual raft of scary coincident reports. Nor will a new
book, *The Sixth Extinction*, by Elizabeth Kolbert, which attempts to
switch the focus of climate catastrophe to the loss of biodiversity.

The American Association for the Advancement of Science,
AAAS, (described by the *Guardian*, in a magnificent Freudian slip,
as "The American Association for the Advancement of Scientists")
issued a statement this week that there was growing risk of "abrupt,
unpredictable and potentially irreversible changes" from man-made
climate change. Addressing them, according to the AAAS, would be
easy, just like wearing seat belts or bike helmets.

Next up this week was news of a study sponsored by NASA (and
again eagerly reported by the *Guardian*) suggesting that industrial
civilization could be headed for "irreversible collapse" due to unsustainable resource exploitation and "inequality," which rather gave the
ideological game away.

The study looked back to previous "complex" civilizations that
had collapsed, such as those of Rome, and noted how "fragile and
impermanent" they were. But that's about as insightful as a golf commentator saying "that putt was always going to the left." Which, come
to think about it, also happens to be the way environmental policy is
always going.

NASA's climate star, you might remember, used to be James
Hansen, the man who described coal transporters as "death trains,"
and accounted for the lack of warming in the past sixteen years by
claiming that the heat was "building up" in the oceans at the rate of
"400,000 Hiroshimas" a day.

The malign hand of industrial man is also now being talked up
as a whole new geological epoch, the "Anthropocene," a term coined
by Dutch Nobel prizewinning chemist Paul Crutzen. (Another, more
revealing, name suggested for the epoch is the "Catastrophozoic.")
The concept plays a prominent role in Ms. Kolbert's book.

For those unfamiliar with her work, Ms. Kolbert, from her perch
at the *New Yorker*, issues some of the shrillest squawks of climate

alarmism. Her book takes us on a gripping tour through dusty museum backrooms, venerable scientific institutions and drizzly Scottish vistas in pursuit of mastodon teeth and field fossils, but her ultimate destination – and conclusion – is never in doubt: capitalism sucks, and is heading for a global man-made Pompeii.

Ms. Kolbert notes that extinction is a relatively modern idea, whose great promoter was the French zoologist Georges Cuvier. She suggests that Cuvier is neglected while Darwin, who regarded extinction primarily as a side effect of evolution, is feted. There is in fact no contradiction between Darwin and Cuvier, even if Darwin didn't know about mass extinctions. But Cuvier is a useful entry point for suggesting that man's impact on earth comes into the same category as the six-mile-wide asteroid thought to have wiped out the dinosaurs.

Humans have certainly played a role in extinctions, likely of megafauna such as the mastodon, and certainly of the passenger pigeon. However, we have arguably now swung to the other extreme: cost-blind hypersensitivity.

This leads to the *T. Rex* in the catastrophist's lab: the assumption that impending disaster implies clear and present managerial policies. All that's needed is to chain capitalism, ditch democracy, torque the cost-benefit analysis, and summon good old political will.

Not surprisingly, Al Gore is an unabashed fan of Kolbert, claiming that she has "developed a distinctive and eloquent voice of conscience on issues arising from the extraordinary assault on the ecosphere." But while man's current impact on the ecosphere is undoubtedly unprecedented, that doesn't necessarily equate to "assault," much less catastrophe.

In his review of Kolbert's book, Gore points to the "psychological barriers" of deniers, and to manipulators of the status quo, but it never seems to occur to catastrophists such as Gore that they might have some psychological issues of their own, including the role that self-interest might play in their subconscious calculations. Subsidized solar hedge funds anyone?

For Gore, the problem isn't just the huge increase in human population and technology, it's "the emergence of a hegemonic ideology that exalts short-term thinking and ignores the true long-term cost and consequences of the choices we're making..."

Yet again, capitalism did it. Or is about to.

There was also praise for Kolbert's book in Monday's *Post* from eminent law professor Ian Hunter. Like Gore, Professor Hunter spewed large, perspective-free numbers into the atmosphere. "[S] ince the industrial revolution," he wrote, "we have burned enough fossil fuel to add 365 billion metric tonnes of carbon to the atmosphere. About a third of that has been absorbed in the world's oceans, which are dangerously acidified."

But apart from what represents "dangerous," which certainly requires consideration, here is another way of looking at that increase in carbon dioxide: if the contents of the atmosphere were presented on a chart three times the height of the Empire State Building, the increase in carbon dioxide since before the Industrial Revolution would amount to the height of a coffee mug.

None of this is to deny the potential impact of human emissions, or that small increases might have big results, it's just to note that disembodied big numbers don't bring any perspective.

Climate science certainly needs assiduous and objective study, but what we have had in recent decades is fashionable, ideologically driven hysteria that has already led to lousy policies, and threatens worse.

No wonder the public has switched off, and climate negotiators are threatened with extinction.

Breaking fake eco news
26 July 2017

There seems to be a radical disconnect between the claim – splashed breathlessly atop the front page of *The Globe and Mail* on Monday – that Canada is failing to protect its environment and the fact that securing approval for any piece of hinterland development these days amounts to a slog through an endless bog of regulation, review and protest.

According to the *Globe* story, which was based on the annual report conveniently leaked to it by the Canadian Parks and Wilderness Society, CPAWS, Canada is lagging commitments made under the UN's Convention on Biodiversity. Since 2010, its "protected" areas have increased from "only" 9.6% to 10.6% of the country, versus the commitment of 17% by 2020 made by the Harper government.

The first question is why the Harper government would have allowed itself to be roped into such an exercise in subversive calculation. All such commitments really do is to provide a fundraising soapbox for radical environmental NGOs.

Meanwhile, the concept of "protection" demands more thorough analysis. What it means is declaring great swaths of the country off limits for investment and job creation, on the ideologically skewed assumption that development and a healthy environment cannot coexist.

Alarmists play on the bogus assumption that since "only" 10% of Canada has been sanitized, 90% must be in danger of being turned into an oilsands Mordor. However, for some much-needed perspective, the amount of urban land in Canada is around one-quarter of one per cent of its landmass. Oilsands development has been projected to disturb just 0.02% of the boreal forest over 40 years. Meanwhile, claims that Canada is a "laggard" are dubious to say the least. According to the report, the leader of the protection pack is green-crazy Germany, which has protected 37.8% of its lands and waters. But we might note that Canada's 10% is three times the size of all of Germany, so that means that Canada has protected close to 10 times as much land as the German "leader."

CPAWS peddles the notion that nature "needs" 50% of lands and waters to be put off limits if she is to survive, but this "half for nature" meme is entirely bogus and fundamentally anti-human.

Until recently, I lived in a house in Toronto that was 300 meters from the busiest highway in Canada. Well over 50% of my lot was devoted to nature. I had abundant flora, dozens of beautiful bird species, and no shortage of raccoons, squirrels, chipmunks, and possums. Meanwhile, nature was constantly seeking to reclaim more of her domain by swallowing my house in ivy and creepers.

If you walk any part of the beautiful trail on Lake Ontario between the iconic industrial cities of Oshawa and Hamilton, you will find magnificent parks and wetlands. But, for the likes of CPAWS, the Greater Toronto environment has been raped and pillaged.

While people may feel uneasy about the hysterical claims and increasing power of alarmist ENGOs, they are reluctant to speak out, partly because anybody who criticizes ENGOs will immediately be screamed down as being "anti-environment."

CPAWS knows a good deal about pack hunting because it was among the ENGO signatories of the rancid 2010 Canadian Boreal Forest Agreement, which was the result of do-not-buy campaigns that threatened leading forestry companies' business, and which gave ENGOs a veto over development in large parts of the boreal forest. Governments, local communities and native groups played no part in this shakedown, which collapsed earlier this year.

Like "the environment," "biodiversity" is a term where the ideological devil is in the details. As humanity has flourished and spread over the earth, it has inevitably converted wilderness. However, humans are unique in actually being concerned about their impact on nature.

The richer they become, the more concerned they are, but also the more likely not just to demand, and get, higher standards, but to support environmental extremism out of guilt and/or ignorance.

Radicals declare that we are responsible for a "wave of extinction," and that thousands, or tens of thousands, of species are being driven out of existence annually. In fact, the recorded number is in the low single digits. But like the environment more generally, biodiversity is a useful weapon for those who seek global control of human affairs, a political thrust with the UN at its epicentre.

The Biodiversity Convention – like the climate policy fiasco – came out of the UN's 1992 Rio Summit, which was masterminded by the late great Canadian eco-doomster Maurice Strong. Strong may be gone, but his sub-species of power-hungry environmental alarmists is growing like an invasive weed, choking development in the process.

The Harper government sought, with spectacular lack of success, to streamline the environmental approval process. The Trudeau Liberals have promised to make it even more unwieldy, not merely by incorporating "traditional" – that is, non-scientific – knowledge into the process, but also by "connecting" human no-go areas. But whatever this sock-puppet Liberal government does, we may be sure it won't be enough for the radicals, or for their mainstream media handmaidens.

7
Uncivil society

UNCIVIL SOCIETY

Environmental non-government organizations, ENGOs, have pro-
liferated enormously in power and importance in recent decades.
This isn't solely – or indeed even – due to increased public environmental concern. It is because they have been cultivated as a key part
of a radical strategy to pressure governments and corporations to
adopt "sustainability" and promote "Global Governance." Their radical presence has been very deliberately injected into the policy process, and their activism is funded not merely by governments and
giant anti-capitalist capitalist foundations but by the corporations
they shake down.

All power to the NGOs!
26 January 2000

Seattle Sea Turtles versus the Washington Tear Gas
6 April 2000

CSR's dirty secret
26 January 2005

Earth Hour's soft fascism
26 March 2008

Don't lie down with pandas
28 March 2008

All power to the NGOs!
26 January 2000

The World Economic Forum, that annual gathering of the Great and the Good, which starts tomorrow in Davos, claims to be "independent and impartial," but any organization that promotes a centrally planned "global agenda" has a very partial view of the way the world should work.

One purpose of the WEF is to infect corporations and the media with the Global Governance view of things: that the world is going to environmental hell in a child labour-made handbasket unless "we" (that is, the WEF) take control.

Forum founder and aspiring global puppeteer Professor Klaus Schwab notes that globalization is leading to the loss of national government power. What the world thus needs, he claims, are "networks, flexible networks, where you put together governments, international organizations and business to look at the new issues on the global agenda." In other words: rule by global technocratic elites.

Meanwhile, according to Prof. Schwab: "You have to integrate the media because you have to make this process transparent – and you have to integrate civil society at large."

The notion that the media should be "integrated" into the WEF's agenda is appalling, but perhaps more significantly scary is his reference to "civil society." Prof. Schwab has always been a big fan of a very particular segment of civil society – radical non-governmental organizations, NGOs – although he admits that his support "irritated" early business forum participants. Not anymore. According to the WEF's website: "Corporate attitudes have changed slowly, but in the wake of a number of highly visible damaging incidents, perceptive CEOs realize that they need to engage civil society rather than scorn it."

When he refers to "damaging incidents," the good professor is presumably referring, for example, to the way cyber-empowered NGOs stopped the Multilateral Agreement on Investment, thus retarding job-creation in poor countries. He also presumably believes that those who have to be "engaged" include the NGO performance artists who last year scuttled the WTO meetings in Seattle and were this week wandering around Montreal banging on drums as their contribution to rational debate over genetically modified food. The message/threat is clear: appease the NGOs or they'll close you down. Appease the NGOs, or you'll be considered an "unperceptive" CEO.

"There can be no doubt," according to the WEF, "that NGOs are now influential actors in every major policy debate on the global agenda." But how did they become so influential? Because they have been sponsored and promoted by the WEF and the UN.

The WEF has long been a focus for conspiracy theories, and it's easy to see why. Maurice Strong – roving ambassador of doom and long a powerful figure behind the scenes at the WEF – once suggested a fictional "plot" under which the public-spirited (such as himself) would kidnap everybody at Davos and bring the industrial world to a halt in order to save it from environmental apocalypse.

Strong believes economic growth is a "disease." He has also long been a powerful promoter of NGOs, to whom he has diverted large amounts of taxpayer and foundation money. Why? Paranoid conspiracy theorists might try the following on for size.

According to the historian Paul Johnson, the Soviets that gave their name to the Soviet Union were spontaneous committees of workers that first appeared in 1905. Although their call was for reform, not revolution, Lenin saw how they might be infiltrated and used to subvert parliamentary democracy. By April, 1917, his Bolsheviks were calling for "the rapid transfer of all state power into the hands of the Soviets." By September, Lenin declared "All power to the Soviets." He then seized power via a coup but, as Johnson points out, he "astutely made the greatest possible use of the spurious legitimacy conferred upon his regime by the Soviets." The rest, as they say, is history.

What a ridiculously paranoid parallel! Still, perhaps it might be worth bearing in mind the next time we hear the message that NGOs must become "partners" in everything from boardroom decisions to the United Nations' General Assembly.

All power to the NGOs!

Seattle Sea Turtles versus the Washington Tear Gas
6 April 2000

The Seattle Sea Turtles are due to descend on the US capital next week for a meeting with the Washington Tear Gas. Fresh from their victory over the WTO Globalizers last year, the Sea Turtles are planning to shut down the annual meetings of the World Bank and IMF. All welcome. No violence, please, but bring a brick, just in case.

Last December's successful disruption of the WTO meeting by a ragtag group of retread '60s radicals, student rebels-looking-for-a-cause, environmentalists and labour unions was motivated by a combination of well-intended economic ignorance, Internet-spread anxiety and cynical self-interest. The self-interest came primarily from the labour movement, which wishes to impose restrictive labour standards on the Third World so as to cut down on competition for its own workers.

Perhaps the most intriguing aspect of the Seattle riots is how their perpetrators, in particular non-governmental organizations, NGOs, far from being condemned, are being hailed as the voice of "Civil Society," which must urgently be allowed into the evolving process of "global governance."

The reason everybody from Kofi Annan, the Secretary-General of the United Nations, to Romano Prodi, the head of the European Commission (which, in ideological terms, is a very short distance) is jumping on the civil society bandwagon is because if there is one thing that this very specific segment of civil society is overwhelmingly in favour of, it is more regulation and control.

Read virtually any speech by a political leader or head of an international organization these days and you will find a grovelling reference to the need to accommodate the forces of Seattle, which are being conflated with democracy. These forces are in fact tools for overturning representative democracy.

In a speech last week, Prodi spoke of "[a] new generation of civil groups and NGOs in which activists, mostly young, are campaigning for a wide range of social and environmental progress. These people must be brought into the decision-making process alongside experts in all fields."

As for the WTO, an organization already paralyzed by the need for consensus even without latter-day hippies preventing delegates getting to meetings, it is, strangely, also calling for more civil society input. In a speech in early March, Director-General Mike Moore declared: "If the WTO is to succeed, it must reinforce its democratic credentials. It must engage the confidence and support of civil society, it must respond to their needs and interests." Moore's motto seems to be: If they look like beating you, have them join you.

Where this is coming from, and going, was clearly indicated at an otherwise doleful meeting in New York last week of the Socialist Scholars Conference. One of the few rays of light seen by the apparatchiks was reportedly the "Seattle streetfighters." When the president of the EU, the Secretary-General of the UN, the director-general of the WTO and the Socialist Scholars Conference are all promoting the same group, alarm bells should be ringing.

CSR's dirty secret

26 January 2005

It is ironic that a campaign to cut down on allegedly wasteful use of paper should take a full-page ad in *The New York Times*. Last Friday, however, a radical San Francisco-based organization named ForestEthics bought such an ad, featuring a sultry model wearing fluffy wings and carrying a chainsaw. The heading was "Victoria's Dirty Secret." The alleged secret? That the famous lingerie company and its parent, Columbus, Ohio-based Limited Brands, print 398 million glossy catalogues annually.

Apparently "two years of investigative research" had established that these catalogues come from paper, and paper comes from trees, and those trees happen to grow in forests, and not just any forests, but "old growth and Endangered Forests in the Canadian boreal, the third-largest forest wilderness in the world and a critical regulator of global climate."

ForestEthics' objective is to force Victoria's Secret to use more recycled paper and less "virgin fibre."

The Times apparently had a few problems with the ad being even more unbalanced than the paper's own environmental coverage, not to mention "violent." However, the latter element was taken care of by drawing in a cartoon chainsaw rather than having the model carry a real one. Go figure.

But is Canada's boreal forest really under threat? Are forestry companies acting irresponsibly? Does the use of more recycled paper make economic – or any other kind of – sense? And finally, and perhaps most relevant, who the hell is ForestEthics?

Canada's boreal forest is unquestionably huge. ForestEthics likes to point out that it is home to three billion birds. That doesn't sound very much like an ecosystem under threat. But what about individual species? Those woodland caribou of the Alberta foothills are much invoked, but to the extent that they are endangered, how culpable are forest companies? Forestry companies point out that the herd has not shrunk in the past 20 years. Nevertheless, those companies still mostly trip over themselves to meet the ever-expanding concerns of their environmental critics. Somehow it's never enough. That's because the critics operate in a cost-free world; that is, the costs of catering to their demonic notions about capitalism are not borne by them, but by shareholders, employees and the other "stakeholders" about whom they tell us they are so concerned. Well, maybe not shareholders. Indeed, costing shareholders money is regarded as a key measure of success.

As a survey in the latest *Economist* points out, notions of corporate social responsibility, sustainable development and the triple bottom line are based on a fundamental failure to grasp the significance of Adam Smith's "Invisible Hand." The most amazing aspect of this way of non-thinking is that it has been embraced by so many muddled/vain/scared/hypocritical corporate "leaders."

The environmental movement's bland disregard for costs was nowhere better indicated than in a campaign last year, based on allegedly "saving" the same forests, which accused manufacturers of bath-room tissue of "flushing ancient forests down the toilet." Greenpeace, which mounted the campaign, rated the "environmental friendliness" of different brands. Most highly recommended was a brand called "Seventh Generation" because of the "high recycled or alternative-fibre content and clean, chlorine-free production." At the other end of the spectrum was Life brand, not recommended because it con-tained "endangered forest fibers." Twenty-four rolls of Life brand cost $6.99. Four rolls of Seventh Generation cost $4.49. In other words, the "environmentally sensitive" brand cost four times as much.

And what does Victoria's Secret have to say about the catalogue campaign, which has been underway for several months? Typically, it has gone straight into grovel mode, pointing out that it does use some recycled paper already, and will try much harder in future. Such a weak-kneed response indicates a further retreat in the war on common sense.

There is much talk about corporations operating under broad "social licence." In many ways this is true, but nobody appointed For-estEthics the licensing authority.

A modest proposal: it's about time that the corporate sector got off its hypocritical rear end and started to stand up for the capitalist system. How to start? What about a certification system for environ-mental NGOs, which goes into the objective validity of their claims, whether or not they use violent or coercive tactics (as ForestEthics has done), and whether they have the slightest clue about how an economy works.

Very few would wind up certified. Which might make it a little easier to tell them to go take a hike in the boreal.

Earth Hour's soft fascism
26 March 2008

Light, both natural and artificial, has traditionally been associated with The Good. A critical element of civilization has been the development of ever brighter, more flexible and more reliable forms of illumination, from the tallow candle, through whale oil and kerosene, to Thomas Edison's marvellous invention of the electric light bulb.

Conversely, the absence of light is associated with primitivism and ignorance. Is it not significant, therefore, that radical environmentalists are seeking to persuade citizens to flick the switch? Toronto, Ottawa and Vancouver are among the cities planning to dim their lights this coming Saturday between 8 and 9 pm, as part of "Earth Hour."

Masterminded by powerful ENGO the World Wildlife Fund, WWF, this stunt is allegedly to raise awareness of climate change, but what needs raising is not so much awareness as knowledge. People are woefully ignorant both about the uncertainties of climate-change science and the implications of climate-change policies. However, the WWF has no interest in discussing or debating the issue. According to them, we should "stop talking and start acting."

Far from being a harmless gesture of support for the environment, Earth Hour is symbolic of a spreading soft eco-fascism, aided by well-meaning individuals and cynical and/or scared corporations. Indeed, what is truly astonishing, and disturbing, about this turn-out-the-lights exercise is how many businesses and corporations have signed on to it. According to WWF Canada, they haven't had one "no" from any company they've approached.

Loblaws, the supermarket chain – which is already seeking environmental salvation by bold strategies such as depriving its customers of plastic shopping bags – is now to deprive them of adequate lighting too. Molson-Coors and McDonald's are on board. Both the Air Canada Centre, ACC, and the Rogers Centre will turn off their external signage and spotlights this Saturday. Although the Leafs are

playing the Habs, the lights in the ACC washrooms will be turned
down. So get ready, as the Aussies say, to "splash your boots."

That is perhaps appropriate since Earth Hour was pioneered last
year in Sydney by WWF Australia, advised by advertising giant Leo
Burnet. Leo Burnet's chairman, Nigel Marsh, declared: "I'm an opti-
mist about climate change. The human race eventually abolished
slavery and gave women the vote. We eventually work it out."

Get the implication? "Deny" the dubious science or dangerous
politics of anthropogenic climate change and you're the kind of person who would support slavery and keep women barefoot and pregnant in the kitchen.

The presence of Leo Burnet indicates that this is very much
about big business and branding (a bit ironic for the No Logo crowd,
surely). Guidelines about how the Earth Hour brand must be used
are available on the WWF Canada website, along with the information
that: "The Earth Hour tone of voice is human, optimistic, inclusive,
passionate and caring. The Brand should never appear to be aggressive or use scare tactics to incite participation."

How this squares with climate change as the greatest-threat-
the-world-has-ever-seen escapes me, but what the hell, this is about
fund-raising and power, not logic or truth.

The mythology about Sydney is that it was a "great success," and
that no less than 2.3 million Sydneysiders happily participated, along
with a couple of thousand businesses, and that there was an energy
saving of 10.2% during that hour-of-no-power.

The endlessly regurgitated 2.3 million figure comes from a poll
taken by the *Sydney Morning Herald*, which just happens to belong to
Fairfax Group, which just happened to sponsor the event (and pulled
in a lot of guilty green advertising in the process). How this figure
gels with the number of Sydneysiders who actually signed up with
WWF Australia to express support, reportedly not much more than
50,000 – i.e. around one-fortieth the number of "participants" – isn't
clear.

And as for those energy savings, subsequent studies suggested
that the actual savings from the event – in which external lights on
the Sydney Opera House and Sydney Harbour bridge were doused

– amounted to 2.1%. Even the most optimistic estimates, that is, those put out by the WWF, suggest that the energy saved had been the equivalent of taking 48,000 cars off the road for an hour. Sounds mildly impressive, until you express this statistic in another way: it was the equivalent of taking one car off the road for five and a half years.

The WWF claims that Sydney demonstrated what we can do by voluntarily pulling together. Indeed it did. Nothing. Meanwhile, following the event, the head of WWF Australia immediately got on a plane to Singapore to discuss the event going global.

On a plane. To Singapore.

Eco Main Chancers in London followed up with "Lights out London." The illuminated ads on Piccadilly Circus were switched off for the first time since the Blitz. Coca-Cola, McDonald's, Samsung, TDK, Sanyo and Budweiser all dimmed their messages. Buckingham Palace went dark, along with Westminster Cathedral, the Houses of Parliament, and Canary Wharf.

The tabloid *Sun's* page 3 pinup backed the move. "If we work together we can massively reduce climate change," she said. "It takes very little effort to be green."

WWF Canada, supported by – among others – *the Toronto Star*, Virgin Mobile, the City of Toronto, Toronto Hydro and Canwest's Global TV (Canwest owns this newspaper), is using Earth Hour as an opportunity to take its environmental indoctrination deeper into schools. It suggests that schools hold an event this Friday, and perhaps turn their gyms into cinemas, where they might show films such as – you guessed it – *An Inconvenient Truth*!

I would suggest that the biggest current threat to our planet is not either climate change or the financial "crisis," but the mindless conformist tendency to support ideas such as Earth Hour, which are aimed at the levers of both electrical and political power.

If you love civilization, freedom and the use of reason, keep on all the lights you need on Saturday. Take Back the Night.

Don't lie down with pandas
28 March 2008

Earth Hour's primary purpose is not to "raise awareness" about climate change, or give people an opportunity to see the stars, but to demonstrate the power of ENGO organizer WWF. Such power comes attached to the potential for earning big bucks. I came across an example of the WWF's earning power at the recent Globe conference in Vancouver.

The Cement Association of Canada had just produced its second "Sustainability Report." At a related session, earnest industry representatives emphasized the many steps they were taking to reduce their environmental footprint. What intrigued me about the session was the appearance of Michael Russill, president and chief executive of WWF Canada. His tone was quite unlike that of the other panel members. He was not there to grovel, or to struggle with practical issues. He made clear that he was not an "advocate" of the cement industry, but noted that WWF International had a "partnership" with French-based cement giant Lafarge, one of whose North American executives was on the panel. According to Russill, Lafarge had come to the WWF for help with work on restoring quarries, and this relationship had "expanded." One of the WWF's "stretch targets" for Lafarge was a reduction in its carbon dioxide emissions from developed countries by 10% below 1990 levels by 2010. "We are demanding and challenging and pushing," Russill said. The WWF, he said, saw its job as "raising the bar." (So much easier than having to jump over it.)

Russill – a former oil industry executive – laid out the "rules of engagement" with Lafarge. The "dialogue" had to be "CEO to CEO." Moreover, the parties had to be free to criticize each other. The WWF insisted on "transparency" and on third-party auditing.

In the interests of transparency, I decided to ask three questions: What was the cost to Lafarge of meeting the WWF's demands? How much was Lafarge paying the WWF? And, since the freedom to criticize was such an important part of the partnership, what criticism did Lafarge have of the WWF's approach?

The Lafarge executive on the dais looked like a deer in the headlights. He didn't have a clue what meeting the WWF's demands was costing. Moreover, he would presumably rather have chewed off his own arm than criticize the WWF. It was left to Russill to reveal the price that Lafarge had to pay to have the WWF hold its feet to the kiln: 1 million Euros; that is, around $1.6 million. Subsequently, however, I discovered, when speaking to Olivier Luneau, Lafarge's head of sustainability and public affairs in Paris, that the figure was actually 1.5 million Euros; that is, $2.4 million, annually, over three years. In terms of WWF targets, Luneau said, Lafarge was on the way to meeting the intensity reduction of 20% by 2010, but was only halfway to meeting the absolute reduction figure of 10% in developed-country operations.

Luneau claimed that he didn't have a figure for the cost of meeting the WWF's demands (beyond what Lafarge would have done anyway). However, he stressed that Lafarge's link with the WWF was valuable in terms of the company's credibility, especially when it came to input into the policy-making process.

Luneau said that the WWF's "stretch targets" were useful in getting the company prepared for a carbon-constrained world: a little toughening up for a more draconian future.

The WWF thus seems to have found a very profitable niche for itself, both as guardian of the planet and consultant on how to deal with guardians of the planet. This unusual combination means that it can happily bite the hand that feeds it; then its corporate "partners" can proudly display the bite marks as proof of their environmental commitment. It couldn't work anywhere but in the environment business.

8

The war in the woods

Canada's forests have been a focal point for radical environmentalists since the protests at Clayaquot Sound on Vancouver Island in the early 1990s. Buoyed by their success in bringing forestry companies to heel there, ENGOS such as Greenpeace and ForestEthics (later renamed STAND.earth) sought to expand their control of Canadian forestry via intimidation and do-not-buy campaigns, leading to forced "agreements" with cowed companies.

Forest shakedown
19 May 2010

Boreal is beyond the law
12 March 2014

At last, a corporate hero
22 July 2015

Tzeporah and the Great Bear
15 July 2016

Good riddance to a bogus boreal forest "agreement"
1 February 2017

Greenpeace's Hachette job
28 June 2017

Forest shakedown
19 May 2010

Behind all the feel-good eco-speak of this week's Canadian Boreal Forest Agreement lies a simple bargain: the forest-products industry gets a bunch of NGOs off its back (at least for the moment); the NGOs get to demonstrate their ability to bring the forest industry, or indeed any industry, to heel.

As Todd Paglia, the executive director of ForestEthics, one of the NGO signatories, noted a few years ago, "We are going to provide these companies with an option of doing it the easy way. If they want to do it the hard way, we can see a tremendous amount of negative press and damage to their brand."

So the Forest Products Association of Canada (FPAC), which signed this deal with nine NGOs on behalf of its 21 members, has effectively cried "uncle" and called it accommodation.

"While the future of forestry and conservation in Canada's Boreal Forest rests primarily with governments," notes the agreement's accompanying blurb, "both industry and environmentalists have a shared responsibility to help define and realize that future."

But whoever elected, or appointed, the environmentalists?

Not, mind you, that governments are going to squeak too loudly. They are under NGO pressure too. Why else would chemophobic Ontario be covered in dandelions? Now logging is to be suspended on 29 million hectares of boreal forest.

This week's deal will undoubtedly mean fewer jobs, higher prices and zero impact on the climate, but it was hailed by its signatories as a success because it would "conserve significant areas of Canada's vast boreal forest, protect threatened woodland caribou and provide a competitive market edge for participating companies." But neither the boreal forest nor the woodland caribou are under any realistic threat. Meanwhile the "competitive market edge" refers to the fact that the eco storm troopers will now call off their "Do Not Buy" campaigns. When is someone going to launch a "Do Not Donate" campaign against these green extortionists?

Now the NGOs will be able to slap a "Do Not Buy" order on any company accused of having lower standards than the open-ended ones in the agreement. Indeed, the extortionists will be fervently cheered on by the FPAC. Otherwise its members will be, as it were, out on a limb. But if the industry really imagines this will end NGO pressure, they are dreaming in Technicolor.

FPAC head Avrim Lazar, who can be seen walking onto the screen to grovel about environmental matters each time you go to the organization's website (Sample: "We all know that if we are going to keep the planet for our children, we are going to have to consume a little less"), declared that: "The importance of this agreement cannot be overstated...Together we have identified a more intelligent, productive way to manage economic and environmental challenges in the boreal that will reassure global buyers of our products' sustainability."

When I asked Lazar how much the agreement would cost in terms of jobs, profitability and higher consumer prices, he almost begged me to understand that the deal was "economic." After all, presumably the threats to jobs, profitability and consumers would be even greater from ever-escalating campaigns of misinformation.

According to Greenpeace's Richard Brooks, spokesman for the NGOs who signed the agreement, "Concerns from the public and the marketplace about wilderness conservation and species loss have been critical drivers in arriving at this agreement."

More hooey is hardly conceivable. Where did such greatly exaggerated "concerns" originate except in the campaigns of Greenpeace and Co.?

Depressingly, but typically, the NGO side of this campaign was funded by the Pew and Ivey Foundations. The Pew Foundation – which was built on the fortune of the stout free-enterprisers who developed the first commercial Athabasca oilsands plant – has been called "perhaps the most egregious violation of donor intent in existence."

A few years ago, the FPAC put out a statement refuting many of ForestEthics' claims about the boreal forest. Lazar then described ForestEthics' version of forestry management as "simplistic and biased." Now he claims that the FPAC, too, might have been "simplistic and biased. That's what happens when you are fighting. We were always playing defence."

Better, apparently, just to give in.

This agreement is a shakedown, and a dark day for Canadian business.

Boreal is beyond the law

12 March 2014

I have no doubt that the Mining Association of Canada's *Towards Sustainable Mining* program is a model of environmental and community responsibility. The Canadian mining industry is here, as in many other respects, a world leader. Where I beg to differ with the association is in the nature and significance of its relationship with an ENGO called the Canadian Boreal Initiative, CBI.

The response, co-authored by the Mining Association and the CBI, to one of my recent columns suggests that "dialogue" is an important part of the "privilege to operate." But surely it is strange to regard the creation of jobs, growth and tax revenue as a "privilege," which requires "licence" from foreign-funded groups such as the CBI, especially as those groups require no licence of their own.

Without such ENGO licence, however, a company or industry opens itself to potential "reputational damage;" that is, the spreading of disinformation about it, and the harassment of its customers. Such harassment was important in forcing the forest industry into the 2010 Canadian Boreal Forest Agreement, CBFA, which was promoted and "brokered" by the Philadelphia-based Pew Charitable Trusts.

This is relevant because the CBI happens to be the Canadian arm of Pew, and a signatory of the CBFA, which has been in turmoil for over a year. One of the CBI's ENGO cohorts, Greenpeace, left the agreement to mount a campaign against one of the corporate signatories, Resolute Forest Products, who then sued Greenpeace for defamation and malicious falsehood.

Greenpeace, rather than offering a defence, has gone back to harassing Resolute's customers, and seeking to promote so called SLAPP (Strategic Lawsuits Against Public Participation) legislation in Ontario, which amounts here to a licence to lie. Another significant development, given the trend to outside certification, is that Resolute suddenly found some of its certification under the Forest Steward-ship Council, FSC, withdrawn. Hardly by coincidence, Greenpeace was one of the founders of the FSC, which is ardently supported by the CBI. This confirms that ENGO-related certification is a tool for bringing companies to heel rather than burnishing their triple bot-tom line.

The Mining Association seems to feel that it should be con-gratulated for getting "ahead of the curve" and going "beyond the law." Some companies may well see competitive advantage in doing so. Nevertheless, this is potentially dangerous territory if the route is being dictated by ENGOs who have agendas beyond responsible development.

Meanwhile, why is the CBI not subject to audits of its own activi-ties, starting with its attachment to objectivity? The CBI claims it "has been recognized as a credible, fair and science-based organization." But by whom? Here is CBI head Alan Young in the *Huffington Post* last July: "The dramatic and expensive floods, storms and wildfires expe-rienced by many Canadian cities in recent months are a reminder of our ties to the boreal. As the world's largest storehouse of carbon, it helps mitigate the effects of climate change."

Even if the science of climate were "settled," the integrity of the vast boreal forest – and its status as a carbon sink – is under no con-ceivable threat, so this statement is pure alarmist propaganda.

The CBI is also closely allied with groups that have demonized the oilsands – the biggest mining project in Canada – and who seek to hold up new pipelines. It supports the "protection" of at least half of the vast boreal, but protection from what? What happens to the people who live in the sanitized area? Are they to be the first genuine "climate (policy) refugees?" Most important, why do we need extra legal forces, particularly foreign-funded ones, to protect the environ-ment? Canada already has a comprehensive – indeed arguably over-elaborate – system of environmental legislation and regulation.

The *Towards Sustainable Mining* programme may indeed present Canadian miners with valuable tools. The concern is how far it might present the miners' "partners" with strategic weapons.

At last, a corporate hero

22 July 2015

Two weeks ago, Todd Paglia, executive director of us-based radical environmental organization ForestEthics, sent a letter of warning to Richard Garneau, CEO of Montreal-based Resolute Forest Products. Paglia declared that he was effectively banishing Resolute, a forestry giant with 7,700 employees and 19 pulp and paper mills in Canada, the us and Asia, from the Canadian Boreal Forest Agreement (CBFA). The CBFA was cooked up five years ago by ForestEthics and fellow radical ENGOs following campaigns of harassment.

It was a shakedown, as we noted in this space at the time.

In a July 10 letter to Garneau, Paglia declared that Resolute had refused to "cooperate" and had achieved "rogue status." Thus, the company would come under renewed attack. He went on to accuse Resolute of being "litigious" because it had brought suit both against Greenpeace and one of its certifiers under the so-called Forest Stewardship Council, FSC, itself another tool of control by environmental radicals.

Garneau's response was, to say the least, refreshing. He strongly disputed the notion that ForestEthics was in any position to throw Resolute out of the CBFA; Resolute had been a major supporter of the agreement, while the actions and demands of ForestEthics and its fellows threatened thousands of jobs. Paglia's letter, alleged Garneau, merely threatened the same old "bully tactics" based on a business model of "extortion."

Paglia responded last week with a second "Dear Richard" note accusing Garneau of "inaccuracies...too numerous to mention" but admitting that Resolute had in fact contributed to the CBFA. He rebutted many points that Garneau had never made, and declared ForestEthics prepared to work on "win–win solutions." A Resolute spokesman subsequently said that the company "stands behind every word" of its response to Paglia's initial letter.

Rarely, if ever, has a corporate executive dared to call an ENGO shakedown what it is. Richard Garneau is thus almost unique among executives. In a corporate world dripping with bogus "business ethics," Garneau, a quiet and modest man who lives in the boreal, has demonstrated some true moral backbone, refusing to bow to what he sees as lies and intimidation. And while his fellow corporate executives are missing in action, more and more Northern communities, aboriginal groups and unions are beginning to stand up against the anti-development bullies.

You'd think that the Canadian media – given to celebration of local exceptionality in any way, shape or form – would be keen to report on Garneau, but he is exceptional in an area where the media almost never dares to tread, either because it is part of the radical environmental crusade itself, or because it too is scared.

Some of the world's biggest media companies – including Hearst Corp., Time Inc. and *The Globe and Mail* – have become overseers of the CBFA, even though, as noted, it was signed under duress. Paglia copied his letter to these overseers, the Boreal Business Forum, BBF, so they can hardly claim to be ignorant of what is going on. Meanwhile another BBF monitor is Limited Brands, which, significantly, was ForestEthics' first major scalp when it launched a campaign against its Victoria's Secret subsidiary 10 years ago. Paglia's most recent conquest is Post-it conglomerate 3M.

The CBFA gives the lie to the stock leftist claim of vast corporate "power." Forestry companies and their customers have appeared almost defenceless against the ENGO onslaught, ostensibly persisting in the delusion that if they keep dancing to ENGO demands they will be granted "social licence."

One of Garneau's boldest moves was that lawsuit, launched two years ago, against Greenpeace, a close ally of ForestEthics. Greenpeace, an original signatory of the CBFA, had exited at the end of

2012, claiming frustration with the process, and redoubled its campaign of misinformation against Resolute. Garneau, throwing away the script which required appeasement, sued.

Greenpeace has been writhing to avoid a trial date ever since, even as it has continued trying to destroy Resolute's reputation. However, its appeals have been knocked down one by one, bringing it ever closer to proceedings that could expose not merely Greenpeace Canada's dirty tactics but its collaboration with its parent and other ENGOS. Resolute wants to frame Greenpeace's activities within the context of its parent's global campaigns, which, Resolute points out, often involve breaking the law. Meanwhile "interference with economic relations" could carry a hefty price tag. When it launched its suit, Resolute named a figure of $7 million, but it could go higher. Plus costs.

In the context of the lawsuit, one of Paglia's letter's most bizarre claims was that do-not-buy campaigns had not impacted corporate operations. However, at the end of last year, electronics giant Best Buy, after coming under Greenpeace harassment, clearly stated that it was diverting orders from Resolute. Indeed, at the time, Paglia had said "Best Buy is just the beginning."

Although his stance looked very lonely at the beginning, Garneau has, as noted, at last begun to receive vociferous support from Northern communities, aboriginal groups and unions. Even the federal and provincial governments, who have been culpably silent on the CBFA, have started to speak up in defence of the industry, which is in fact one of the most stringently regulated in the world.

Last October, Quebec officials travelled to New York, Denver and Atlanta to meet with major forestry clients such as Hearst, the *New York Times* and Home Depot. "There were some surprises," noted Quebec Forestry Minister Laurent Lessard. "It's not what they'd been told by certain groups. The facts had been distorted."

Governments are also beginning to address the fact that foreign-based organizations such as the Forest Stewardship Council, FSC, with no political legitimacy, are "certifying" Canadian forestry practices, and then using such certification as a weapon. Lessard said last October that he would be meeting with representatives of the FSC "to set the record straight." He cited in particular the FSC's withdrawal of licences from Resolute. Licensing, Lessard noted, better late than never, was governments' business.

In May of this year, more than 20 mayors representing Northern communities in both Ontario and Quebec went to Ottawa with forestry representatives to condemn what they called "eco terrorism" by ENGOs who, they noted "misinform, mislead and threaten customers of their local forest industries." They singled out Greenpeace, and accused the ENGOs of using bogus science.

Peter Politis, the mayor of Cochrane, noted the influence of ENGOs on government policy, but asked "Who is keeping the focus on the hundreds of thousands of families who not only live harmoniously with nature in the vast majority of Canada's geography, but who are as much part of the ecosystem as any other species in it?" In June, Politis and Roger Sigouin, mayor of Hearst, joined the Kapuskasing local of the United Steelworkers at Resolute's shareholder meeting in Augusta, Georgia, to deliver "a clear message" to Greenpeace.

Most recently, at their meeting in Thunder Bay, the Canadian Council of Forest Ministers acknowledged that it was time to stand up and recognize "the significant economic implications of misinformation." Canadian embassies have also finally begun to get the facts out.

Paglia concluded his threatening letter to Resolute by suggesting that while it planned to exclude the company from the CBFA, it would itself continue to meet with Canadian governments on policy issues. But what is a radical US-based organization doing dictating Canadian policy? ForestEthics has been a fierce campaigner against the oilsands and was also behind a lawsuit against the Harper government over Ottawa's desire to streamline resource regulation.

ENGOs have been given far too easy a ride because they hide behind speaking up for Mother Nature, but their real cause is power via protection racket. They suck in naïve and well-intended young people to do their unseemly work.

Richard Garneau, as a genuine proponent of sustainability – defined as balance between economic, social and environmental concerns – exposes the fact that the ENGO's approach is quite unbalanced. However, his willingness to confront misinformation does not necessarily endear him to his corporate fellows, since it exposes their own cowardice. Like kids faced with a schoolyard bully, they have been eager to keep their heads down lest they be noticed.

I called the Forest Products Association of Canada last week for a comment on Paglia's letter. They did not respond.

As one person close to the situation put it, "Profiles in Courage wasn't written about the corporate suite." Thanks to Garneau, however, the radical ENGO shakedown – and its part in a more sinister global agenda – may at last receive the public scrutiny it has so long avoided.

Tzeporah and the Great Bear

15 July 2016

Justin Trudeau keeps saying that British Columbia's Great Bear Rainforest is "no place for a pipeline." This assertion has no more rational basis than "Four legs good, two legs bad," or "Because it's 2015." It does, however, reflect the extraordinary success of the radical environmental movement in controlling, or stopping, economic development by rebranding – or claiming guardianship over – great swaths of Canada, and infiltrating the political system.

Trudeau's chief advisor is Gerald Butts, former head of WWF Canada. Go to the WWF's website and you will find the claim that the Great Bear Rainforest is – guess what – "no place for an oil pipeline."

Radical greens scored another, and closely related, victory this week with the appointment of Tzeporah Berman, co-founder of ForestEthics (now known as STAND.earth) and former co-director of Greenpeace's global climate and energy program, as co-chair of the panel appointed by the Alberta NDP government to look at how its cap on greenhouse gas emissions will work. That cap, again, was the result of "negotiations" with radical ENGOs, including STAND. The Great Bear Rainforest was in fact the creation of Berman and her fellow eco-warriors. It was conceived in the early 1990s in the wake of the environmental movement's success in bringing loggers to heel at Clayoquot Sound on Vancouver Island. Clayoquot, where Berman began her ascent to becoming the Canadian Queen of Green, was the start of a co-ordinated series of campaigns to control Canadian resource development, principally through the (Anti) Tar Sands Campaign and the Canadian Boreal Forest Agreement. Both were, and are, based on misinformation and intimidation.

The Great Bear Rainforest was created by drawing a line on the map around what had previously been known – less romantically – as BC's "mid-coast timber supply area." Its 6.4 million hectares stretch from the north of Vancouver Island to the Southern tip of Alaska. According to Berman, in her autobiography *This Crazy Time*, the new name was dreamed up in a "cheap Italian restaurant." Significantly, the restaurant was in San Francisco.

"I knew we needed a name that was iconic and created an image in people's minds," she wrote. "We wanted the next Amazon. We wanted people to hear the name and be mad as hell that anybody could turn it into toilet paper." She and her fellow diners picked the Kermode, or "spirit" bear (an albino black bear) as the campaign's requisite donation-inducing piece of "charismatic megafauna," and then they started harassing customers of the big BC logging companies. Greenpeace helped co-ordinate blockades.

BC premier Glen Clark called the activists "enemies of the state." Besieged corporations dubbed them "eco-terrorists." Local aboriginal bands branded them as "eco-imperialists."

But the ENGOs won.

The Great Bear "agreement" was announced at the beginning of February, when BC Premier Christy Clark claimed that it might be a model for other resource agreements. But the Great Bear is in fact a model primarily of how to use coercion to hold up development, at the expense of jobs and local First Nations. It also projected the cause of pristine nature across the path of any pipeline, and in particular the Northern Gateway proposal. Northern Gateway, which was launched by Enbridge 12 years ago, now appears deader than Monty Python's Norwegian Blue parrot. Having been approved by the

National Energy Board with 209 conditions, then given two thumbs up by Stephen Harper's Cabinet in 2014, the project was harpooned this year by the federal Liberals' decision to ban tanker traffic on the northern BC coast. Then it was eviscerated by the Federal Court of Appeal's recent 2-1 majority decision that cabinet had approved the project without sufficient aboriginal consultation.

In January, the Trudeau government introduced a raft of new regulatory and oversight provisions, including on greenhouse gas emissions, ostensibly designed to re-establish the credibility of the pipeline approval process. But the approval process was only incredible to radicals, and how much credibility does Justin Trudeau have as a mouthpiece for an environmental marketing campaign? By the end of the year, we will find out if there is any place for a pipeline in Canada. The federal cabinet is to decide then on Kinder Morgan's TransMountain expansion, which is essential if production is to increase towards Alberta's emissions cap. Trudeau can hardly say that the TransMountain route is "no place for a pipeline" because a pipeline is already there. The proposal involves trebling that line's capacity, to 890,000 barrels per day, and would require additional tanker traffic in Vancouver Harbour, through which oil from Trans-Mountain has been passing without incident for 60 years. However, the Usual ENGO Suspects and their political patsies – including Vancouver mayor Gregor Robertson – remain resolutely opposed to the project.

As for appointing Tzeporah Berman co-chair of the Alberta emissions cap panel, putting the fox in charge of the henhouse doesn't even begin to describe it.

Good riddance to a bogus boreal forest 'agreement'
1 February 2017

The Canadian Boreal Forest Agreement (CBFA), one of the most ignominious deals in Canadian business history, is being quietly euthanized. Last week, its Ottawa-based secretariat was closed, without fanfare or eulogy. However, most of the agreement's signatories seem as reluctant to admit its demise as they have been silent about its true nature.

According to Derek Nighbor of the Forest Products Association of Canada (FPAC), which led the industry into the deal in 2010, the agreement isn't really dead; it is "transitioning to a new model." Nighbor, who has been head of FPAC for less than a year, claims that the CBFA has had its successes, and that forest companies are keen to "leverage the good learnings" from six years of "investment in bilateral decision-making."

Lorne Johnson, a green consultant who was not merely a "facilitator" of the CBFA but its secretariat's first co-executive director, agrees that "death" isn't really the right word. It's more a "recalibration of the delivery model."

The man who as head of FPAC led the industry into the CBFA was Avrim Lazar who, as an Ottawa bureaucrat, had helped draft Canada's suicidal climate commitments under Kyoto. He seemed typical of the tendency of industry to hire representatives who think more like their opponents than themselves.

Did Lazar lead FPAC into the boreal agreement after negotiating the best deal he could, or was he a Judas goat? Whose side was he on? Whatever the answer to that question, there is no doubt that Canada's most prominent forestry companies had been browbeaten by the "market campaigns" of a pack of rabid ENGOs, led by Greenpeace and ForestEthics (now STAND.earth).

Since leaving FPAC, Lazar has become a radical environmental advocate, calling for the movement to rise up in an "Environmental Spring." He was also instrumental in trying to persuade the oil industry to "collaborate" with ENGOs along the lines of the CBFA. The poisoned fruit of this approach was the 2015 agreement to cap oilsands emissions, an agreement that split the industry.

The boreal covers an area 13 times the size of California and is one of the best-managed in the world. It is under zero threat of deforestation, so the CBFA was somewhat like an agreement to protect the sands of the Sahara. It was nothing less than an attempt by unelected, mainly US-funded groups to seize control of Canadian environmental policy, and maybe a whole lot more.

According to Lazar at the time, "The importance of this agreement cannot be overstated...Together we have identified a more intelligent, productive way to manage economic and environmental challenges in the boreal that will reassure global buyers of our products' sustainability."

Put more frankly, the deal would give corporate signatories a "competitive edge" in much the same way, say, as not having your legs broken by the mafia might give you a competitive edge in a foot race.

Equally disgraceful, a number of forest industry customers – including media giants such as *The Globe and Mail* – agreed to join something called the Boreal Business Forum, which would hold the forest companies' feet to the fire if those feet failed to dance to the ENGOS' tune. *The Globe* wrote editorials praising the CBFA to the skies, despite the fact that an unpublished internal analysis by KPMG revealed comprehensive internal discord and few, if any, achievements.

This discord erupted into the open toward the end of the agreement's original three-year term, when ENGO signatory Greenpeace – an organization that was "post-truth" decades before the term was invented – broke away to attack leading corporate signatory, Resolute Forest Products, with a truckload of misinformation. Another ENGO signatory, Canopy, departed claiming that "The disappointing reality is that not one hectare of forest has been protected and species and ecosystems are still at risk." Apart from revealing hysterical absolutism, this statement in fact contradicted the stance of the other environmental signatories, who declared that great progress was being made, but that the only problem was Resolute. All the ENGO signatories conspicuously suspended dealings with the company, gathering in a pack for what they hoped would be the kill. The FPAC was nowhere to be seen.

However, throwing out the playbook of corporate appeasement, Montreal-based Resolute, led by intrepid CEO Richard Garneau, decided to fight back by suing Greenpeace. Early last year, Resolute upped the ante by bringing a racketeering case against Greenpeace in the US. Meanwhile, forest communities and aboriginal groups were also beginning to kick back against the investment and job costs of the spreading Green Blob.

Most of those officially involved averted their gaze from Resolute's unseemly display of backbone, pretending that everything was proceeding swimmingly. Typical was a panel session on the boreal at the biannual Globe conference in Vancouver last year. Aran O'Carroll (who lost his job last week as executive director of the CBFA's secretariat) acknowledged that the agreement had been preceded by some "adversity," but said that corporations' "good behaviour" had led to "recognition in the marketplace." He made no mention of the ENGOs' outrageously bad behaviour in the marketplace, but then O'Carroll had previously been employed by one of the ENGO signatories.

Paul Lansbergen, then acting head of FPAC, described the agreement as a "journey of collaboration," a bit like a marriage, where you had to learn to live with your "new life partner." But if marriage was an appropriate analogy, it was of the forced and/or abusive variety.

Nobody on the panel mentioned Resolute or Greenpeace, or why another of the original signatories, the David Suzuki Foundation, had quietly exited the year before (the Suzuki Foundation didn't respond to an inquiry about why it left).

Behind the scenes, meanwhile, the great collaboration had ground to a standoff. It was decided – although when and by whom is unclear – to let the CBFA fade away. Undoubtedly Garneau's resolve had stiffened some spines. When somebody reportedly suggested to the CEO of another forestry company that what was needed was "CBFA 2.0," the CEO responded that what was actually needed was "CBFA 0.0."

FPAC's new head, Nighbor, claims, as noted, that the CBFA is not really dead, *per se*. Meanwhile, don't forget those "successes." For example, there are "methodological frameworks" that Nighbor admits are beyond him, but which apparently couldn't have been hatched without ENGO guns to corporate heads.

After that boreal session in Vancouver last year, I introduced myself to someone who worked for one of the corporate signatories of the CBFA. "I love your stuff," the executive said. "You write what we can't say." After we parted, the individual came after me and said "You won't quote me on that, will you?" None of this is to say that all environmental organizations are wicked, or that there are no environmental issues, or that responsible ENGOs have no role to play. But any free and democratic society should fiercely resist forced arrangements about which people are scared to speak the truth. The sooner the CBFA is buried the better, but it would be foolish to bury its lessons, or fail to register the dangers that irresponsible and destructive radical ENGO power – supported, ironically, by US and Canadian foundations built on capitalist fortunes – continues to pose for Canada.

Greenpeace's Hachette job
28 June 2017

Montreal-based Resolute Forest Products has distinguished itself in the corporate community by being prepared to take on the lies and intimidation tactics of radical environmental juggernaut Greenpeace, but the price is having to suffer repeated low blows and threats to its business.

The latest came when Greenpeace pressured Arnaud Nourry, the head of Paris-based publishing giant Hachette, a major Resolute customer, to write a letter that appeared to threaten Resolute's business with Hachette.

Greenpeace has for years been fundraising by harassing Resolute as a "Forest Destroyer." Four years ago, Resolute CEO Richard Garneau threw away the usual playbook of corporate appeasement and sued Greenpeace for malicious defamation. Last year he upped the

ante by bringing suit against Greenpeace in the US under RICO racketeering laws.

Greenpeace has writhed to avoid its day(s) in court, mainly by
turning up the heat on Resolute's customers, but it has also tried to
claim that the case is really all about free speech, which has allowed it
to apply particular pressure to publishers. As part of this campaign,
the environmental NGO has recently recruited lefty Canadian literary
celebrities – such as Margaret Atwood and Naomi Klein – to sign a
"pledge" for free speech. It also published newspaper ads indicating
support from 90 other lefty organizations – from the Broadbent Institute through the Pembina Institute to 350.org – for the notion that
Resolute was "trying to sue Greenpeace and STAND.earth (formerly
ForestEthics) out of existence. This is all about trying to silence anyone who disagrees with Resolute. It's an attack on public discourse,
free speech and the very heart of our democratic society."

Hooey. Resolute just wants these shakedown merchants to stop
destroying value, jobs and northern communities by telling lies.
Canadian forests are the best protected in the world. Resolute has
won numerous awards for its stewardship.

Greenpeace's greatest recent coup is that letter from Hachette's Nourry to Resolute's Garneau, even though Nourry explicitly
acknowledges in the letter that he doesn't understand what the case
is about. He writes "I have no intention of getting involved in the
dispute, for as publishers, we have neither the expertise nor the
resources to forge an educated opinion as to who is right and who is
wrong in what seems to be a complex set of highly technical issues."

To call this disingenuous is to give it far too much credit. By writing this letter, Nourry became involved front and centre. As he well
knew, his pathetic disclaimer would be ignored and the letter would
be trumpeted by Greenpeace as evidence of support.

Nourry goes on to tie himself further in knots by writing "The
other point I would like to make, not as a customer but as a publisher
and a citizen, is that the vigour of your legal response to Greenpeace
under RICO statutes strikes me as excessive."

But how can Nourry make any comments about the appropriate
level of Resolute's response if he admits that the case is too complex

for him to understand? Perhaps his most disgraceful claim/threat is that "an escalation of the legal dispute could cause some authors to decline having their books printed on Resolute's paper, further complicating the situation."

Bizarrely, Nourry brings in the Trump administration's withdrawal from the Paris accord on climate, thus allegedly rendering the role of "independent NGOS such as Greenpeace" more important. One's head spins at the *non sequitur*. Nourry seems to be saying that because the US is abandoning Paris, Greenpeace should be allowed to ride roughshod over truth and jobs, and Resolute should not defend its reputation in court. Nourry's reward for his collaboration was to be instantly both hailed and misrepresented by Greenpeace, who suggested that he had called on Resolute "to do better for the forest in the strongest possible terms."

Meanwhile there is indeed an issue of free speech here, but it is Greenpeace who is trying to crush it. What are the chances that any of Hachette's imprints are now going to publish books exposing, or even criticizing, Greenpeace, whose campaigns against chlorine and genetically modified foods have cost not just jobs, but lives? This is not the first time that the corporate media has been cowed and co-opted by Greenpeace.

That CBFA has now dropped like a rotten fruit, but corporations remain scared, vulnerable and reluctant to take on Greenpeace and its ENGO comrades.

If Greenpeace believes its tactics against Resolute are legally defensible, why is it so frantically pursuing this huge extra-legal campaign to get Resolute to drop the cases? Perhaps because, as part of its defence, it has already admitted that its claims are "non-verifiable statements of subjective opinion and at most...rhetorical hyperbole...not intended to be taken literally."

In other words, Greenpeace is trashing Resolute, but don't take their accusations "literally."

Then again, if Greenpeace's case is so weak, why aren't Resolute's corporate fellows lining up to support the company? The simple answer is that they are too scared. Free speech requires that Greenpeace be brought to justice.

9
Oilsands sheikdown

CALLING ALL ENVIRONMENTALISTS

DIVEST NOW!!

DO I HAVE TO?

YES! IT'S TIME TO LEAD BY EXAMPLE. SO...NO MORE TV, NO MORE INTERNET, NO MOBILE PHONE, NO HEATING (EXCEPT WOOD BURNING, OBVS), NO FRIDGE, NO MEDICINES, NO CAR, NO FLYING, NO ASPHALT ROADS

NOW, DON'T YOU FEEL GOOD?

*ALL MADE FROM OR DEPENDENT ON FOSSIL FUELS

The Alberta oilsands are one of the largest and most demanding petroleum deposits on earth. Their development is a monument to corporate commitment and technical innovation. However, open pit mines and their allegedly "dirty" oil proved an irresistible target for global climate campaigners, who have peddled hysterical misinformation and mounted multiple legal challenges.

239

Bath bombs hit oilsands
9 June 2010

A new Marx attacks oilsands
12 August 2010

Conflict bananas
29 December 2011

Oilsands dialogues of the deaf
16 October 2012

Moral sediments
30 January 2013

Tom Steyer's anti-Canada crusade
13 September 2013

Oilsands should stay out of the dark ENGO forests
6 December 2013

Neil Young hits low note with oilsands assault
13 January 2014

Demonization and divestment
10 October 2014

Welcome to Peaksville, Alberta
27 May 2015

Pipeline dictators
31 August 2016

The Deep Liberal State bites back
19 July 2018

From Petro-Canada to Pipero-Canada
27 July 2018

Bath bombs hit oilsands

9 June 2010

A UK bath products company called Lush is today asking its North American retail staff to take to the sidewalks, dressed only in barrels, to protest the wickedness of the Alberta oilsands.

That hardly places the company out on a limb when it comes to eco-posturing. Still, Lush isn't like those other companies that promote trendy causes for fear of NGO "Do Not Buy" campaigns. Its orientation comes from its founder, British "bubble bath baron" Mark Constantine. Constantine is the true heir of the late cosmetic hypocrite-in-chief, Anita Roddick. Ms. Roddick, founder of the Body Shop, was one of the originators of hiding high margins behind even higher humbug.

Constantine has provided support for a number of activist groups, including Plane Stupid, which specializes in disrupting UK airports, and Sea Shepherd, which likes nothing better than a good naval battle. In Canada, his company has organized campaigns against the commercial seal hunt. In 2008, it produced a "Guantanamo Garden foaming bath ball," which released pictures of US detainees into the tub.

Anyway, mix in a pinch of Al Gore and you get some idea of the toxic mental stew that permeates the marketing of Lush's Fair Trade, vegan, "fizzing bath bombs, bubble bars, shower jellies, solid body butters and solid shampoo bars."

For the next two weeks, Lush's shop windows across North America will showcase images of deforestation and open-pit oilsands mining. Staff in the US will hand out postcards to be sent to President Obama "to fund green, renewable energy and put an end to government support for the Canadian tar sands oil." In Canada, the postcards will be for Stephen Harper.

The company claims that the oilsands are a bigger environmental catastrophe than the BP Gulf spill. "If left unchecked, the project will turn Alberta into a toxic moonscape." A video on the company's web-site claims that the oilsands represent a "toxic sacrifice zone the size of England," and that "tar sands kill people," so "Shut the F*cker down."

To demonstrate its commitment, Lush has created "a limited edition Wild Rose Country bath bomb," scented with bergamot oil and rose absolute, the proceeds of which will go to the anti-oilsands campaign of the ENGO Rainforest Action Network, RAN (motto: "Environmentalism with teeth").

According to Lush "Campaigns Manager" Brandi Halls, "The future has to be one without oil, and we need the government to help us get there by pushing for clean, renewable energy."

I called up Brandi to ask how much solar and wind Lush used in its operations. She explained that their role was not so much to use these alternatives themselves as to pressure governments to subsidize them. I asked her how they shipped their product. After a detour about how they were working with ForestEthics to wean themselves off the evil substance, I got her to admit that the motive power for transporting Lush's products was, well, oil.

I asked Brandi what percentage of total carbon dioxide emissions came from the oilsands. She didn't have a clue, but she did declare unequivocally that their production emitted three times the CO_2 of conventional oil. I asked Brandi if she knew anything about rules for land reclamation. She said her "sources" had told her it wasn't happening fast enough.

Although the industry is traditionally as nimble as a 5000-tonne oilsands dragline in dealing with such attacks, the Canadian Association of Petroleum Producers (CAPP) managed to produce a press release yesterday pointing out that the planned protest was "based on misinformation and rhetoric, not facts." It then proceeded into a typically guarded statement questioning Lush's claims (which had all been provided for it by RAN and Greenpeace). CAPP pointed out that the amount of land disturbed by oilsands over 40 years represented 0.02% of the boreal forest; future development would not be based on strip mining; land had to be reclaimed under rigorous regulations.

As for producing three times as much carbon dioxide, "We see a range among producers and cite oilsands as 5% to 15% more carbon-intensive on a life-cycle basis than the average barrel imported into the US today." Mmm. Not very punchy.

The release then droned on about carbon levies and extensive consultation, and water quality. CAPP head David Collyer's name was attached to a typical boilerplate quote at the end: "Experience shows that collaboration, not confrontation and rhetoric, is the most direct path to results."

The problem is that for radical groups such as RAN and Greenpeace, confrontation and rhetoric have proved the direct path to forced collaboration. RAN is supported by the Pew Foundation – the perverted child of capitalist success – which three weeks ago scored a stunning victory in forcing the Forest Products Association of Canada to sanitize great chunks of the boreal forest and accept a group of radical NGOs as partners in anti-development. But while the NGOs are happy merely to bring the forestry industry to heel, they want to close the oilsands down.

Are Lush's customers too dumb to realize what that would mean to jobs and livelihoods? Surely somebody might show up at the Lush store at the Market Mall in Calgary to express their displeasure. Or what about starting a Facebook page to boycott the company that wants to destroy Canadian jobs by spreading lies?

A new Marx attacks oilsands

12 August 2010

A recent survey of 4000 Canadians, Americans and Brits reported a precipitous fall in participants' willingness to visit the province after seeing a *Rethink Alberta* video that peddles untruths about the province's oilsands.

The oilsands have become the focus of a worldwide campaign of demonization and misinformation by activists whose motives are a stew of reflexive anti-developmental Suzuki-ism, cynical fundraising, and aspirations to Global Governance. The *Rethink* campaign, which has been underway for several weeks, seeks to link the oilsands to the

BP Gulf blowout. Billboards in Seattle, Portland and Denver point to "Alberta: The other oil disaster." The campaign also wants to kill TransCanada Corp.'s Keystone XL pipeline extension, part of a system to take diluted bitumen from Alberta to the refineries of the US Gulf Coast.

The *Rethink* campaign peddles the lie that the oilsands are destroying an area the size of England, which conflates the total size of the deposits with the much smaller area being mined (and which has to be reclaimed). It ignores the fact that most future extraction will take place underground. It also regurgitates spurious claims about local pollution and sickness, and implies that the industry is virtually unregulated.

The campaign is masterminded by a California-based organization called Corporate Ethics International, CEI, which is the brainchild of one Michael Marx, a name almost too ironic to be true, since he spouts so much anti-capitalist claptrap. Marx claims that the US is a corporate plutocracy, and that CEI's mission is "to bring corporations back in service to and under the control of the citizenry," although only, presumably, if the citizenry happens to think the same way as Marx.

Marx was previously an executive of the Rainforest Action Network (RAN), another peddler of environmental whoppers. Not surprisingly, RAN is part of this campaign, along with shakedown artists ForestEthics, the anti-everything Polaris Institute, and Friends of the Earth, who have rarely betrayed themselves as Friends of Mankind.

According to Marx, the campaign was launched "to expose the fact that Alberta, in aggressively promoting its tar-sands industry, is interfering in Canadian, US and European efforts to end the world's addiction to oil and transition to cleaner energy sources."

The *Rethink* website features an Orwellian "pledge" to halt oilsands expansion, stop PR campaigns that would keep the US "addicted to dirty Tar Sands oil," and take meaningful steps to promote "clean energy alternatives."

Unfortunately, this coincides with a great deal of ill-informed US political opinion. It also fits with President Barack Obama's fantasies of green industrial strategy as a job creator.

Both Alberta and the oil industry seem to be particularly bad at countering disinformation. One problem is that ponderous Alberta Premier Ed Stelmach would be the last man you'd pick to sell anything.

Ultimately, Corporate Ethics and its cohorts are motivated by the alleged vices they project onto corporations: the lust for power and money. Those taking the new Marxist "pledge" are required to give their names and email addresses. How long do you think before they get an appeal to send cash?

If *The Communist Manifesto* were to be issued today, it would be called *The Green Manifesto*, dominated by the environment, and appear on a website with a link to PayPal.

Workers of the World donate!

Conflict bananas

29 December 2011

Ohio-based Chiquita has discovered that kowtowing to eco-fascism is not without its costs. The famous banana company is facing made-in-Canada outrage for caving in to NGO ForestEthics by committing not to use oil from the Alberta oilsands, and to "expose" those that do.

The oilsands has become the main target (and fundraising opportunity) for radical green groups. The recent decision by the US administration to hold up approval of the Alberta-to-Gulf-Coast Keystone XL pipeline was a major coup, and has encouraged radical NGOs to up their campaigns of lies and intimidation.

One well-worn technique is to demand of US companies – "When did you stop beating your wife?"-style – whether they are using "dirty" oilsands oil. Last year, ForestEthics, a veteran of anti-corporate thuggery, sent such a demand to Chiquita. Senior vice-president Manuel Rodriguez sent a grovelling response committing "to directing our transportation providers to avoid, where possible, fuels from tar sands refineries and to adopt a strategy of continuous improvement towards the elimination of those fuels." ForestEthics released Rodriguez's letter with much fanfare.

For once, however, there was some pushback. The Canadian organization EthicalOil.org – which was set up to make the case for the oilsands – launched a radio attack ad against Chiquita and organized a protest outside an Edmonton Safeway store, complete with sombreros and ponchos. The ad called Chiquita a "foreign bully" (a particularly sensitive point given the company's "banana republic" past as the United Fruit Company), and pondered whether Chiquita preferred oil from "OPEC dictatorships." Prime Minister Stephen Harper and several Cabinet ministers denounced the company and the Alberta Enterprise Group called for a boycott of its products. The Canadian Association of Petroleum Producers wrote to Chiquita asking where it was getting its (mis)information.

Although touting the moral credentials of commodities is a potential minefield, it is difficult not to cheer the ethical oil initiative. California-based ForestEthics, an anti-capitalist organization that is – ironically but not untypically – supported by money from capitalist foundations, has run roughshod over truth and jobs for too long. Its previous corporate victims included US clothing giant Limited Brands, which was brought to heel for the crime of using paper in its Victoria's Secret catalogues. Rather than attempt to refute ForestEthics misrepresentations, Limited Brands paid to "work with" the NGO, thus setting a precedent for green extortion. Earlier this year, ForestEthics released an ad featuring California grocery chain Trader Joe's acquiescence in the anti oilsands campaign. It didn't bother to ask Trader Joe's permission. Did Trader Joe's complain? No. It was obviously too scared. ForestEthics has other campaigns going to force Walmart and Safeway to condemn the oilsands.

This kind of "corporate social responsibility" has – as Milton Friedman famously suggested – always been a slippery slope. Every time a corporation caves in, it opens the door to further demands. For example, ForestEthics used Chiquita's letter to bolster its attack on rival fruit company Dole. "Dole Bananas: Brought to you by dirty

Tar Sands oil," claims the ForestEthics website, inviting its acolytes to use social media to pressure Dole. Dole's response? To grovel. The company's vice-president of worldwide corporate responsibility and sustainability, Sylvain Cuperlier, went on YouTube to claim that the company didn't use oilsands oil, as far as it knew, but begged Forest-Ethics to "share information" with them.

ForestEthics' response was that this just wasn't good enough: "[A] business as large as Dole is filthy with Tar Sands unless, like Chiquita, they are actively working to get it out of their footprint. ForestEthics has repeatedly asked Dole to disclose the refinery sources of origin for the fuel they use, but they haven't."

By what right does ForestEthics demand information from anybody? Who gave them, or any of their fellows, a "social licence?" In the interests of transparency, let's have a full accounting from Forest-Ethics of all the money they have received from the corporations who have been bullied into "working with them."

Meanwhile here, in all its tawdriness, is "stakeholder capitalism:" green-cloaked shakedown artists dictating corporate policy on the basis of misinformation and intimidation.

Four years ago, Chiquita paid a stiff fine for buying mafia-style "protection" from South American thugs masquerading as freedom fighters. Is trying to buy protection from the mendacious green lobby any different?

Oilsands dialogues of the deaf
16 October 2012

Rick George, the former head of Suncor, is one of the most talented and successful of Canadian businessmen. On the basis of a single insight, he transformed the economics of the Alberta oilsands. He repatriated and reprivatized Suncor. He absorbed Petro-Canada in the biggest merger in the country's history. And yet George was also apparently slow to see, and perhaps naïve in dealing with, the environmental whirlwind that would be unleashed by his oilsands success. This appears evident in his newly published autobiography, *Sun Rise: Suncor, the Oilsands and the Future of Energy.*

George's tale of business success is often inspiring, if somewhat guarded, but that part of the book contrasts markedly with the account of his well-intended but often muddled and contradictory approach to dealing with the environmental movement's massive international campaign of misinformation about the oilsands.

The fact that President Barack Obama nixed (at least temporarily) the Keystone XL pipeline – which was designed to take diluted oilsands bitumen to the refineries of the US Gulf Coast – while the other main oilsands export routes – to the west coast – are being resolutely opposed by environmental NGOs, aboriginal groups and BC radicals, suggests that George's fervent belief in "dialogue" failed to produce the required results. Indeed, it is never quite clear if his policy was to keep his enemies close, or to be eaten last.

First the inspiring bit. George was born in a small town in Colorado, became an engineer, joined Texaco, expanded his perspective by qualifying as a lawyer, then went to Philadelphia-based Sun Oil, where he starred in the company's North Sea operations.

In 1991 he moved as heir apparent to the company's Canadian subsidiary, whose perpetual corporate headache had been its oilsands operations. George's light-bulb moment was to see that the company was using a flawed production process. The open-pit operation depended on massive bucket wheels to dig out the unyielding oil sand, which was then loaded onto conveyor belts to be taken to a processing plant. This method had originally been developed to produce soft coal.

Frozen oil sand was a whole different bucket load, and led to endless shutdowns. George's deceptively simple answer was to replace the bucket wheels with mechanical shovels and the conveyor belts with trucks. The result was a $5 per-barrel reduction in production costs; a proverbial "game-changer."

His corporate parent in Philadelphia saw profitability as an opportunity to sell, as did the government of Ontario, which had decided in the early 1980s, after seeing the "success" (i.e. public popularity) of state-owned Petro-Canada, to buy 25% of its own "window on the industry."

Apart from inspiring many other companies to move into the oilsands, George also greatly expanded Suncor's operations. This success attracted the attention of the environmental movement, for whom the oilsands were an easy target.

Perhaps the industry's first strategic mistake was to be frightened away from even addressing the climate science on the basis of which "dirty oil" was condemned. George asserts that nobody has a "permanent and practical solution to the current state of global warming," but he nowhere tells us what the current state of global warming is, although he claims that he doesn't "question its predicted effects."

He should.

George's firm, rationalist belief in dialogue, meanwhile, not merely failed to appease the ENGO enemies of petroleum, it gave them legitimacy.

George appears to step outside his "let's-dialogue" persona in launching attacks on, respectively, the wild exaggerations, cluelessness and hypocrisy of NASA official James Hansen, actress Daryl Hannah and film director James Cameron, but where are his exposés of the misrepresentations of the David Suzuki Foundation or the Pembina Institute? Oh, that's right, Suncor likes to dialogue with them.

George fails to make much sense when it comes to recommending a vague national energy strategy, except that it will be "well constructed" and all about responsibility, sustainability and carbon management. He even makes the astonishing suggestion that "some long-term policy decisions are too important to leave to the federal government if it appears reluctant or too distracted to deal with them."

One doubts that such a view would find much favour with Stephen Harper, whose name, strangely, does not appear in the book, except by implication as the figure culpable of failing to deal with climate "concerns."

George wants a carbon tax, which the Conservatives have firmly rejected. He also calls for (more) government subsidies for alternative energy, noting that Suncor has dived into wind and biofuels via its "Parallel Paths" strategy, which sounds like something dreamed up by the Chinese Politburo. He supports the "freedom…to make moderate use of energy derived from fossil fuels," without apparently realizing that introducing the word "moderate" risks waving goodbye to "freedom."

Supreme optimism and faith in ingenuity of the kind displayed by George are, when combined with his extraordinary talents, a gift to Canada and to the global economy more broadly. Unfortunately, optimists tend not to grasp the motivations of those who use pessimism in pursuit of power. George claims that one of his greatest strengths is the ability to listen. The problem may have been his inability to hear what his diehard foes are saying: that they have no interest in dialogue, except as a weapon.

Moral sediments

30 January 2013

Whatever the state of "the science," even greatly expanded oilsands development could have no significant impact on the global climate. However, oilsands' possible local effects require sound and objective study. The problem is that some of the leading researchers in that area are themselves also climate alarmists and political activists.

A recent example of how ideology may be corrupting science – and how eagerly a crusading media regurgitates alarmism – came with the release of a study of the impact of emissions from the oilsands on nearby lakes. The study appeared three weeks ago in the *Proceedings of the National Academy of Sciences.* Most of its authors were from Environment Canada, but its chief promoter was Queen's University professor John Smol, Canada Research Chair on Environmental Change.

Queen's issued a press release on the paper with the headline "Oilsands study shows negative impact on lake systems." In fact, the study – which analyzed sediments in lakes close to the oilsands for deposition of polycyclic aromatic hydrocarbons (PAHs) – didn't show any such thing. Moreover, the release was issued without being vetted by Environment Minister Peter Kent's office. Perhaps Smol was eager to avoid what he has called the Harper government's "tongue police."

The study, by going back in time through core samples of lake beds, did indeed demonstrate that PAH levels had increased, and that the increase was linked to bitumen production rather than natural sources, such as forest fires. However, levels were similar to those in other remote lakes, with the exception of one lake – "NE20" – which was very close to two oilsands plants, where the government's interim standards (the lowest level of concern for toxicity) had been exceeded since the 1980s. However, they were still well below the levels at which there was a chance of "probable" environmental harm.

Certainly, the issue of whether further depositions might cause harm requires examination, but the study in fact demonstrated little to justify Prof. Smol's assertion in the Queen's press release that "Combined with the effects of climate change and other environmental stressors to aquatic ecosystems, these results are worrying."

Prof. Smol then proceeded in media interviews to talk up the study and even misrepresent its conclusions. He suggested that "back of the envelope" calculations pointed to problems with oilsands expansion. "We might well be close to significantly higher levels and more dangerous levels very quickly," he said.

In fact, NE20 was the only lake in which sediment levels might reach guidelines for "possible" harmful environmental effects, but that would depend on emissions and depositions ramping up in tandem with oilsands expansion, and ignored the likelihood of further scrubbing of emissions.

On US National Public Radio, Prof. Smol declared "I'm not saying that these lakes are toxic pools. The contaminants in these lakes are now about the same level that you might see in a lake, you know, in an urban...setting."

In fact, this statement contradicted the report's own finding, which was that PAHs in the six lakes "were within the range typical of remote lakes but substantially lower than lakes in urbanized catchments."

Meanwhile, this was only one of several occasion on which Prof. Smol noted that the lakes were not "poisonous" or "toxic" pools. This seemed like telling a child at bedtime that there is no monster in the closet. It plants the idea of a monster.

The media obliged with a raft of scary headlines – "Toxic tar sands." "Oilsands polluting nearby lakes: study; 'smoking gun.'" "Rising contaminant levels forecast unprecedented change in oilsands area lakes."

Prof. Smol has never made any secret of his fervent belief in the dangers of catastrophic man-made climate change. He has – like other prominent Canadian scientists such as David Schindler and Andrew Weaver – also been sharply critical of the Harper government and its alleged agenda of "pushing through" oilsands development.

Last year, in a joint editorial with Schindler, Smol declared that: "The embarrassment over our present-day selfish and non-evidence-based environmental policies has grown as quickly as our environmental footprint." The authors suggested that "Canadians have been lulled into a Faustian bargain whereby promises of economic prosperity today are traded for a burden on future generations and an expensive environmental debt."

Prof. Smol was recently featured in a remarkable newspaper ad attached to the Queen's University fundraising "Initiative Campaign." It claimed that global temperatures had increased "alarmingly" in the past century, asked "Who cares?" and recorded that John Smol did, and intended to do something about it.

It is difficult not to conclude – given the way he has presented the lake pollution paper – that the "something" he had in mind might include retarding oilsands development. While Prof. Smol is quite justified in holding this as a personal stance, there is a problem when it perverts science.

This study, and the way it has been reported, raises doubts over whether the joint federal provincial monitoring agency, which is currently being constructed to look at the impact of the oilsands, can ever hope to establish objectivity.

This week, Prof. Smol was quoted as saying "A storm is developing, and the wind is blowing in the direction of the oilsands." One can't help thinking that he sees himself as a puffy-cheeked god helping those winds along.

Tom Steyer's anti-Canada crusade
13 September 2013

Who is Tom Steyer? The California-based US billionaire has suddenly emerged as a high profile, and rabid, opponent of TransCanada Corp's Keystone XL pipeline. He was recently responsible for a television ad that portrayed TransCanada CEO Russ Girling as a cross between Snidely Whiplash and the guy riding the intercontinental ballistic missile in *Dr. Strangelove*. He has just launched another series of misinformation-filled ads.

Steyer is conventionally described as a major financial supporter of President Obama, but a long article in this week's *New Yorker*, by Ryan Lizza, suggests that Steyer is more like Obama's nemesis, hoping to embarrass the President into a symbolic gesture that would do nothing for the climate, damage relations with Canada, and establish not Obama's resolve, but the fact that he is in thrall to an out-of-control, elitist, billionaire-funded environmental movement.

It has been suggested that Steyer – who made his money managing a hedge fund – and his law professor brother, Jim, might be "the Koch brothers of the left." However, Steyer angrily dismissed the parallel on the basis that the Kochs – who are to the environmental movement what Emmanuel Goldstein was to the totalitarian rulers in *Nineteen Eighty-Four*: a focus of demonic hatred – are only interested in profits, while he stands selflessly for US citizens.

This level of power-blinded self-delusion is almost comical. It is also hypocritical. Not only did Steyer make lots of money out of investing in fossil fuels, but through his new organization, Next-Gen, he is involved in clean energy investment funds whose fortunes depend significantly on legislation that cripples fossil fuels.

Steyer's guru is environmental activist Bill McKibben, who runs 350.org. That organization takes its name from the claim of leading climate hysteric James Hansen that any concentration of carbon dioxide in the atmosphere above 350 parts per million threatens a climatic "tipping point." (It wouldn't have been quite so dramatic to call the organization 0.00035.org, which would represent the actual proportion of the atmosphere that 350 parts per million represents.)

Steyer was reportedly deeply impressed by an article that McKibben wrote for the *Rolling Stone* in 2012 called "Global warming's terrifying new math." It should have been called "Global warming's terrifyingly bad math," since it was filled with mystic numerology and false claims, such as that humans are responsible for all the 0.8 degree Celsius rise in global temperature over the past century. The article might have been weak on science and logic, but it was very clear on policy. What "the movement" needed was "an enemy."

Steyer invited McKibben on a hike in the Adirondacks, and came down from the mountain full of McKibben's terrifyingly politically useful math. Henceforth he dedicated himself to killing Keystone by stoking moral outrage via the "liberation technology" of social media, and using his wealth to punish politicians.

Steyer has made the bogus claim that Keystone XL would enable the oilsands to be developed three times faster, and that it would "dramatically increase greenhouse gas emissions." In fact, it would carry less than 1% of global oil output and be responsible for much less than one thousandth of man-made emissions of carbon dioxide.

Certainly, cancelling Keystone XL would slow the pace of oilsands development, but the oil will find its way to markets by other means. To the extent that other forms of transport, primarily rail, are more expensive, they will undoubtedly affect the oilsands' economics, but they might also wind up producing more emissions than if the pipeline were built. That, however, is the sort of math that opponents are unwilling to countenance.

In the first part of Steyer's new four-part, million-dollar anti-Keystone ad campaign, he claims, from a boat near a Gulf Coast refinery owned by Royal Dutch Shell and Saudi Refining, that America would not profit from Keystone, whose oil would go "through, not to" the nation. He suggests that only foreign companies would benefit and that refined products would be exported to China to make products to ship back to the us, thus taking American jobs.

But even if Keystone oil were refined only at foreign-owned refineries, which it won't be, are not the workers in those refineries overwhelmingly American? That all the refined products would be exported is highly improbable, but if they were, so what? They would only be exported if the profits to be made – to the benefit of America – were higher. Moreover, refined product exports are dictated by the global refined product market, not where the oil originates. Steyer made no mention of the thousands of American jobs that building the pipeline would create, nor that Keystone oil would displace imports from suppliers such as Venezuela and Russia.

What is truly fascinating is that an allegedly sophisticated businessman should spout such populist nonsense in pursuit of power. What is psychologically intriguing is that he might genuinely believe that he is motivated only by the "public good."

Oilsands should stay out of the dark ENGO forests
6 December 2013

Machiavelli is credited with the insight that you should keep your friends close but your enemies closer. However, the suggestion that the oilsands industry might deal with its public perception problems by climbing into bed with its fiercest detractors is little short of suicidal.

The industry has been the subject of a global campaign of demonization, disinformation and intimidation, executed by a wide range of interlinked ENGOs. That campaign has been based on false or grossly exaggerated allegations of toxicity, sickness and environmental destruction, in particular regarding the significance of the oilsands for global warming. And it has been highly effective.

Its greatest success has been in pressuring President Obama to hold up approval for the Keystone XL pipeline. It has also stirred alarm about the construction of new – or "looped" – pipelines through BC to the west coast, using aboriginal discontent about treaty issues to make them partners in opposing development. It also stands against the movement of oilsands oil to the east, and is behind EU initiatives to ban diluted bitumen.

None of this is to say that there are not very genuine environmental issues of pipeline and tanker safety, but rational examination has been polluted by hysteria, and attempts to unclog the regulatory system have been met with lawsuits and bogus claims of silencing dissent.

Some are now proposing that rather than counter misinformation, the industry should legitimize it by sitting down with its ENGO tormentors. Even more bizarre is the suggestion that the industry might use the Canadian Boreal Forest Agreement, CBFA – which embedded activists at the heart of Canadian forestry policy – as a model.

Certainly, the response of both governments and industry to the ENGO assault on the oilsands has at times looked shambolic. A bewildering proliferation of monitoring agencies and industry technology initiatives – plus a reflexive tendency by the industry to apologize and say it will "try harder" – merely appears to confirm that the existing systems are inadequate.

The CBFA does indeed offer lessons, but rather of which path to avoid. Radical ENGOs have a distinct advantage when it comes to negative marketing. For any corporation, a necessary emphasis on the bottom line means that they tend to avoid controversy and buy off potentially costly attacks rather than fight them. For ENGOs, by contrast, stoking controversy is often the main source of both their income and their very real coercive power.

Some shills for the ENGOs, such as Avrim Lazar – the former eco-bureaucrat and enthusiastic promoter of the CBFA when he was head of the Forest Products Association of Canada – suggest that it doesn't matter how the ENGOs came by their power; since they have it, they have to be dealt with. But do we want to live in a society where power and influence is acquired by disinformation and intimidation?

The situation with the oilsands is in any case markedly different from that of forestry, where the ENGOS claimed that their concern was "responsible development." When it comes to the Athabasca region, the ENGO pack hunters make no secret of wanting to close down development altogether, on the way to a UN-mandated, globally governed, low-carbon future, whatever the impact on jobs and freedom.

Significantly but not surprisingly, the most vociferous anti-oilsands ENGOS were also signatories of the CBFA; not just Greenpeace, but ForestEthics and the David Suzuki Foundation.

Does the industry really want to sit down with these thugs and negotiate its own death sentence?

Neil Young hits low note with oilsands assault
13 January 2014

The first performance by environmental supergroup Suzuki, Weaver and Young – at Massey Hall in Toronto on Sunday afternoon – was more entertaining and thought-provoking than anticipated.

The venue was to hold a concert by rock legend Neil Young in the evening as part of his four-city Canadian "Honour the Treaties" tour. All proceeds were to go to a legal fund for the people of Fort Chipewyan, which is 220 kilometers north of Fort McMurray. Young is hardly the first celebrity to join the pack assault on the oilsands and to pick the downstream community of Fort Chipewyan as a focal point, although he seems to have been the first to suggest that the development looks like Hiroshima.

His backup group of David Suzuki, as "moderator," and climate modeller-turned BC Green Party politician Andrew Weaver, were there to amplify Young's castigation of greed, corporations and the Harper government. But the pregnant question raised by the conference was the extent to which native people might be more badly served by their "friends" than their alleged enemies.

The afternoon's standout performance came from Athabasca Chipewyan First Nation chief Allan Adam, a tough-looking but earnest man who, while obviously frustrated, revealed the complexities of his situation. Chief Adam suggested – according to script – that oilsands development was like a "runaway train," but he also acknowledged that his mandate was to climb aboard. He said that his life became a good deal more complicated due to a health study that claimed to find alarmingly high cancer levels among his people. While he did not elaborate on the study and its aftermath, it is in fact central to the enormous pressure that has been put on Fort Chip by environmental activists.

The study to which Chief Adam referred was done by a physician named John O'Connor, who was subsequently sanctioned by the provincial College of Physicians for serious inaccuracies. The study's conclusions were also refuted by an expert panel from the Royal Society of Canada, which suggested that anxiety was being caused in Fort Chip by environmental alarmism.

That alarmism had been cranked up further by two studies co-authored by David Schindler, which indicated elevated levels of some toxic compounds in spring runoff around the oilsands. The studies didn't say that the levels were dangerous, but they were peddled around the world as evidence that those downstream of the oilsands were being recklessly endangered.

Fort Chip's unwanted fame was ratcheted up another notch when film maker James Cameron visited. It was also the subject of a severely-slanted CBC documentary, *Tipping Point*, featuring David Suzuki.

On Sunday, Young inevitably brought up the community's alleged cancer problems, and Chief Adam spoke movingly of his neighbours' recent deaths from cancer. The only problem is that these deaths apparently have nothing to do with the oilsands.

There are certainly major problems in how governments and industry have mishandled their dealings with aboriginal peoples, and have failed to establish the credibility of their monitoring regimes, but the best hope for those who live in remote communities such as Fort Chip lies in resource development. Indeed, the oilsands are already the largest employer of native people. Chief Adam acknowledged that his community had seventeen companies involved in the oilsands, which were "economically critical."

This message clashed alarmingly with the policy visions of Weaver, who appears unfazed by the fact that climate models (including his own) have performed so badly in the past two decades. He proceeded to bash the Harper government on its climate policy and suggested that the route to "clean tech" was clear, but has he looked at the results of Ontario's Green Energy Act? More relevant, does he think Fort Chip might have a future manufacturing solar panels?

Everybody had really come to listen to Young, who, dressed in buckskin and a cowboy hat, proceeded to spray vitriol and ignorance in all directions. Fort McMurray, he said, stands for disease and pollution. It's all about marketing and big money for big corporations, and the oil's all going to China anyway. Reclamation is impossible; it would be like turning "the Moon into Eden."

Like Weaver, Young concluded that there were alternatives to a "dirty future...a door into the sunshine." Again this raised the issue of Fort Chip's prospects in solar panel assembly, but also of just how helpful the environmental supergroup – and their activist cohorts – really are to Chief Allan Adam and his people.

Demonization and divestment
10 October 2014

The latest front in the war against the oilsands is the divestment movement. Next month, in Montreal, an organization called the Canadian Youth Climate Coalition, CYCC, is set to hold a "convergence" on pressuring institutions such as pension funds and university endowments to ditch their shares in Canadian oil and gas companies.

"Oh those students!" you might say, "always protesting about something." But the CYCC isn't some Quixotic group of young idealists. Its divestment thrust is the offshoot of an international campaign – backed by big US foundations – to "dismantle the fossil fuel industry and create a transition to a clean and just energy economy." Its targets include all the major Canadian oil companies.

CYCC is part of the same movement that recently saw the Rockefeller Brothers Fund declare its intention to sell its fossil fuel interests. That announcement was more PR than substance. Still, divestment agitation is growing. Bizarrely, one of the most prominent Canadian agitators is Thomas Van Dyck, a senior executive in the Wealth Management division of the Royal Bank of Canada, RBC. CYCC has also been supported by the TD bank. What are these banks, heavy lenders to – and investors in – the oil industry, thinking?

The Divest-Invest movement was inspired by American Bill McKibben, founder of 350.org, which CYCC acknowledges as its partner in the "Fossil Free Canada" initiative. McKibben is the alarmist guru of billionaire activist Tom Steyer, who has been using his money to influence the US mid-term elections and, in particular, "punish" those who refuse to fall in line on climate. Both men have been rabid opponents of the Keystone XL pipeline, and important in forcing President Obama to delay its approval.

In January of this year, Ellen Dorsey, executive director of the Washington-based Wallace Global Fund – a major backer of radical environmental groups – launched Divest-Invest Philanthropy, supported by seventeen foundations, including the Schmidt Family Foundation, an institution started by Eric Schmidt, the executive chairman of Google.

The Divest-Invest movement claims that fossil fuel divestment is analogous to the divestment movement against South African apartheid (Archbishop Desmond Tutu is an eager supporter). In fact, the comparison is inappropriate because climate change is a scientific issue with possible moral implications depending on its causes and future course, both of which are highly uncertain.

Even a "little bit" of apartheid is morally repugnant, whereas a moderate amount of global warming would be beneficial. Ironically, meanwhile, South Africa is among those countries that desperately need more fossil-fuel-based energy to grow and relieve poverty.

According to the CYCC, "the divestment movement is the fastest growing front in the fight to take on the fossil fuel industry." It seems peculiar therefore that Canadian banks that finance fossil fuel companies might be connected to it. Indeed, RBC's Van Dyck is not just involved, he is a "leader."

Van Dyck, billed as a senior vice-president of RBC, appeared earlier this year on the Bill Moyers TV show in the US, along with Ms. Dorsey of Divest-Invest. Moyers introduced them as "leaders of this new divestment movement." Van Dyck claimed that, "Fossil fuel companies receive $1.9 trillion in subsidies globally on an annual basis. So here's this very, very profitable industry being funded by governments around the world…" The problem with that $1.9 trillion figure is that it is a pure concoction, generated from an IMF study that indicates that the actual amounts of financial subsidies to oil companies in advanced economies are minuscule. The only real number is $480 billion, which are subsidies that overwhelmingly go to people in poorly governed oil-producing countries. That number is quadrupled by cost-benefit hocus pocus about "externalities."

Van Dyck, an investment specialist with RBC, nevertheless suggested that governments might take this non-existent $1.9 trillion and transfer it to "clean technology."

"These are very, very wealthy companies," he declared, "which is one of the reasons why we're trying to turn them into a moral pariah." But these moral pariahs, we might recall, are among his bank's biggest clients. Along with apartheid, Van Dyck invoked the Civil Rights movement and Vietnam.

Both Ms. Dorsey and Van Dyck peddled the claim that the movement was being led by students, but CYCC seems to have a lot of non-youth organizations pulling the strings, including major anti-development groups such as US-funded Tides Canada. The CYCC's other "friends and supporters" include, or have included, the Canadian Auto Workers union, the Pembina Institute, the Sierra Club, the Council of Canadians, the United Church of Canada, the WWF, and the TD bank's Friends of the Environment programme.

I put in a call to RBC asking how one of their senior employees could so vigorously attack their clients. In an email, the bank responded that "Tom's stated views are his own," which I guess is something of a relief, although Van Dyck's bank credentials are on public display and contribute to his credibility. The email went on to stress that the bank's energy clients were "working hard to become more sustainable" and "to supply the world with energy in an environmentally and socially responsible manner." Such grovelling before the vacuous gods of sustainability and social responsibility almost make it sound as if Van Dyck has a point. I also called the TD, who said they couldn't get me a response by my deadline. But then what could they possibly say?

Welcome to Peaksville, Alberta

27 May 2015

One of the greatest episodes of that iconic series *The Twilight Zone* concerned a six-year-old boy named Anthony, who combined super-human powers with the temperament of a truly evil Bart Simpson and the aspirations of a President Obama (Anthony could change the weather).

Having isolated his town, Peaksville, Anthony controlled everything, and everybody. The citizens dare not even think negative thoughts about him, because he could read minds. They told him that everything he did was "good," from fear of being dispatched to something called "the cornfield."

Anthony came to mind while reading recent remarks by Steve Williams, the CEO of oilsands pioneer Suncor, Canada's premier integrated oil company. Just like the citizens of Peaksville, the Alberta oilpatch, with Williams as its spokesman, is circling Rachel Notley's new NDP government with scarcely concealed fear.

Notley, I'm sure, is a lovely person – nothing like Anthony – but the NDP have many items on their agenda that could send the Alberta economy into the cornfield, including higher corporate/carbon taxes and royalties, and forced local upgrading of resources.

Adopting the role of the "Rachel Whisperer," Williams' speech to a Calgary audience last week was a masterpiece of carefully crafted platitude. The one necessary piece of ugly reality was his suggestion that emissions taxes must be aimed primarily at consumers rather than industry (he'd never win an election on that platform). He declared that climate change was happening and that inaction was not an option. He did not say exactly where it was happening, or why. Nor did he acknowledge that any action that Alberta – or indeed Canada – might take wouldn't make the slightest difference.

He pointed to seat-belt legislation as an analogy to climate policy. Perhaps a more accurate analogy would be forcing all pedestrians to wear helmets and body armour. Just in case.

Williams is on the advisory board of the Ecofiscal Commission, the self-appointed group of alleged policy mavens that has promoted the barmy idea that the provinces should each go their own way in climate legislation; let all the cats out of the policy bag and maybe you can herd them towards a coherent national policy at some later date.

The immediate source of industry concern is the expiration of Alberta's Specified Gas Emitters Regulation, under which small levies are made on companies that fail to reduce their emissions intensity by 12% annually. The fear is that something much more draconian is in the works, hence Williams' urgent appeal for the province to take the time to get the policy "right."

Nevertheless, a policy with teeth is allegedly required to help the industry gain "social licence" from those standing in the way of new pipelines. Unlicenced NGO licensing authorities have a lot in common with Anthony.

The industry's immediate concern is to make sure that the new Alberta government does as little damage as possible. The one thing of which everybody can be certain is that no policy will have the slightest impact on the climate, unlike little Anthony, who made it snow in Peaksville, with disastrous implications for the local farm economy. But the terrified Peaksvilleans still said it was "good."

Pipeline dictators
31 August 2016

There are multiple connections between Justin Trudeau's first Prime Ministerial visit to China and protesters shutting down the National Energy Board (NEB) hearings on the Energy East pipeline in Montreal this week.

In China, the state shuts down individuals. In Canada, individuals can apparently shut down the state. Or at least they can shut down any state apparatus they don't like. But then the Liberal government has already undermined this particular piece of apparatus by declaring that the NEB needs to restore a credibility that has been dented by...the Liberal government!

There has been much criticism of how two NEB panel members met privately with former Quebec premier Jean Charest while he was consulting for Energy East sponsor TransCanada Corp. An error of judgment, perhaps, but surely it is far more significant that a self-righteous beefy brawler can shut down public hearings by rushing the panel like an irate baseball batter charging the mound. Then there was Montreal mayor Denis Coderre, who had come not to offer input to a process of weighing costs and benefits, but to just say no.

Certainly, M. Coderre and his fellow mayors democratically represent the people of the Montreal region, but they and their constituents have been sucked into anti-pipeline hysteria promoted by radical groups who have as little regard for democracy as they have for truth. Which brings us back to that China trip.

While human rights will hopefully be high on Trudeau's agenda ahead of the G20 meeting in Guangzhou next weekend, climate policy looms above all else as a threat to both wealth and freedom, while pipeline policy – or lack of it – is a particular irritant to Sino-Canadian relations.

The Chinese hardly have to play a hypocritical game when it comes to climate. President Obama was so desperate to push his legacy as the modern King Canute that his "landmark" agreement with China, announced two years ago, involved the Chinese committing to nothing. Ontario premier Kathleen Wynne made a big deal about closing two provincial coal plants, at significant cost, while China continues to build hundreds annually.

It is unimaginable that Chinese megaprojects would be held up – at least for too long – by protesters. We might then think that this week's scenes in Montreal are to be celebrated as a welcome display of free speech, but they are the opposite: a determination to silence all opposing points of view. For the kind of people who want to shut down the Canadian fossil fuel industry, totalitarianism is not the enemy, it is the model.

Three years ago, Trudeau enthused about how Chinese dictatorship made it easier to pursue climate goals. The remark may have been off the cuff, but it represented a conviction that he would have absorbed at his father's knee. Pierre Trudeau was a long-time Communist sympathizer who, like all Fellow Travellers, found it easy to ignore state murder and oppression. It was the same arrogant mindset that led to an economic assault on Alberta in the form of the 1980 National Energy Program.

Fossil-fuelled capitalism remains the enemy, but the rationale for the assault has changed. In the NEP era it was the alleged threat of foreign – that is, mainly American – control of Canadian resources, and of Alberta having "more than its fair share" of Canada's petroleum patrimony. Now it is the alleged existential threat of greenhouse gases. The guilty parties are the same, as is the policy solution: more bureaucratic control of economic activity, only now at a global level.

State control has never gone out of fashion in China, but the country's enormous success is due to unleashing the Chinese entrepreneurial spirit. Unfortunately, that success has enabled the recrudescence of imperial ambitions.

Meanwhile, Chinese economic interests and those of "Junior Trudeau" are hardly consistent. The Chinese are upset that the tens of billions of dollars they have poured into the Alberta oilpatch are showing significant losses, not just because of low prices but because Alberta oil is being blocked by the same forces that closed down the Montreal hearings. The same anti-development groups have also stood against west coast liquefied natural gas (LNG) plants. LNG could replace Chinese coal and thus address real environmental problems (as well as lowering emissions).

The Harper government adopted a pragmatic – that is, deliberately vague – policy towards further takeovers by Chinese state-owned enterprises, or SOEs. It has been suggested that Trudeau might relax those rules this week as a goodwill gesture, but one doubts there are too many Chinese SOEs interested in pouring more money into the oilsands. What China wants is for roadblocks to new pipelines to be removed. By contrast, everything the Trudeau government has done so far serves to reinforce those roadblocks. That beefy brawler in Montreal was really just part of the program.

The Deep Liberal State bites back
19 July 2018

The Trudeau Liberals, like the old comic-strip character Pogo, are discovering that when it comes to pipeline policy, the real enemy is themselves. Their acquisition of the TransMountain pipeline is yet another example of their progressive pretensions colliding with economic reality. The contradictions of their climate and energy policies have put them in a mighty pickle, after they effectively killed all other new domestic alternatives to take diluted bitumen from the Alberta oilsands to tidewater.

Justin Trudeau's bland declaration in 2015 that "The Great Bear Rainforest is no place for a pipeline" has returned to haunt him in the form of a much more valid criticism: a pipeline is no place for a government. But that is almost a peripheral issue. At some stage – assuming TransMountain survives endless court challenges and the diehard opposition of the BC government – push will come to shove. Literally, when protesters hurl their bodies in the pipeline's path.

Ironically, Justin Skywalker is about to discover the figure inside that Darth Vader suit – the Dark Force of eco-extremism now fighting his pipeline – is...his father! That's because one of the main nodes of opposition to construction is funded by a government entity that was created when Pierre Trudeau was prime minister. A sizable portion of opposition to TransMountain is being funded by a grant from the Social Sciences and Humanities Research Council, the SSHRC, an entity set up as part of what might be called the "Deep Liberal State" – that is, permanent Liberal government-funded institutions created to make sure that the progressive agenda continues, whatever that agenda happens to be at the time, and whichever government happens to be in power.

The SSHRC doles out hundreds of millions of dollars in academic research grants with a distinctly left-liberal bias. The council received unwelcome attention last year when it turned down a research grant to celebrity anti-progressive academic Jordan Peterson (who had received considerable previous funding) suspiciously soon after he had refused to be forced to use gender-neutral pronouns.

How dare ze!

Three years ago (significantly when Stephen Harper was prime minister), the SSHRC gave a hefty $2.5-million grant for a six-year study to expose the supposedly insidious political power of the fossil-fuel industry. Other entities, such as union giant Unifor, kicked in an additional $2 million to the project, which was called *Mapping the Power of the Carbon-Extractive Corporate Resource Sector*. It was to be "hosted" by the University of Victoria, the Parkland Institute at the University of Alberta (the place where they think David Suzuki is worthy of academic honours), and the Canadian Centre for Policy Alternatives (which we usually describe here as the Canadian Centre for Alternatives to Good Policy). The academic leader of the study is an old UVic Marxist named William Carroll.

Visit the power-mapping project's website today and you will find a picture of Justin Trudeau alongside the words: "Power and influence in the fossil fuel industry today place sharp limits on our democracy." The juxtaposition might suggest that the words are a quote from the PM. They are not. Still, one must admit that the observation is insightful – except the power really undermining democracy is coming from radical environmentalists entirely unconcerned that a majority of both Canadians and British Columbians support building TransMountain. The radicals' idea of "democracy" is, more accurately, minority rule by social-mediated mobs.

That brings us to the power-mapping project's activist bit: its plan for the "Development of an open source, publicly accessible corporate database and training program for citizens and civil society groups..."

Although they are still working on the database, it's starting to become clear just what sort of training they're offering citizens and civil society groups. Earlier this year, the project co-sponsored a presentation in Vancouver by US activist Winona LaDuke. Since twice running on the Green Party's vice-presidential ticket alongside Ralph Nader, LaDuke has featured prominently in protests against Enbridge's Line 3 replacement in Minnesota and the illegal week-long sit-in against the Dakota Access line, in which Enbridge also has a significant stake.

LaDuke declared in her Vancouver speech that Canada was a "petrostate," and that she "understood" that climate change would cost 20% of global GDP "in a few years."

That's a pretty serious misunderstanding. Another term for it might be "monstrous lie."

After running through the stock litany against GMO foods and fracking, she proposed a locavore society where everybody would live on solar power and grow their own crops. "You don't need a lawn. Grow food," she lectured. "Be smart," she said, "like Denmark and Germany" (whose off-carbon transition policies are comprehensive disasters).

LaDuke also declared her determination to continue fighting Enbridge in the US, and ridiculed the company's efforts at appeasement. She urged Canadian activists on in their fight against TransMountain. LaDuke concluded by demanding the audience not relinquish power to "the one per cent."

In reality, it is LaDuke and her ilk who represent the grossly disproportionate power of the one per cent of radical activists. They are funded not only by the American 0.0001 per cent, made up of billionaires and foundations who think Canada should be one big national park, but, thanks to Pierre Trudeau's SSHRC, by Canadian taxpayers, too. And those government-funded radicals are about to bite Trudeau *fils* in the butt.

From Petro-Canada to Pipero-Canada
27 July 2018

Justin Trudeau's Liberals are about to undertake their first significant piece of energy nationalization in three decades, and it's going to get ugly. Their imminent $4.5-billion takeover of the Trans-Mountain pipeline and its $7-billion-plus expansion proposal has its nearest historical counterpart in the acquisitions made by Pierre Trudeau's state oil company, Petro-Canada, in the 1970s and 1980s. But the attitude of the second Trudeau regime to nationalization could not be more different from the first. The good news is that the acquisition of TransMountain is attached to no grand xenophobic industrial strategies (although it exposes the hypocrisy of Ottawa's commitment to a low-carbon "transition"). The bad news is that it amounts to an act of sheer desperation by a government that finds itself up climate-policy creek in a barbed wire canoe, without a paddle.

In fact, the lessons of Petrocan appear entirely forgotten, if indeed they were ever widely known. Petrocan was taken over by Suncor almost 10 years ago and is now known by most people merely as a gas station brand that sponsors sports on the CBC. Suncor runs Petro-Canada now as a respectable business, but given its history, it is remarkable that the brand should exist at all. Anybody who kept around "Titanic," "Edsel" or "Enron" as brand names might be thought deranged, but it's in the same category that Petrocan belongs.

The state oil company's very expensive lesson was that government can't run things, can't compete with the private sector, can't resist using such instruments for political reasons, and is inevitably bamboozled by its own creations. Petrocan did however run a very successful Olympic torch relay to Calgary in 1988.

Do we need any more lessons in government incompetence? The federal Liberals' announcement in May that they would buy Trans-Mountain coincided with an auditor general's report that Canada has a "broken government system." Among the many other things it can't do is refurbish bridges (the Champlain bridge in Montreal), or organize payroll systems (Phoenix).

Bizarrely, however, the fact that the government can't run anything in particular has transmogrified – thanks to the manufactured climate crisis – into the claim that it must "sustainably" regulate everything. This megalomanic aspiration is just one part of a program of global governance co-ordinated by the utterly corrupt and incompetent United Nations. Predictably, that system is crashing the world over, and not just because of President Donald Trump's denialist deplorables.

When Finance Minister Bill Morneau announced the Trans-Mountain deal a couple of months ago, he couldn't stress too strongly how the government had no intention of being in the pipeline business long term. Part of the deal was that the project's parent, Kinder Morgan, would help the government look for another private investor to whom to pass the parcel. The period for Kinder's assistance ran out last weekend, just after the cabinet reshuffle that saw Edmonton MP Amarjeet Sohi take over the Natural Resources portfolio, along with responsibility for TransMountain. Sohi politely declared that he had "big shoes to fill," but the most important feature of the ministerial footwear inherited from his predecessor, Jim Carr, is that it is nailed to the floor.

As the former minister for infrastructure, Sohi knows something about handing out government money, but TransMountain is not a problem that can be solved simply by throwing taxpayers' cash at it, although that was inevitably the government's first resort.

Meanwhile the Liberals' infrastructure plans have been treading water in concrete overshoes. Ironically, in their desire to shovel money out the door, they abandoned a provision that projects should be checked out for their potential as public–private partnerships. That's because governments are far more efficient at spending money, but not spending it efficiently. However, the Liberals would love a private pipeline partner right now.

Ottawa has been peddling the notion that lots of companies have been looking at TransMountain, and that it may have snapped up "a bargain" but, despite the offer of government indemnities, nobody has stepped in. Any investor that did so would be rash indeed, for the more funds the government has to pay out to cover court delays and civil disobedience, the more the investor will be pilloried as an incompetent corporate-welfare bum. Certainly, all sorts of investors would be interested in buying the system once – or rather if – the expansion were completed.

It is difficult to imagine how TransMountain will not remain a political albatross, although the Liberals obviously made the political calculation that buying it was better than simply having the project die immediately due to their startlingly muddled policies on energy and the environment.

It is hardly good news for the Liberals that TransMountain is likely to be overshadowed by the even larger – but very much related – fight over carbon taxes, as provincial premiers, reflecting the belated awakening of their electorates, fight these economically destructive and environmentally pointless burdens.

Under government ownership, pressure is bound to increase for indigenous interests to be given an equity interest. That in fact may be inevitable, but there will surely also be other pressing Trudeaupian issues, such as how many women there will be on the TransMountain board, and whether the company's procurement is suitably supportive of racial, gender and every other form of diversity.

While it should be of concern that the "learnings" of Petrocan have never been absorbed, TransMountain is about to provide a whole new set of lessons about government support for the fatal contradictions of pretentious environmental progressivism.

10

Unsustainable subversion

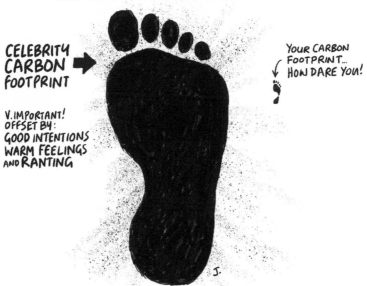

KNOW YOUR CARBON FOOTPRINT
LEARNING TO SPOT THE DIFFERENCE

CELEBRITY
CARBON
FOOTPRINT

YOUR CARBON
FOOTPRINT...
HOW DARE YOU!

V. IMPORTANT!
OFFSET BY:
GOOD INTENTIONS
WARM FEELINGS
AND RANTING

"Sustainable Development" and "Sustainability" have become the great weasel concepts of our times, incessantly parroted by United Nations poobahs, politicians, corporate chieftains and ENGO activists. Everybody feels compelled to support such notions but nobody is quite sure what they mean; but then who could favour "unsustainability"? SD is designed -- as with most parts of the Global Governance Agenda -- not to promote thought but to preclude it.

273

Nothing to fear from Bigfoots

25 October 2006

It seems that by the year 2050, the human race is going to be a planet short of its resource needs. I know this because I heard it yesterday morning on the CBC news. I was still reeling from the previous night's revelation on the CBC's *The National* that the Canadian Prairies are – due to global warming – heading for a massive drought. But then what is mere drought compared with a missing planet?

The CBC's story was based on the World Wildlife Fund for Nature's (WWF) 2006 *Living Planet* report. According to the report, "The world's natural ecosystems are being degraded at a rate unprecedented in human history." But surely this is simply a function of the fact that there are more humans living better than at any time previously. Isn't that a good thing? And is "degraded" the right word?

Not merely do professional alarmists refuse to countenance the lessons of economic history, they staunchly avert their eyes from examining why doleful projections have been wrong in the past.

The father of all such thinking was Thomas Malthus, who contended 200 years ago that the mass of humanity was destined to live at the level of subsistence because of their inability to stop breeding. It was simple arithmetic: agricultural land expanded only gradually, in a linear fashion, while human mouths grew exponentially. Only a fool could fail to see a future of misery.

Malthus was proved wrong by a combination of astonishing increases in agricultural and industrial productivity, and the ability of an increasingly educated and healthy population to control its fertility. And yet two centuries later the end is still always nigh.

We have been hearing the modern drumbeat of gloom and doom for more than 40 years. In 1972, the much-praised book *The Limits to Growth* projected that we would run out of gold by 1981, of mercury by 1985 and of zinc by 1990.

In 1968, Paul Ehrlich, who the last time I looked still hadn't been ridiculed to another planet, wrote *The Population Bomb*, which foresaw global famines well before the end of the past century.

The dangerous depletionism argument has gone global since the mid-1980s, with the spread of the deeply flawed and subversive concept of "sustainable development," which implies that mankind is incapable of tying its collective shoelaces and thus must be led by unredeemed socialists into a resource-constrained future. Its latest variant is peak-oil theory, which contends that a maxing out of oil production will lead to the "end of economics."

The WWF report emphasizes two allegedly dire sets of statistics. The first is that there are 30% fewer of 1300 chosen vertebrate species around now than there were in 1970. Note that this does not mean a 30% decline in the number of species but in the numbers of particular animals and fish.

If humans were intent on driving species to extinction, we might have cause for worry, but humans in developed countries are more sensitive to the natural environment than ever.

The second index of horror is that of humans' "ecological footprint," which, according to the WWF study, tripled between 1961 and 2003. Again, is this bad or surprising? The WWF's Top 10 Bigfoots include not merely the United States, Canada and Australia, but also Sweden and Norway. So doesn't that mean that a big footprint is good? Not according to the WWF. That's because our collective footprint "exceeded biocapacity" by 25% in 2003. Clearly, if that is true, it is "unsustainable." But what happens when something is unsustainable? It stops. We don't go marching on brainlessly to oblivion like some out-of-control herd of island-bound ungulates. The notion that an extra planet or two might be required is intended to demonstrate that economic growth is unsustainable, but what it really emphasizes is how ridiculous are linear projections that take no account of markets' feedback effects.

The market gives price signals, articulates demands and promotes and rewards ingenious solutions. Denizens of market economies, since they tend to be democratic, also exert powerful political pressures when they become convinced of environmental problems. But of course that leaves them open to being fed alarmist junk.

Power-hungry Jacobins such as the WWF are always talking about the pressing need for us to adopt "new" values and lifestyles, but they don't believe that this is going to happen voluntarily. What is needed is always "political will." We must be forced to change by wise governments. The problem is that wise governments are as mythical as spare planets.

Unsustainable bureaucracy

18 May 2007

When Francis Nhema, Zimbabwe's Minister for Environment and Tourism, was elected last Saturday to head the UN Commission on Sustainable Development (CSD), there was a torrent of righteous criticism.

Nhema is a member of the tyrannical regime of Robert Mugabe, who has turned the "breadbasket of Africa" into a basket case, halving the life expectancy of its benighted population in the process. Nhema himself has presided over the ruin of a rich and productive farm that the government stole – sorry, "repatriated" – from its white owner. He has also overseen the collapse of the country's wildlife sanctuaries.

While most pundits agreed that the appointment of Nhema was a farce, few suggested that the CSD is an equally surreal joke. Instead, the commission was generally referred to as if it were a valuable and worthwhile organization that, if only it had a more credible leader, might do some solid good for the wretched of the earth and the future of the planet.

The UK's Minister for Africa, Lord Triesman, declared that Nhema's appointment "damages the credibility of the commission." But what credibility? London's *Observer* claimed that the commission "should be an institution of some importance and authority," but it didn't say why, or how. *The Times* of London admitted that sustainable development is "an opaque coinage," but went on to suggest that Nhema's appointment had "failed Africa." A short editorial in *The Globe and Mail* declared that: "The UN commission deserves better than a repudiation of everything it stands for." But for what, exactly, does it stand?

The conventional definition of sustainable development – meeting the needs of the present without jeopardizing the needs of the future – was hatched by the UN's 1987 Brundtland Commission. The definition manages to be at once bland, meaningless, utopian and dangerous.

Inevitably, Canada's maestro of multinational multi-tasking, Maurice Strong, was a key member of Brundtland. The CSD was set up following the anti-capitalist carnival at Rio in 1992, which was orchestrated by Strong. It is essentially yet another of the sleeper cells created to pursue his impossible autocratic dream.

If anthropogenic global warming represents the alleged mother of all "collective action problems," sustainable development represents the matriarch of all political pretensions. It is the notion that, as Strong has said without attracting sufficient laughter, what the world needs is a UN-based system to manage literally everything.

But if Africa's problems can be linked to any concept, it is surely that of sustainable development, which is based on emphasizing the alleged dangers of private property and free markets, and suggesting that what is needed to save the world is yet another dose of comprehensive planning and forced redistribution.

Sustainable development, like its semantic sister, corporate social responsibility, is merely the failed socialist wolf in the emperor's new green sheepskin.

The reason that sustainable development has spread like wildfire throughout the world's governments and bureaucracies is because it gives them a rationale for expansive – and expensive – meddling. It is high on the agenda of next month's G8 summit. British Foreign Minister Margaret Beckett this week suggested that it was an area in which China might provide a leading role (after all, they are communists, and Maurice Strong is, significantly, holed up in Beijing).

Sustainable development also appears to have extraordinary attractions for those leaving office under an ethical cloud. Outgoing French president Jacques Chirac is to head a new foundation that will focus on sustainable development "with a particular emphasis on Africa." Indeed, we might now suggest – with all due respect to Dr. Johnson – that it is not patriotism that is now the last resort of the scoundrel, but sustainable development. (Apparently, the first step in Chirac's new concern for the environment is the vigorous composting of documents in the Elysee Palace, since he will, after leaving office, no longer have immunity from prosecution.)

Fortunately, Nhema is about to head an organization that has no operational targets, just a never-ending list of areas in which to meddle. One of its latest is global road safety. Two weeks of UN gabbing ahead of Nhema's election (it was Africa's "turn") produced no consensus about the CSD's agenda. So it will just float on downstream, populated by time-servers and leftist intellectuals, soaking up wads of laundered tax dollars and organizing pointless conferences that contribute millions of tons of carbon dioxide to the problem about which it claims to be so deeply concerned.

Ironically, Nhema won't be able to travel to Europe because the entire Zimbabwean government is under a travel ban. Perhaps this will encourage the commission to start teleconferencing to reduce its "footprint." But I doubt it.

Cuba's carbon bootprint
21 June 2008

Cuba was crowned two years ago as the model for "sustainable development." Its unique status as the only country that "enjoys" sustainability was first celebrated in the World Wildlife Fund's *The Living Planet Report 2006*. The island gulag is the only state whose "ecological footprint" and level of "human development" (according to the UN's peculiar scale of values) are both within the tiny box in which humans are to be allowed to live.

The concept of the ecological footprint was first developed in 1993 by the University of British Columbia's William Rees and his student Mathis Wackernagel. It claims to quantify the area of land needed to support an individual within a particular nation using available technology. Based on a number of assumptions, humans allegedly have some 1.8 hectares of planet each. If your lifestyle requires more, you are taking "more than your fair share" and contributing to "ecological overshoot."

Such thinking is a stew of hunter-gatherer egalitarianism, neo-Malthusianism, economic ignorance and Soviet planning. It gives rise to the bizarre statistic of the Earth equivalent ratio, or EER, which indicates "how many earths" would be needed if everybody was to live at a particular nation's lifestyle. Since we only have one earth, such flights are designed to shock us at the unfairness of it all, plus establish that it is physically impossible for poor people to achieve the lifestyles of the rich and greedy. If everybody was to live at the per capita standards of the US, we would need more than five earths!

Where Cuba scores is that if everybody lived like Cubans (not the Castros, of course, but the average benighted José or Maria), we would only need one earth. But shouldn't we also note that Cubans have lived under a Communist dictatorship for almost fifty years? Apparently, that doesn't matter, at least not if you look at the other axis of Cuba's sustainable virtue. Cubans are doing well according to the UN's Human Development Index, HDI, which is based on weighted rankings for longevity, literacy, years of schooling and per capita Gross Domestic Product. Naturally, democracy doesn't get a mention, and income is underplayed, as is the fact that Cuban schooling means indoctrination. Nevertheless, if you want to live a long life without being threatened by obesity, cell phone addiction or thought, Castro's Cuba is the place for you.

Wackernagel claims that a combination of his footprint and the HDI enables him to give a "robust measure" for sustainable development. It is defined as having an HDI of at least 0.8 and a maximum EER of 1. Too low an HDI means "underdevelopment;" a greater EER means your nation is "gobbling up too many resources." Cuba is thus the Goldilocks of nations, the only one, according to the *New Scientist* magazine, which is moving in the "right direction."

Wackernagel admits that Cuba didn't achieve ecological virtue without a little push. According to him, Cubans were "forced into a smaller footprint because of the oil embargo." That's right, US hegemony played its wicked part in achieving this noble end. Strangely, however, Wackernagel doesn't mention the role of Communism in forcing Cuba into a bicycle- and ox-powered economy (which has been lavishly praised by David Suzuki, who is – now here's a surprise – on the Science and Policy Advisory Council of Wackernagel's Global Footprint Network).

The Cuban regime – ever on the lookout for rationalizations of its repression – has been quick to leap on footprintthink. Earlier this year, Ricardo Alarcón, the unctuous liar who is the regime's third-in-command, was challenged during an appearance at a Havana university on why Cubans weren't free to travel (the questioner was, of course, subsequently detained). His response: "If all the world, some six billion people, could travel whenever they wanted, the jam in the skies would be enormous." We'd need the airspace of another dozen earths!

Sustaina-bull

16 August 2008

This week, petroleum giant Royal Dutch Shell had its knuckles rapped by the UK's Advertising Standards Authority (ASA) over claims that its Canadian oilsands operations were "sustainable." There is a certain rich irony in Shell being hoist on its own environmental petard. The company's former CEO, Sir Philip Watts, once claimed that Shell's commitment to sustainable development and corporate social responsibility were what elevated it above its rivals. That was before he was thrown out of the company for cooking the financial books.

For years, Shell has been kowtowing to the environmental movement, and has featured a rogues' gallery of board members and executives who ranged between green radicalism and abject appeasement. Typically, as it groveled to defend itself in the ASA case, it quoted a report by the World Wildlife Fund, wwf, the very organization that had challenged its ad in the first place. One can't help conjuring up the image of a dog licking the hand of its vivisectionist.

The first Shell chairman to go conspicuously native was Sir Mark Moody-Stuart, who was to be seen cavorting with environmental radicals in that anti-corporate snuff flick, *The Corporation*. Sir Mark also got himself involved in promoting poverty-inducing alternative energy projects in the third world, and was fingered by *The Economist* as a leading sell-out to csr.

Then came Lord Oxburgh, an academic geologist who was appointed non-executive chairman and proceeded to rail against markets, preach environmental doom and gloom, and express deep faith in wise and expansive government: the Useful Idiots' trifecta. The true Knight of Hypocrisy was the above mentioned Sir Philip Watts, who perpetually bleated about the need to earn a "licence to operate" from "stakeholders" such as the wwf, but neglected to tell the truth to shareholders. Meanwhile he wasn't just any old hypocrite; he was the chairman of the World Business Council on Sustainable Development, the very Round Table of Useful Idiocy.

Executives at Shell's Canadian operations have also shown gung-ho support for suicidal policies. When Nicholas Stern, author of the appallingly skewed uk report on the economics of climate change, came to Toronto to speak, he was introduced, and lavishly praised, by Clive Mather, the head of Shell Canada.

Sir Philip Watts claimed that sustainable development had become "central to how we do business." But this week's ruling indicates that Shell doesn't actually understand what sustainability means. But then nobody does.

The asa case was based on an ad in the *Financial Times* to coincide with the release of Shell's 2007 financial results. There, Shell declared that "the challenge of the 21st century is to meet the growing need for energy in ways that are not only profitable but sustainable. As our 2007 results show, we're investing heavily in new technology and assets to safeguard the interests of our shareholders and future generations."

Seems pretty unobjectionable, but the asa concluded that the ad didn't meet its standards with respect to two of the examples given: the oilsands and Shell's Port Arthur refinery.

The ASA relied for its assessment of the oilsands on a report by Canada's National Energy Board that noted that oilsands development has considerable social and environmental impacts. This is hardly a surprise, but the important point is surely just how considerable compared with the related considerable benefits?

Most pointedly, the ASA objected to Shell's use of the word sustainable because it contravened British government rules against "vague or ambiguous" language in environmental advertising. It concluded that "Because 'sustainable' was an ambiguous term, and because we had not seen data that showed how Shell was effectively managing carbon emissions from its oilsands projects in order to limit climate change, we concluded that on this point the ad was misleading."

However, the ASA report makes major assumptions. The first is that since Shell's oilsands are big, located in the boreal forest, use a lot of water, and emit a calculable portion of Canada's anthropogenic greenhouse gases, then they are somehow unsustainable. More profoundly – and controversially – the ASA implies that Shell could somehow affect the climate by curbing its oilsands' greenhouse gas emissions, which is nonsense.

The oilsands have, for some time, been a focus of a concerted attack by environmentalists, who have concentrated a good deal of their efforts in the UK. A sign of their success was a stunningly ill-informed editorial in *The Times* of London earlier this year that described oilsands activity as a "filthy habit" and called on the next US president to clamp down on imports of their production.

On the bright side, however, this decision might stop companies from flaunting the "S" word, which, as has often been stressed in this space, is both operationally meaningless and politically subversive.

The Sustainable Emperor is stark naked
8 June 2012

The Rio+20 Earth Summit on Sustainable Development, which starts in two weeks, will be a farce, even if everybody keeps a straight face. The grand UN-based system conceived to co-ordinate the activities of all mankind has proved utterly unsustainable, a dysfunctional mess that generates nothing but endless meetings, agendas and reports.

That sustainable development would collapse under its own contradictions was inevitable. What is fascinating is why every country on earth would earnestly have committed to a murky concept hatched by a cabal of ardent socialists. Equally fascinating is the almost universal reluctance to acknowledge the organizational disaster that has ensued.

Welcome to sustainable development's world of devious ideological purpose, ridiculous bureaucratic pretension, bogus "civil society" enforcement, and political hypocrisy.

The phrase "sustainable development" first achieved wide currency as the result of the 1987 report of the UN's all-socialist Brundtland Commission. The vague but subversive concept was rooted in projections of environmental apocalypse due to catastrophic man-made global warming, species extinction, resource depletion, and any number of other apocalyptic scenarios that would be brought about by unfettered capitalism.

What was needed to fix this (projected) mess was greater political oversight and control, which would delicately balance the triple bottom line of the economy, the environment and social issues. As Brundtland commissioner Maurice Strong, who orchestrated the subsequent 1992 Rio conference, declared: "[W]e must devise a new approach to co-operative management of the entire system of issues."

So how is the dream looking after 20 years?

Rio+20's "themes" are "Green economy in the context of poverty eradication and sustainable development" and "The institutional framework for sustainable development governance." Green economies, which are everywhere based on unsustainable subsidy and dead-end technologies, are stumbling throughout the world, but the more intriguing theme is that "institutional framework."

The descent of sustainable development master plans into abject confusion was acknowledged in a widely unread 2008 report from the UN's Joint Inspection Unit. The report noted that the ramshackle sustainable governance "framework" had at least three interrelated masters: the UN Environment Program (UNEP), which had been set up with Strong as its head after the 1972 UN conference in Stockholm; the Commission on Sustainable Development (CSD), which had been created after Rio in 1992; and the UN's Economic and Social Council (ECOSOC), to which the CSD theoretically reported.

The report found these bureaucracies to be disconnected from the ever-proliferating UN secretariats formed to deal with ever-multiplying multinational environmental agreements. Indeed, nobody had a handle on just how many programs, projects and organizations there were within the UN's exploding universe. It ran into the hundreds. The Joint Inspection Unit suggested that taking a basic inventory might be a good start.

The report also found that this unwieldy system, which was meant to impose a godlike "balance," contained no mechanism for assessing whether the environmental benefits of agreements were actually greater than the costs of their implementation. What this uncoordinated hydra-headed UN–ENGO monster was good at, however, was producing an endless stream of voluminous reports. Unlike the organizational mess, these stressed a number of relatively consistent, albeit unworkable, themes, all of which pointed – once you penetrated the Orwellian verbiage – to a comprehensive power grab.

One key theme was that national governments had to sacrifice sovereignty and give more power to radical ENGOs (who had been eagerly promoted – and allowed into the UN process – as the voice of "civil society" by the Brundtland gang and their fellow travellers at nodes such as the World Economic Forum). Another was that the UN needed an independent source of income, perhaps via a tax on financial transactions. Yet another was that the International Financial Institutions, primarily the World Bank, should be pressured both to withhold funds from fossil-fuel development and fund alternatives. There were persistent calls for more money and bigger bureaucracy. The latest demand is a World Environmental Organization. Fortunately, some countries are resisting, among them Canada. Nevertheless, Canada is firmly, and hypocritically, embedded in the sustainability charade.

Starting in 1997, all federal departments had to table sustainable-development strategies every three years. A Commissioner of the Environment and Sustainable Development was created within the Office of the Auditor-General. It was inevitable that the commissioner's reports would be sharply critical of the government's move toward sustainability, because nobody was quite sure in which direction it lay. Year after year, commissioners' reports were critical of governments' planning and reporting for sustainability (which, somewhat ironically, is all about planning and reporting). They cited a lack of clearly defined priorities, metrics, targets, accountability and leadership, as well as failure to achieve other bureaucratic buzz concepts such as "horizontal integration across departments" and strategies that would be "drivers of change." The thorniest issue was climate-change policy.

A 2006 report by then commissioner Johanne Gélinas was useful to the Harper Conservatives because it laid bare that the previous Liberal government had spent billions to achieve zero impact on climate. Not that the Harper government wanted to "achieve" too much either, since sustainable "achievement" tended to be both climatically pointless and economically destructive. Earlier this year, the commissioner again castigated the Conservatives for having no clear plans to meet their carbon dioxide reduction targets by 2020.

Meanwhile, in 2008, after 11 years of sustainably treading water, a Federal Sustainable Development Act was passed (with all-party support), calling for a Federal Sustainable Development Strategy (FSDS). You know, the thing that was meant to have been introduced in 1997, and which had since produced nothing but a digital mountain of departmental reports.

The first FSDS was tabled in October 2010. The impossible dream would be carried forth on yet another wave of good intention and gobbledygook, "An integrated, whole-of-government picture of actions and results."

Canada's "national submission" to the Rio conference is yet another model of bureaucratic pretension and political hypocrisy, in which an ostensibly right-wing government calls for more comprehensive and effective progress toward the socialist dreams of Brundtland and Rio '92.

Although it opposes the creation of a World Environmental Organization, the submission – which one doubts any government minister has even skimmed – appears infinitely amenable to sprucing up dysfunctional organizations such as UNEP and ECOSOC to pursue "more focused" agendas within "more streamlined" and "integrated" formats. It suggests institutional reforms to embed sustainable development even more deeply into UN processes, programs and partnerships, although only in a co-ordinated, coherent, whole-of-government sort of way.

It's time for that little boy in the crowd to state the obvious. The Sustainable Emperor has no clothes.

The Rio future we avoided

22 June 2012

The "failure" of Rio+20 is a cause for celebration, even if you can't afford the champagne and foie gras that ecocrats served themselves while their hopes for "Sustainia" retreated into the policy fog. A mostly "B" list of government leaders (no Barack Obama, no David Cameron, no Stephen Harper, no Angela Merkel) was set to adopt a pablum-filled 283-point "vision" on Friday.

"[N]othing less than a disaster for the planet," declared Nnimmo Bassey, Nigerian poet and chair of Friends of the Earth International. "[A]n epic failure," claimed Kumi Naidoo, Greenpeace International executive director. '[A] colossal waste of time," chimed in Jim Leape, international director-general of the World Wildlife Fund.

An umbrella group of NGOs bemoaned the official text's lack of mention of "planetary boundaries, tipping points or planetary carrying capacity," the very shibboleths of radical environmentalism's zero-sum non-thinking.

Significantly, the mother and father of sustainable development, Gro Harlem Brundtland and Maurice "Chairman Mo" Strong, carped – or should that be gro-aned and mo-aned? – from the Rio sidelines.

According to Ms. Brundtland, Rio+20's failure is due to the eurozone financial crisis and the power of US Tea Party climate deniers. Strong was flown in from China to be regaled by a group of big corporations on Monday as a "very special guest of honour."

One wonders if these aged eco-doomsters were embarrassed by support from Iranian President Mahmoud Ahmadinejad, who called for rich countries to eschew "materialist" desires and pursue "spiritual" development. Ahmadinejad also suggested that "The collapse of the current atheistic order is reaching its time."

Perhaps so – the social democratic replacement for God is certainly proving to have feet of clay – but it is doubtful that Gaia's caliphate will be taking over any time soon.

The high priests of the new green world order crave cash, but calls for humanity to fork over for Gaia's "services" are falling on deaf ears, and not just because of the global economy. One problem is that Gaia has no bank account. UN Secretary-General Ban Ki-moon, while ritually bemoaning the weakness of Rio+20's outcome, declared this week that "Nature does not negotiate with human beings." But then neither does she speak through the UN. Gaia's service fees would wind up in the coffers of the guys and gals who brought you not just oil-for-food, but a human rights system ruled by the world's worst rights abusers, utterly corrupted climate science, and turmoil in Syria.

The failure of Rio does not mean disregard for "The Environment." Environmental protection is an aspect of human protection. The environment has no value except for what it means to humans. The outrage that this observation might promote serves to prove the point. The environment can no more value itself than it can express outrage. Human development inevitably involves disturbance of land and the potential pollution of air and water. The issue is never people versus the environment. It is the interests of some people vs. the interests of other people. The question is one of balance.

Canada under Stephen Harper should be justly proud of being in the vanguard of this return to balance both via its withdrawal from Kyoto and the environmental provisions of Bill C-38, which do not seek to trash safeguards – as alarmists have suggested – but to eliminate duplication, bureaucratic overreach, and the potential for sheer obstructionism.

Naturally, the threat of sustainable ideology is not over. Too many bureaucrats at the international and national level are invested in it. Too many scientists are paid to support it. Too much NGO fundraising depends on it.

Significantly, the official conference text talks of working with NGOs, despite their lack of political legitimacy. It also calls for more power for the United Nations Environment Program. At least there is no mention of a World Environmental Organization, which would have been just as useless but would have threatened endless further negotiations on membership, funding, agenda, etc. etc.

There remain calls to tie down a set of Sustainable Development Goals, which should be good for another hundred reports and a dozen conferences. An Intergovernmental Science-Policy Platform on Biodiversity and Ecosystem Services is also on the drawing board. This will reportedly do for biodiversity what the Intergovernmental Panel on Climate Change did for climate science: pervert it for political ends.

The Rio+20 text was originally sold as promoting "The Future We Want." However, the "we" in question was always a self-selected group of UN bureaucrats, alarmist NGOs, corporate rent-seekers and main chancers whose interests were often sharply at odds with those of ordinary people. Rio+20's failure should be celebrated as "The Future We Avoided." So far.

11

Corporate social suicide

Like its twin, sustainable development, corporate social responsibility, CSR, is a term that sounds unarguable, but is subversive. The great economist Milton Friedman pointed to its dangers almost fifty years ago and has been misinterpreted and condemned for doing so ever since. CSR's definition and obligations are open ended, and it invites an endless parade of meddlesome "stakeholders" – beyond customers, employees, investors and local communities – to have a kick at the corporate can. It has also inevitably become an arena for posturing by businessmen, and for competitive hypocrisy between corporations.

Social responsibility, corporate humbug
23 June 1999

Corporate social responsibility sounds like motherhood. But social responsibility to whom, and for what? Similar unasked questions apply to the related field of "corporate ethics." Both concepts seek to smuggle what Nobel economist Milton Friedman once called "fundamentally subversive" doctrines into society. These doctrines go under the name of "socialism."

Banking – perennially concerned about its public image – has always been particularly vulnerable to CSR and ethics shakedowns. Bankers often show a lemming-like tendency to be the first off the CSR cliff, below which lie a morass of non-business obligations. Current leader of the pack is Citizens Bank, the two-year-old electronic banking arm of Vancouver-based VanCity Savings Credit Union, which is perhaps less responsible lemming than ethical peacock.

Earlier this week, Citizens announced an "Ethical Policy" that brims with humbug. It is against "excessive" environmental harm, but then who isn't? It will have no truck with companies involved in weapons – which, taken to its logical conclusion, means that the bank opposes national defence. It will not do business with those involved in nuclear energy or tobacco products.

Earlier this year, Citizens sought to link its low mortgage rates with child prostitution, promoting in its advertising "two numbers you should know" – one being its 5.9% five-year rate, the other the alleged 0.9% of children between 10 and 17 in Canada who are living as prostitutes. This latter statistic, if true, is appalling, but to link it to mortgage rates is contemptible.

Professor Friedman long ago saw the dangerous drift in CSR. In an article in *The New York Times* in 1970, he wrote: "Businessmen who talk this way are unwitting puppets of the intellectual forces that have been undermining the basis of a free society these past decades."

Prof. Friedman's message is often misrepresented by his opponents. He was not speaking out against social responsibility; he was merely pointing out that such initiatives – already practised on a massive scale by the state via taxation and redistribution, but otherwise an individual and community matter – should not be the province of the corporation. Corporate executives who indulge their personal convictions – or the personal convictions of others – at the expense of shareholders are abrogating those shareholders' rights.

He noted that companies might engage in community activities or even charitable contributions to promote goodwill, but that this was corporate self-interest, not "social responsibility."

The Big Lie at the root of CSR and corporate ethics is that business is fundamentally unethical. But what promotes honest business is primarily competition and the value of reputation rather than fear of prosecution. That is, unless you are a crook.

Prof. Friedman noted the short-sightedness of businessmen who, by donning the heavy mantle of CSR, "strengthen the already prevalent view that the pursuit of profits is wicked and immoral and must be curbed and controlled by external forces."

It is significant that Citizens Bank bills itself as "Canada's socially responsible bank," thus implying its moral superiority to the larger banks. The big banks, meanwhile, are in fact tripping over each other to promote everything from aboriginal achievement to gay pride.

Prof. Friedman noted that the adoption of CSR is a "suicidal impulse." Once corporations start taking on social responsibilities, there is no end to their potential burden. Meanwhile, governments will be only too willing to lumber them with more, ultimately without choice.

Chunky Monkey and hippie hypocrisy
14 April 2000

The announcement on Wednesday that ice cream-maker Ben & Jerry's had been bought by European consumer products giant Unilever for US $326 million sent shock waves through the ranks of the socially concerned. Could the hippie, New Age manufacturer of cutely named desserts such as Chunky Monkey and Cherry Garcia have sold out to The Man? Say it isn't so.

In February, 1998, when it rejected a takeover offer from a California company, Ben & Jerry's declared "it is in the long-term interest of the company and its shareholders, its employees, customers and the Vermont community for the company to remain independent and headquartered in Vermont." They forgot to add: "unless someone with more money comes along."

Not that founders Ben Cohen and Jerry Greenfield didn't go down without a fight. In fact, according to the bafflegab attendant on the announcement, they haven't gone down at all. Two black-gloved fists could be seen poking skyward above the pile of cash thrust upon them by Unilever. According to the co-founders: "Neither of us could have anticipated, 20 years ago, that a major multinational would someday sign on, enthusiastically, to pursue and expand the social mission that continues to be an essential part of Ben & Jerry's."

So that's it. This is really a reverse moral takeover.

The sale marks the removal of another – if not the final – veil in the progressive exposure of a company that became the torchbearer for the evolving values of the '60s; travelling from ignorant self-indulgence to self-righteous environmental alarmism.

The problem with Ben & Jerry's was not that its owners donated 7.5% of pre-tax profits to causes of their choice – that was entirely admirable as long as the shareholders were onside – or that the company held whacked-out annual meetings at which those tie-dyed shareholders listened to Joan Baez before being regaled about the alleged evils of the American defence budget. It was that Ben & Jerry's sought to elevate its own moral status by portraying the rest of business as inherently deficient.

Quite apart from the ludicrous pretension of a "socially positive ice cream business," companies that promise "a new corporate concept of linked prosperity" – as Ben & Jerry's did in its 1988 mission statement – inevitably cast doubt on what the old concept was.

Unilever has meanwhile agreed to subject its worldwide operations to a "social audit" as a condition of the deal. Unilever is not merely saving Ben & Jerry's two faces in going along with the notion that the Vermonters will be "teaching their parents well," as the Woodstock generation might have it, it is inevitably concerned that Ben & Jerry's brand equity remain intact. That could prove problematic if B&J are regarded as sell-outs.

Apparently, the founders will stay on as ambassadors for "caring capitalism" (as opposed to the other, mythical kind, which would presumably manufacture flavours such as "Surplus Product Sundae" and "Immiseration Milk Shake").

At least Unilever won't have any problems with Ben & Jerry's stand against genetically modified food. It has already given in on that.

Going bananas over CSR

30 January 2004

Every good student of anti-capitalist history knows about the United Fruit Company. The banana giant's involvement in the overthrow of the government of Guatemala in 1954 is widely invoked as an example of evil US corporate power. Then there was the great Honduran bribery scandal of 1975, after which the chairman of the company – which had changed its name to United Brands – took a dive from New York's Pan Am building.

In 1990, the company changed its name to Chiquita Brands International and proceeded to attempt to clean up its image. It self-flagellated over its past, and declared a new spirit of "openness." It climbed into bed with the activist NGO Rainforest Alliance on the "Better Banana Project," and subjected its Latin American farms to rigid certification. It adopted tough labour standards. However, the more it tried, the harsher the criticism became. Its ultimate reward was a devastating series of articles about its Latin American operations in its hometown newspaper, *The Cincinnati Enquirer*. Although the story's allegations were subsequently retracted by the newspaper, which was forced to pay the company US $14 million in damages,

Chiquita, like Boxer the carthorse in *Animal Farm*, decided that it just had to try harder.

By 2001, the company's obsessive desire to prove itself a worthy corporate citizen had, as it were, borne fruit. It had won the Rainforest Alliance's "Sustainable Standard-Setter" award. All its Latin American farms were up to Better Banana Project standards. Wal-Mart had awarded it the "Environment Supplier of the Year Award." It had earned the Green Award for outstanding achievements in plastic recycling. It was engaged in an endless round of dialogues with the labour unions and ENGOs. Oh, and it was bankrupt.

In November, 2001, the company was forced to seek Chapter 11 protection, from which it emerged in March of 2002 after its creditors had swallowed US $700 million of bad debts, and its shareholders were all but wiped out.

The company had certainly been damaged by the "banana war" started by the European Union, which gave trade preference to bananas from former European colonies, but a critical question is how far "corporate responsibility" had helped almost put it under.

That issue was conspicuously not addressed this week when Chiquita's new boss, Cyrus F. Freidheim, Jr., spoke to the Conference Board of Canada's conference on Corporate Governance in Toronto. Then again, if there's one thing the CSR movement seeks to avoid, it is addressing the costs of its ever-growing list of demands.

Typical of such busybody concerns was a "consensus" report this week from a mob of academics, government types, NGOs and alleged representatives of business. Entitled *Corporate Responsibility and Accountability in the Global Marketplace*, it alleged that Canada was in danger of falling behind on the ethical standards that similar groups had succeeded in foisting on business in the United States and Europe. The exercise was masterminded by York University's Wesley Cragg, who declared that "Business in Canada needs to understand that ethical standards are a bottom line issue." They certainly are. Just look what they did to Chiquita's bottom line.

Corporate Social Stupidity
3 March 2004

I don't usually recommend reading our media opposition, but this month's *Globe and Mail Report on Business* magazine contains the "First Ever Corporate Social Responsibility Ranking." It is required reading for anybody who wants to understand just how intellectually vacuous and politically dangerous CSR is.

According to the magazine's editor, CSR is "based on the belief that corporations have emerged as the dominant world power." So countries are now redundant? It is companies that wage wars and put people in jail? We are ruled by a General Assembly of United Corporations?

But let's not raise picky facts. After all – as the survey ponderously intones several times – this is the "post-Enron" era. You remember Enron. It committed crimes, got away with it, got bigger and more powerful…Oh no, sorry, that's the Liberal Party of Canada I'm thinking of.

Enron was destroyed. Its senior executives are now either in the hoosegow or waiting to go there. So where's the dominant power?

OK, so that argument doesn't hold up. Nevertheless, CSR "appears," according to the sensitive cultural antennae of the *ROB* magazine, to be "in the ascendant." Moreover, even "the most narrowly focused laissez-faire capitalist" must now realize that time is "running out," and that he has to take a "leadership role."

The survey was masterminded by Michael Jantzi Research Associates. Nowhere – perhaps not surprisingly – is the most fundamental pre-methodological question addressed: who the hell is Michael Jantzi? What we do know, however, is that his Commandments are a meddlesome wish list of highly contentious "indicators" that in many cases defy statistical analysis and certainly cannot be added together. These include charitable donations, aboriginal relations, "controversies" over marketing, "public concerns" over products or services, governance styles, the "work/life balance" of employees, the percentage of women on the board, union relations, a slew of environmental reporting requirements, and fretting about human rights down the supply chain.

Sixty-odd companies agreed to subject themselves to the survey's elaborately biased questionnaires. None survives unscathed. Both mining and the oil and gas industry are declared to be fundamentally "unsustainable." The automotive sector receives a collective slap on the wrist for "introducing too many higher-margin – yet more harmful – large vehicles." Come on you guys, get those margins down!

The banks are tut-tutted for not giving more details out on lending and underwriting. Open up so we can trash you more easily!

Still, in the food and beverage sector the Brewers Retail distribution monopoly is praised because it makes recycling easier. On the darker side, competition (which, of course, is bad) is putting pressure on wages and job security, "leading to confrontations between unions and management."

In the mining sector, "[M]any companies still tend to dig in their heels when dealing with local communities." Such a prudent self-interest is not to be tolerated. Significantly, corporations lose marks for being in any form of confrontation – be it with communities, unions, governments, or aboriginals. They are always and automatically in the wrong.

In the "Food Distribution" sector, companies score marks for responding to hysteria over genetically modified foods, but Loblaws gets a prod for resisting "GM-free" labelling, and is further castigated for not responding more vigorously to bogus scares over farmed salmon. And it's the top-ranked company!

Forest companies are raked over the coals for simply obeying the law rather than kowtowing to activist NGO-enhanced "certification" programs. In insurance, Manulife comes out on top, but suffers because of CEO Dominic D'Alessandro's high salary. He also loses marks for not being a woman.

The survey is filled with NGO Barn Door conventional wisdom: fossil fuels bad/windmills good; SUVs bad/hybrids good. It suggests that "Producing fossil fuels and burning them is inherently harmful to the environment, but most oil and gas producers are at least trying to reduce the damage."

But shouldn't we perhaps remember that burning fossil fuels may also have some benefits, like supporting our way of life and being the engine of economic growth?

Just a thought. Better take it out the back and shoot it before anybody else starts thinking.

George Soros: big money, bad ideas
29 October 2004

The danger of the commercial rich corrupting politics and undermining the state has been a theme of heated debate since before Plato. Plato's answer was to have a ruling class of philosophers who would live in relative poverty. Some hopes.

The Bush administration is portrayed by the left as the culmination of Plato's fears. The United States, they tell us, is run by a plutocracy under which – to take one prominent allegation – the Iraq war was undertaken in order to grab oil concessions and snag contracts for Halliburton.

Certainly, businessmen will usually seek special favours if they are available. The answer to this problem is relatively simple: limit the power of governments to hand out such favours. However, this solution presents a major problem to modern left-liberals, since for them big – and expansive – government is the *sine qua non* of the Just Society. But then George W. Bush can hardly be accused of being a fan of small government.

Since modern left-liberals have no fundamental comprehension of what Hayek called "the extended order" of market cooperation, they believe – or profess to believe – that only a big state can save us from corporate servitude and environmental destruction. Businessmen – in particular, big businessmen – are written off as irretrievable self-seeking hypocrites. And here, perhaps, modern left-liberals have their strongest point, although not quite in the way they think.

One of the most glaring fallacies of the conventional wisdom is that businessmen are supporters of free enterprise. In fact, to the extent that businessmen do become publicly involved in national politics, they are far more likely to espouse some version of special-favour fascism, radically redistributive left-liberalism or environmental alarmism. Take George Soros, the Hungarian-born multi-billionaire investor and speculator who has made the defeat of George W. Bush a personal crusade.

Soros has not just poured millions into a stream of fretful books and support for anti-Bush websites. He has recently been on a 12-city speaking tour, which ended yesterday in Washington. All this to promote his message that President Bush is "endangering our safety, hurting our vital interests and undermining American values."

Now Soros may well have a point. The wisdom and efficacy of the Iraq war is as hotly debated by the right as by the left. Bush's economic policies have been worse than a mixed bag. The President has grown government while handing out subsidies in all directions. Nor do I have objections to Soros spending his fortune promoting his views, but we should look at exactly what Soros stands for.

Soros fancies himself a philosopher, and claims to cleave in particular to the thought of philosopher Karl Popper. He named his main philanthropic organization The Open Society Institute, after Professor Popper's most famous book, *The Open Society and its Enemies*.

Soros's institute has done a great deal of good in aiding the spread of freedom in the formerly Communist nations, but he holds a set of beliefs that are in some respects positively anti-Popperian.

Soros has absorbed the whole anti-market canon, from the allegedly invalidating impact of market "imperfection" to the power of advertising to subvert consumer choice. Worse, he thinks powerful governments can put all this straight. He embraces a more powerful UN and a world monetary authority.

Popper – who was a supporter of free markets and profoundly cynical about all forms of government – would spin in his grave at such notions. He rejected the conspiracy theory of politics that Soros embraces as the "secularization of religious superstition." The "Homeric gods," he suggested, had given way to "powerful men or groups – sinister pressure groups whose wickedness is responsible for all the evils we suffer from – such as the Learned Elders of Zion, or the monopolists, or the capitalists, or the imperialists."

On his website, Soros asks, "Why should you listen to me? Not because I have a lot of money – although it helps to get my message out – but because I have an unusual background and experience that may help throw some light on our predicament…"

But as Prof. Popper once quoted Heraclitus as observing: "Who knows many things need not have many brains." Nor need anybody who has made lots of money.

Why do CEOS sign on to CSR?

27 April 2005

"When ideas fail, words come in very handy."

–Anonymous

I have a modest proposal. I think the term "corporate social responsibility" should be reformulated to more accurately reflect its meaning. I suggest: "A Plot To Seize The Political Agenda By A Small Elite Group Of Environmental Alarmists, Aided by NGO Activist Thugs, Self-Serving Consultants And Pollsters, And Corporate Stooges Who Think They Are Being Smart."

I know that's not quite as grabby as "CSR," but it does get to the heart of the matter.

CSR has nothing to do with responsibility. It is – along with "Sustainable Development" – part of a subversive attack on the Western way of life. So why would CEOS sign on?

Corporate chieftains recoil at the notion that pursuing profits leads them – as Adam Smith famously suggested – to do a "good that is no part of their intention." Businessmen want to be conspicuous for doing more than simply making money. They often eagerly embrace the demonic mythology of capitalism, both because they are ignorant of history and because of a near-universal psychological tendency to elevate ourselves by denigrating our fellows. You will hear certain businessmen wittering on about other businessmen who are greedy, blinkered, environmentally insensitive and obsessed with the short term, but they will rarely name any. That's because such individuals are largely a myth.

The final reason for big companies to support CSR is to gain competitive advantage, both by outposturing their rivals and by hoping that those who refuse to march in the parade will be "punished" by NGO misinformation and a resultant loss of business.

When challenged, devotees of CSR resort to peddling pablum, parodying their opponents, pulling out opinion surveys or quoting the support of business consultants who earn big fees from recycling CEOS' misconceptions.

All these strategies were used in a speech on Monday to the Canadian Club by Paul Tsaparis, the head of Hewlett-Packard (Canada), who is obviously angling to be Canada's CSR champ. He declared that Canada's best bet for global competitiveness was not to lower taxes, reduce regulation or improve education; it was to adopt CSR. Canada, after all, has always been a leader in social responsibility; just take our role in founding the UN and socialized medicine. We should therefore adopt a corrupt and incompetent UN and a crumbling healthcare system as proud models for the corporate sector.

Then there was public opinion. According to Tsaparis, a survey carried out for HP Canada by GlobeScan found that 93% of those surveyed believe CSR should be as important as profits and shareholder values. But then a vast majority of people once believed that the world was flat.

Having corporate policy decided by opinion polls indicates how dangerously far the corporate sector is straying into political territory, which is exactly what CSR promoters want. This survey also reminded me of one taken just before the last election, which claimed that 82% of Canadians supported Kyoto even though only 26% were marginally "familiar" with it (and they were undoubtedly lying). I wonder how many of those surveyed by GlobeScan have any idea what CSR is really about. Certainly, if my alternative wording had been used, I doubt if similar responses would have been forthcoming.

We might also take a closer look at where GlobeScan is coming from. Just last week it produced an alleged survey of "civil society leaders" who believe, according to its president Doug Miller, "that we can no longer wait to save the planet and our civilization." In fact, the "Global Stakeholder Panel" represents a totally unrepresentative, self-selected group dedicated to "building common NGO agendas."

If Tsaparis wants to know where all this is headed, he might look south at what has happened recently to banking giant JP Morgan Chase. This week, the bank introduced an "environment policy" that represents a stunning piece of appeasement. The policy follows a campaign by the San Francisco-based ENGO Rainforest Action Network that featured both executive harassment and the marshalling of schoolchildren. Stunningly, the policy includes the bank's agreement to lobby the White House for action on climate change. This follows similar cave-ins from Bank of America and Citibank.

Tsaparis announced that HP Canada has now set up a CSR website, which it hopes to be a centre for "dialogue." I doubt this article will be included in the conversation.

Saving the Earth, one noodle at a time
11 July 2008

Lee Scott, CEO of retailing behemoth Wal-Mart, deemed the noodles in Hamburger Helper guilty of "unnecessary curliness," so he browbeat their producer, General Mills, into straightening them.

As with so much corporate lunacy these days, this vignette is rooted in the alleged need for corporations to take a conspicuous lead in forestalling catastrophic climate change. You see curly noodles take up more space than straight ones, and thus require larger packages. So, due to Scott's intervention, the Hamburger Helper box is now 20% smaller, with – according to General Mills – an annual saving equivalent to taking 500 trucks off the road. One assumes that Scott's crusade will now bring him into conflict more broadly with the pasta industry, whose products display a shameful array of shapes that leave empty spaces in packaging. He will no doubt be seeking the eradication of the spirals, bow ties and tubes of fusilli, farfalle and penne in favour of more compact spaghetti and tagliatelle. Otherwise we might be forced to conclude that Scott has something against consumers of Hamburger Helper. Let them eat utility pasta! Does he plan to start editing alphabet soup?

I always regarded tales of Wal-Mart's terrifying "power" as nonsensical, based on the automatic leftist conflation of economic heft and political clout. Now I'm not so sure. For Wal-Mart to squeeze its suppliers in the name of customer value and profitability is sound business; to twist suppliers' arms to save the planet drifts into dangerous politics, and potentially lousy economics.

The delightful animated movie *Wall-E* portrayed a world depopulated by crass materialism, of which the main pusher was a monolithic and environmentally feckless nightmare version of Wal-Mart named "Buy n Large." The real Wal-Mart is now determined to portray itself as greener than green. Indeed, its new, Orwellian, motto is "For the Greener Good." And I do mean Orwellian, because Wal-Mart seems to want to play Big Brother to its suppliers.

Straightening out Hamburger Helper is just one example of the use of Wal-Mart's green muscle (perhaps its new symbol should be The Incredible Hulk). Procter & Gamble, too, has apparently been pressured to produce only concentrated detergent.

The problem is that the Hamburger Helper intervention might burnish Wal-Mart's CSR credentials, but it makes General Mills look stupid, and undermines the free market more generally.

General Mills was either deficient in providing its Hamburger Helper in a form that consumers didn't want, and which involved waste packaging, thus damaging its own profitability, or, if its consumers really did like their curly pasta, it has sacrificed them to environmental bullying.

I sent an e-mail to General Mills asking – among other things – about the role of Scott, why Hamburger Helper was curly in the first place, and whether any market study had been done on how consumers felt about the shape shift. The company claimed that consumers were happy with the changes, and ignored the questions about Scott and the pasta's shape. It also asserted that General Mills had been "focused on efficiency and minimizing our impact on the environment for decades." But that's the point. Economizing on packaging and raw materials is a critical aspect of any business, as is responding to, and anticipating, consumer wants.

Green marketing is hardly a new phenomenon. Almost twenty years ago, Dave Nichol, the public face of Loblaw's *President's Choice* brands, said, "I think in the future we're going to look back at this point in time as the start of what is going to be the most important revolution in our society – the politicization of the consumption process."

It was an astonishingly prescient choice of words, although what Nichol was in fact talking about was the power of consumers "to vote for the environment at the cash register." Things have turned out somewhat differently, significantly due to climate change hysteria and pressure on corporations from NGOs. Companies pressure their suppliers as a means of taking the heat off themselves. This thrust is furthered by a growing army of environmental consultants, certifiers and "social licensers" who earn fat fees for nagging their clients, and/or providing them with a Cloak of Green.

Tim Flannery and the weather exploiters
16 October 2009

Tim Flannery, the radical Australian environmentalist, quoted Adam Smith this week during a CBC radio interview, thus surely sending the great economist spinning once more in his Edinburgh grave.

Promoting his latest book, *Now or Never* on the CBC's *The Current*, Flannery cited the Sage of Kirkcaldy's warning against attempts by businessmen to influence policy: "The proposal of any new law or regulation of commerce which comes from this order [merchants or manufacturers], ought always to be listened to with great precaution, and ought never to be adopted till after having been long and carefully examined, not only with the most scrupulous, but with the most suspicious attention."

True indeed, which makes it intriguing that Flannery should regard Al Gore, who has made, and stands to make, hundreds of millions of dollars from promoting government subsidy and regulation, as one of his heroes.

Even more strange, or perhaps just spectacularly hypocritical, that Flannery – whose previous book, *The Weather Makers*, was a bestseller – should head something called the Copenhagen Climate Council, which is a morass of the kind of corporatist influence against which Adam Smith was warning.

The council's members include an association called Combat Climate Change, which represents, among others, GE, Unilever, Citigroup, BP and Siemens. Then there is The Climate Group, whose corporate members include Bloomberg, Coca-Cola, Dell, Google and IBM. Another member is the World Business Council on Sustainable Development, which was set up by the UN's former chief Global Salvationist, Maurice Strong, to push his socialist blueprint. Then we have the World Economic Forum, yet another organization of the self-appointed Great and Good, where Strong again had enormous influence until he was inconveniently implicated in the UN oil-for-food corruption scandal.

The Copenhagen Climate Council's "sponsors" meanwhile consist of a group of mainly Danish corporations who make no secret of their desire to influence policy. "Bioinnovation" company Novozymes declares "[W]e aim at influencing opinion-leaders and... decision-makers towards an ambitious protocol. The [Copenhagen] conference constitutes a unique opportunity to position sustainable technologies, and an opportunity for Novozymes to brand our biotechnologies, our products, our company and our overall sustainability business model."

So, it seems, we should be suspicious of corporations peddling self-interested legislation unless that legislation also claims to be saving the planet.

In her interview with Flannery, which was conducted in the kind of hushed, deferential tones usually reserved for rape victims, *The Current*'s host, Anna Maria Tremonti, served up softball after softball. Was the global situation rather like "The Lorax?" (Dr. Seuss's creature that claims to "speak for the trees" against a greedy businessman). Would we wind up like Easter Island (all stone heads and no vegetation)? Then, Ms. Tremonti lobbed up a question about "The $700 billion bailout of the banks. What does that say to you?"

Apparently it didn't say anything to Flannery, but then perhaps that was because so many recipients of bailout money are represented on his Copenhagen Climate Council.

In this, and at least one other CBC interview this week, Flannery condemned "ordinary" businesses – that is, those that want to make profits and look after their employees – as being like "crime syndicates." His book is full of business demonization. In a Foreword, David Suzuki claims that twenty years ago, "corporations began to spend millions on a campaign to confuse the public" on climate change. No names are given, but the evidence is apparently in a book called *Climate Cover-Up*, by James Hoggan, a close associate of Suzuki.

Flannery claims the coal industry has "lied to the public for decades." Tropical loggers are "thieves…regardless of the letter of the local law." He decries coffee business "middlemen." He conjures a demonic fantasy of a twentieth-century "social model" that marched under such slogans as "survival of the fittest" and "greed is good." These "Cheneys and Bushes" adopted a "dog-eat-dog doctrine: 'We'd better keep others down, keep growing and remain strong, because if we don't, we'll be attacked and destroyed.'"

Flannery's book also contains the usual hysterical pseudo-science. Greenhouse gases are "choking our atmosphere." Humanity is "now between a tipping point and a point of no return." Anybody who questions this science can only do so because of "ignorance, bias or skepticism."

It gets worse. Flannery promotes primitive mysticism in his portrayal of earth's great self-regulating system as "Gaia," a Goddess that, he claims, demands that humans "serve" her. Where this mysticism gets transparent is in the implication that Gaia needs a priestly caste, led by the likes of Flannery, to provide a little help at the altar of planetary self-regulation.

Sounds like the sort of blatant self-interest that should be the source of great suspicion, especially as appropriate legislation would have to be enacted by a collection of what Adam Smith called "that insidious and crafty animal, vulgarly called a statesman or politician, whose councils are directed by the momentary fluctuations of affairs."

Unilever's most dangerous brand
15 February 2013

The Bata Lecture on Responsible Capitalism – named for the great Canadian businessman Thomas Bata – was delivered in Toronto on Thursday night by Paul Polman, chief executive of British consumer goods giant Unilever. Unilever sells brands such as Dove Soap, Axe deodorant and Ben & Jerry's ice cream. Polman's presentation confirmed that he ranks as one of the world's foremost peddlers of "Global Salvationism."

That term was coined by David Henderson, a former chief economist for the OECD, in his 2004 book, *The Role of Business in the Modern World*. Henderson identified the phenomenon as a combination of environmental alarmism, resource depletionism and a guilt-ridden conviction that big business had to devote itself to issues such as global poverty. He noted that this "agenda" – a critical part of which was "collaboration" with the UN and its pet NGOs – was spread via organizations such as the annual World Economic Forum in Davos and the World Business Council on Sustainable Development (WBCSD).

Polman is not only a co-chair of Davos, he is incoming chair of the WBCSD and a prominent member of the UN Secretary-General's "High Level Panel" on the "Post-2015 Development Agenda." His speech ticked all the boxes of what Henderson also called "new millennium collectivism." Polman denigrated business "short-sighted-ness," promoted climate catastrophism and suggested that what was needed was a "new model" of capitalism in which giant corporations would sacrifice shareholders in order to solve global problems.

Although he did not mention him on Thursday, Polman stoutly opposes the great economist Milton Friedman's concern that such "corporate social responsibility" is dangerous. In fact, Prof. Friedman never said that corporations should not take a long-term perspective, as Polman has claimed. More significant, Prof. Friedman acknowl-edged that community activities or charitable contributions might well make sense in terms of a corporation's self-interest, but that to dress up such activities as "social responsibility" was "hypocritical window dressing."

Such window dressing has now taken on global pretensions. In his 1957 book, *The Hidden Persuaders*, Vance Packard noted that soap marketers could multiply the price of a bar of soap if they could convince women consumers that it made them not merely clean but beautiful. A sign of The Beauty Myth times is that Dove is now aimed at the non-beautiful. That is clever marketing, but Polman's claim is that another of the company's brands, Lifebuoy, is "no longer just soap, it's a movement to improve lives."

Unilever brands more generally are described as "movements for social change." You don't just sell toilet cleanser any more, you have to promote a "World Toilet Day."

Polman knows he is riding a tiger in courting the NGOs, but has little choice. Social-mediated do-not-buy campaigns and consumer boycotts are powerful new weapons. Polman noted that – with the help of social media – the government of Egypt fell in just 17 days. Companies, he suggested, could fall in a matter of hours.

He did not dwell on how inappropriate it might be to compare a corporation to a repressive government (although Occupy-inclined denizens of Facebook might not think so), or on how what followed the Egyptian uprising might turn out to be worse.

Some may raise the objection that it is inappropriate to criticize Polman because he runs a company that is performing relatively well on the stock market. This is all the more remarkable because he has suggested that shareholders should not rank above other stakehold-ers, and that he doesn't even want "speculators" and hedge funds – who he said would sell their grandmothers for profit – buying Unilever shares. He does not give earnings guidance to analysts, and has stopped giving quarterly earnings reports, which he has dubbed "three-month rat races." But we should also remember that he is sit-ting atop brand values that have been built over many decades. One danger is that consumers may tire of not being able to buy shampoo, ice cream or toilet cleanser without having to lug home some great "social" cause in their reusable shopping bags. Holier-than-Thou marketing may eventually be hoist on its own petard.

Polman acknowledged that Thomas Bata and William Lever, one of the brothers who founded Unilever, were great contributors to society. Indeed they were, but it was their exceptional achievements in generating profits by serving consumers that gave them the where-withal to pursue their broader philanthropic interests. The problem of the modern corporation is not that it forces single-minded devo-tion to the bottom line on its managers, but that it gives them too much leeway to dabble with dangerous fads. Meanwhile, those who spout about a "new model" for capitalism invariably hold an inac-curate and demonic image of the (relatively) free-market original, which is still the only truly "sustainable" version.

Polman suggested on Thursday that it was time to take "the road less travelled." We should be concerned that it might be the road to serfdom.

George Mitchell and the limits to thinking

2 June 2015

One of the great paradoxes of the fracking revolution is that its "father," the late George P. Mitchell, was a fan of sustainable development. This might not quite rank with cotton manufacturer Friedrich Engels supporting Karl Marx, but it comes pretty close.

That's because if sustainability has one key tenet, it is that the fossil fuel industry must be killed to save the planet. Instead, fracking has revitalized it.

Mitchell symbolizes an understandable public confusion: that capitalism is somehow synonymous with the weird, anti-market ideas that capitalists often embrace. Businessmen tend not to be fans of competition and often seek government favours. One of the great current examples is Elon Musk, the entrepreneur who has received billions from governments desperate to promote the climate agenda.

Great capitalists also sometimes have strange views that have little or nothing to do with their business success. Henry Ford was profoundly anti-Semitic. Bill Gates, the richest man in the world, has fallen victim to the notion that corporations should be dedicated to solving the world's social problems. Ted Turner is among those promoting sustainability and population control while leaving a massive personal carbon footprint and having a large family. In a world when climate skepticism is claimed to be a product of fossil-fuel industry misinformation, billionaires such as Michael Bloomberg and Tom Steyer receive only praise for supporting alarmism. But few businessmen held views as paradoxical as Mitchell, who died a couple of years ago.

Mitchell allied himself with the outer fringe of catastrophists and depletionists – in particular the authors of *The Limits to Growth*. That book claimed, in 1972, to have studied the future "with the aid of a giant computer" and projected unarguable resource exhaustion, ecological "overshoot" and civilizational collapse (funny how current official climate models are claimed to predict something similar).

According to *Limits*, it would all be over before the end of the twentieth century unless mankind engineered a "totally new form of human society" and imposed a "sustainable...global equilibrium." That equilibrium required the sacrifice of "certain human freedoms" and rigid control of population and investment.

Mitchell embraced these views and supported conferences to promote them, even as he was part of the – relatively – free-market process that ultimately made *Limits*' projections as wrong as its policy recommendations were repugnant.

Mitchell pioneered fracking, which involves pumping high-pressure liquids into horizontally drilled wells and thus releasing vast amounts of petroleum that were previously considered uneconomic. The technology is responsible for reversing the decline of oil and gas production in North America, and for a sharp drop in global petroleum prices. The cheap natural gas bonanza has revitalized the US manufacturing sector and led to a projected boom in liquefied natural gas trade. It has pulled the already tattered rug from under renewables, such as solar and wind, and caused turmoil in Russia and throughout the nations of OPEC.

Fracking has been fiercely opposed by anti-development ENGOs, who have thrown every form of junk science at it, from claims of flaming tap water to earthquakes. Craven politicians have banned it, or put moratoria on it, rather than confront social-mediated mobs.

The irony is that the man who perfected fracking embraced many of the same alarmist notions and simplistic top-down "solutions" as those violently opposed to his innovations.

Mitchell was the embodiment of the American Dream. The son of a poor Greek immigrant, he not merely created a successful petroleum enterprise but also built a model community in Texas, helped revitalize Galveston, and was a generous contributor to university research, as well as signing Bill Gates' Giving Pledge.

Some claim that Mitchell, like Musk, could never have done it without US Government geological mapping and R&D credits (indeed, President Obama – the most anti-petroleum president ever – has claimed credit for the fracking revolution). Certainly, governments are unavoidable in the business sphere, and perpetually seek to associate themselves with business success, but whether their impact is a net benefit is another matter entirely. History would suggest otherwise.

Mitchell's son, Todd, admitted the "Mitchell Paradox," based on the fact that his father supported population control but had ten children, and was a champion of sustainability although he never invested in renewables.

Dennis Meadows, lead author of *The Limits to Growth*, has continued to peddle the same old catastrophism, simply kicking the doomsday can down the road. Two years before Mitchell died, Meadows gave a speech in Ottawa in which he claimed it was "too late for sustainable development." During the question period, somebody was impolite enough to point out that Meadows had suggested a decade earlier that Canadian natural gas production had peaked. Meadows squirmed. Ironically, the man who had made him wrong – yet again – was George Mitchell.

Level heads have suggested that the shale gas revolution offers a "bridge" to a more sustainable future, but this argument tends to be angrily disputed by environmental radicals, who would prefer to blow up such a bridge.

Mitchell is particularly fascinating because his belief in the need for anti-market sustainability was refuted by his own ingenuity, and yet he seemed to fail to grasp that minds such as his own, as the great economist Julian Simon noted, are the "ultimate resource."

12

The great green non-transition

I THOUGHT THEY
WERE SUPPOSED
TO SAVE THE PLANET
NOT RUIN IT!

WAITING FOR GREEN GODOT

The transition to a low-carbon (dioxide) "green economy" has become an article of faith rather than a subject of debate. This transition is claimed by the politicians, bureaucrats, NGOs and businessmen to be both inevitable and a job creator. So far all it has led to is less reliable and more expensive energy, while having zero impact on the climate. It is the very last thing the world can afford as it struggles to deal with the economic damage of COVID-19.

315

Hypercar trip to energy neverland
19 October 2000

The emperor's new car
5 December 2002

Why state R&D flops
7 January 2009

A transition to be avoided
9 August 2016

Waiting for green Godot
22 November 2018

Hypercar trip to energy neverland
19 October 2000

Amory Lovins first achieved fame in the 1970s as the guru of small, renewable, decentralized energy: the "Soft Path." A windmill on every rooftop, a biogas digester in every backyard. By the year 2000, he predicted, the United States would produce 35% of its commercial energy "softly." How wrong was he? Calculated generously, by a factor of 10. Less generously, maybe 100.

Lovins continues to be hired as an advisor by numerous multinational corporations, national governments and international agencies, but his emphasis has changed. He has gone from anti-nuclear Luddite to technological fantasist. In particular, he is the father of the "Hypercar," a concept he liked so much that he slapped a trademark on it.

Last Sunday, in Montreal, Lovins, founder of the Rocky Mountain Institute, was the keynote speaker at a "High-Level Seminar" (altitude is essential for the international wonkasphere) on "Cleaner Production" sponsored by the UN Environmental Program (UNEP). There's nothing the UN loves more than to rush to the head of a well-established long-term trend in free markets – namely, the reduction in energy usage and pollution per unit of output – and claim its guidance is needed. According to current UNEP head Klaus Toepfer, "to a large extent we have built the worldwide consensus on cleaner production. However, we have certainly not reached the end of the road, and we must foster greater commitment." Wow. Who would believe a bureaucrat could go so far out on a limb?

Lovins was the keynote speaker presumably because he makes the most outrageous claims for cleaner production, thus establishing that those who live in the real world just aren't displaying enough "commitment." According to Lovins, the world could increase its energy efficiency by a factor of 10, and all within a generation!

Key to the practicality of this claim is Lovins' Hypercar, a vehicle of mythical characteristics in every sense. Lovins recently told *Fortune* magazine: "It will be roughly four to eight times as efficient as a car of comparable size. You can make it a 110-mile-to-the-gallon large SUV or a 200-mile-per-gallon family sedan. In either case it will perform like a Jaguar." In a recent book, he declared that the wonder vehicle would combine "Lexus comfort and refinement, Mercedes stiffness, Volvo safety, BMW acceleration [and] Taurus price."

Oh, and by the way, the fuel-cell-powered vehicle would be a source of energy, too. Instead of plugging it into your house, you would plug your house – or workplace – into it. As for emissions, there would only be pure water, which led Lovins to suggest that the Hypercar might be equipped with on-board espresso machines. But then, why not espresso machines? Indeed, why not an on-board banana farm similar to the one Lovins has at his ultra-high-efficiency (and ultra-high-cost) house in the Rockies? When you're having a fantasy, why not go all the way?

Perhaps the most far-fetched assertion made by Lovins is that the billions of dollars that auto companies are spending on alternative vehicles are somehow due to his innovative ideas. The real reason is the threat of draconian legislation such as California's demand for zero-emission vehicles by 2003. The auto giants aren't pouring billions into fuel cell and electric cars because they make any economic sense, but out of fear and desperation. According to Lovins, their main problem is not technical or economic, it's cultural.

In technical terms, Lovins has very few ideas at all. Just assume fuel cells work, ignore the costs of a hydrogen-fuelling infrastructure, use all the lightest and most expensive materials, then declare blithely that "scale" will bring costs down. Way down.

In fact, here on planet Earth, automakers are facing all kinds of technical and economic problems with alternative vehicles. Battery-powered cars have proved, yet again, to be a dud. Earlier this year, GM scrapped its EV1, a very expensive car that took you not very far, not very fast. The new breed of "hybrid" gasoline/electric cars, such as the Honda Insight and the Toyota Prius, are again expensive. They get good mileage but at the slight expense of not being able to take too much in the way of either passengers or luggage. Meanwhile, the truly astonishing advances continue to be made in conventional cars and the internal combustion engine, which, through upgraded catalytic converters, improved computer control and enhanced air-fuel mixtures, will soon be able to achieve 99% less smog-forming emissions than in the 1960s.

But where's the environmental fantasy – not to mention the consulting fees – in that?

The emperor's new car
5 December 2002

Many, many, years ago, when I was a mere cub reporter on Fleet Street, I used to be the *Financial Times'* deputy motoring correspondent. Part of my job was testing cars in which the motoring correspondent wouldn't be seen dead. That was how I found myself one day manoeuvering a leaden tortoise named the Enfield 8000.

"If the Ford Motor Company," I wrote in my review, "suddenly revealed that it was to launch a revolutionary small car which could carry just two passengers at a top speed of 40 mph over a maximum range of 55 miles and require eight hours to refuel…the public might with some justification feel that the strain of coping with the dismal car market had finally been too much for the management's sanity."

I thought I was being witty, but a quarter-century later that is exactly what Ford did. It bought a Norwegian company that manufactured a plastic-bodied two-seater with performance comparable to that of the Enfield 8000, invested us $100 million in it, leased it to adventurous but soon-disillusioned guinea pigs, then abandoned the whole idea. Ford was, nevertheless, able to say that it had made the effort. For its part, General Motors has so far flushed us $1.25 billion down the toilet to prove that electric cars won't sell.

Why would the automobile giants invest in dead-end technology? Primarily because of California legislation threatening a "zero-emission" mandate. It wasn't that the car companies wouldn't, they just couldn't. Faced with reality, California merely tinkered with the legislation. GM and DaimlerChrysler have now sued to have the law overturned. This week saw the latest episode in the great California zero-emission fandango, as the phenomenon of automobile sticker shock entered a whole new dimension. Toyota leased a handful of its fuel cell hybrid vehicles to the University of California and to the Japanese government for a knock-down price of just under US $10,000 a month. Honda leased a single FCX fuel-cell passenger car to the Japanese government for a bargain US $6,600.

But why would Toyota and Honda be charging governments or universities anything? Even at these prices, the recovery from these leases are mere drops in the bucket of research costs. Moreover, Toyota is effectively subsidizing the University of California to pay for these leases through research grants. Why not just give them the cars? Could they be sending a subtle message? "Remember that somebody has to pay for these things."

The message is intended primarily for the government of California. More generally, it is aimed at those whose grasp of economics is perennially clouded, if not completely eclipsed, by their moralistic approach to environmental issues.

Urban pollution is indeed a real problem. Catastrophic projected global warming is much more debatable (although you are not allowed to debate it), but real solutions must be based on science, costs and benefits. To mandate the makeup of state-wide vehicle sales to solve a Los Angeles smog problem makes no sense. Pouring money into fuel cells is analogous to the drunk who is looking for his car keys under the street lamp, not because he dropped them there, but because that's where the light is. All technologies are improved over time, but the fuel cell, like the battery, requires a quantum leap that is by no means guaranteed, or even probable.

The fuel cell is feted because it helped take man to the moon, but that's exactly its problem. It's an incredibly expensive – and aged – technology that was used in a project where expense was no object. Automobiles are different. In most cases, individuals have to pay for them directly.

Many commentators assume that because governments everywhere are pouring money into fuel cell technology, often at the behest of corporations, that indicates their potential viability. No way. As I concluded in that review of the Enfield 8000 all those years ago, if you want to appreciate the gasoline-powered automobile, just look at the alternatives.

Why state R&D flops
7 January 2009

A key part of president-elect Barack Obama's plans to "stimulate" the US economy involves funnelling US $150 billion over 10 years to the development of "green" technologies.

Those inclined to give credence to such grandiose plans would be well advised to read a recent book entitled – somewhat misleadingly – *Sex, Science & Profits*, by British academic Terence Kealey. The book deals with the nature of science, the history of technology and the role of governments in promoting economic growth. It provides a devastating critique of states' failure to fund economically useful knowledge, and suggests that all spending on "technologies of the future" is likely to wind up down the drain.

Professor Kealey is not promoting some off-the-wall, right-wing economic theory. A comprehensive 2003 study by the Organization for Economic Co-operation and Development entitled *The Sources of Economic Growth in OECD Countries*, found that the only useful R&D came from private sources and that public R&D funding tended to have negative consequences.

Professor Kealey provides the history and psychology behind this inconvenient truth, and sets out to explode the pervasive notion – first propounded by the prototypical 17th-century English policy wonk, Sir Francis Bacon – that science is a "public good" that needs to be promoted by governments.

In a sweeping analysis, Professor Kealey notes that advances in both science and technology have – from the steam engine to radio astronomy – come overwhelmingly from the private sector. "Powerful" states, from ancient Egypt through China to Soviet Russia, have held up technological advance rather than promoting it. The vast US expenditure on research in the wake of the Sputnik scare in the 1950s managed to put a man on the moon, but has (strategic considerations to one side) done little or nothing for the wellbeing of the average American.

Professor Kealey supports the wisdom of Adam Smith, the 18th-century Scottish economist, who suggested that technological advance was a natural consequence of market specialization, which could not be improved upon by governments, except when it came to national defence.

The Industrial Revolution in Britain was promoted by the political freedoms consolidated by the "Glorious Revolution" of 1688. Its agents were eminently practical private tinkerers who had little or nothing to do with government or the educational institutions of the day. France, by contrast, was dripping with state-funded agriculture and science, but lagged Britain severely.

Professor Kealey explodes the notion of private "underinvestment" in R&D, which is based on flawed economic theory rather than historical fact. He also highlights the counterproductiveness of government technological promotion, using two prominent British examples. Before he became Prime Minister, Harold Wilson, in the early 1960s, promoted the "White Heat" of technological revolution, using the Soviet Union as a model. His Labour government greatly increased public R&D spending, which yielded the first commercial nuclear reactor, the first jet passenger aircraft, the first commercial computer and (half of) the first supersonic commercial aircraft. What all these "achievements" had in common was that they were financial disasters, and accompanied a decline in the British economy.

Margaret Thatcher, by contrast, was castigated for cutting government R&D, but her cuts were more than compensated for by increases in private spending, confirming that government R&D merely "crowds out" the private version. Government R&D also tends to be counterproductive because it emphasizes political priorities.

One of Professor Kealey's most fascinating revelations is the astonishing success of promoters of publicly funded science and technology in bending history to suit their prejudices. The advance of privately funded British science has for two hundred years gone hand in hand with constant predictions of decline. The experience of post-war Japan was comprehensively falsified. In fact, Japanese government support for R&D has almost everywhere proved counterproductive. State agencies opposed the development of cars, electronics and cameras, while government promotion of "fifth generation" computers, and the space and nuclear industries has been a bust. To the extent that Japan was successful, it was due to private R&D.

Again, Germany's post-war success was not due to government but to the state's abandonment of so-called "Rhenish capitalism," with its cartels, tariffs and subsidies, and the adoption of the "Ordo-liberalism" of Ludwig Erhard, who established an independent central bank, reduced government controls and liberalized trade.

Professor Kealey notes that government funding tends to corrupt science, but unfortunately does not go into the currently most dangerous example: that of state-funded "climate science" – although he does refer to the establishment pogrom against the environmental skepticism of Bjorn Lomborg.

Bold presidential technological commitments such as those of Obama have – with the exception of the moon shot, which could not have been less commercial – a depressing history. If Obama is channelling any former president right now, it is the hapless Jimmy Carter, who, in the 1970s, invoked the "moral equivalent of war" to promote energy alternatives. Professor Kealey's book explains why he – inevitably – failed.

A transition to be avoided

9 August 2016

"The transition to a low-carbon economy" is a truism/mantra intoned by almost every political party, environmental group, global bureaucracy and media outlet. It is invoked not just as a policy prescription but as a moral imperative. However, like all the catchphrases of the Big Green Agenda – sustainable development, corporate social responsibility, climate crisis, environmental justice, social licence, etc. etc. – it demands close analysis.

Free markets are always "in transition" due to innovation and ingenuity, but the low-carbon transition is to be forced. Its great proponents are the enforcers, and we are talking about something far more radical than merely the way we generate energy. Leading transitionistas admit that they want a fundamental change in the global economic and political system.

Whenever I hear such people assert both the necessity and viability of the Great Transition, I think of the introduction to my old paperback copy of Joseph Schumpeter's great book, *Capitalism, Socialism and Democracy*, which was first published in 1942.

In that introduction, written in 1976, British Marxist academic Tom Bottomore declared that the book's popularity was explained "by the fact that it undertakes a serious and thorough examination of the great social transition of the present age, from capitalism to socialism." Bottomore, failing to see Schumpeter's ironic subtext – "Socialism is coming, and won't you be sorry when it arrives" – went on to praise Soviet satellite Yugoslavia as a likely model for the state enterprise that would bring about heaven on earth.

Fast forward 40 years and both the Soviet Union and Yugoslavia have disintegrated, but radical socialism has far from disappeared. It has simply gone green. The transition to a low-carbon economy is still code for a transition to more political control, less freedom and less wealth.

Fortunately, like that "inevitable" transition to socialism circa 1976, the transition to the low-carbon economy has profound practical problems. Unfortunately, the public's slowness to grasp those problems will prolong the pain, although the pain is already being felt in much of Europe and in the People's Republics of Ontario and Alberta.

The natural tendency of markets is always to use less energy per unit of output. ExxonMobil, the now criminally persecuted Great Satan for the radical green movement, projects that global GDP will be 80% higher per capita by 2040, but this will require only a 35%

increase in energy use. That energy won't be wind and solar. According to optimistic projections from the International Energy Agency, (which, like all multinational bureaucracies, is full of transitionspeak), wind and solar will account for just over 2% of the world's energy needs in 2040, when the use of fossil fuels will be, as noted, significantly greater. How does that equate with the alleged essential reduction of greenhouse gas emissions by 80% by 2050? It doesn't. Despite the success of radical greens and their political puppets in bringing new pipelines to a halt in Canada, the fossil fuel industry shows no prospect of dying either here or elsewhere. Ironically, thanks to the fracking revolution, US output has enjoyed a resurgence under the most anti-petroleum president ever. Oil production in 2015 was 72% higher than in 2010. Natural gas production was also at a record.

According to Harvard guru Michael Porter, not only does cleaner-burning natural gas promise further to lower emissions, but its sudden abundance and cheapness has revitalized the entire US economy. If lowering emissions really is the radicals' priority, natural gas should be their ideal transitional fuel. Thanks to the shale gas boom and the (market-based) switch from coal, the US is leading the world in emissions reductions. But ENGOs are not delighted at the fracking revolution. They hate it, and have pulled out every piece of fearmongering and misinformation to close it down, particularly in Europe, where they are eagerly supported by Vladimir Putin. They want fossil fuels dead, and they want them dead now.

Schumpeter was among those who warned of the dangerous leftist trends that were building during and after the Great Depression. His work was followed by similar warnings in Friedrich Hayek's *Road to Serfdom* and fictional works such as *Nineteen Eighty-Four* and *Atlas Shrugged*. And yet societies continued down paths warned against by those authors for three or four more decades before socialist economic policies were exposed as disastrous. Exposed, that is, to everybody but dedicated socialists, who continue to strut and fret in countries such as Venezuela, or seek new rationalizations, such as catastrophic climate change.

Schumpeter wrote that capitalism was doomed partly because it funded a "scribbling class" of leftist intellectuals and academics committed to its destruction. These "judges," he wrote, "have the sentence of death in their pockets."

The immediate economic costs of the new transition to green socialism are already clear in soaring energy bills and sluggish economies, but the faithful – including the mainstream scribblers – claim the problem is merely one of denialism, obstructionism and, ultimately, moral turpitude. To them, "the transition" is still inevitable, and the sentence for capitalism is still death.

Waiting for green Godot
22 November 2018

Amid hundreds of graphs, charts and tables in the latest World Energy Outlook (WEO) from the International Energy Agency (IEA), there is one fundamental piece of information that you have to work out for yourself: the percentage of total global primary energy demand provided by wind and solar. The answer is 1.1%. The policy mountains have laboured and brought forth not just a mouse, but – as the report reluctantly acknowledges – an enormously disruptive mouse.

The IEA has in recent years become an increasingly schizophrenic organization. As both a source of energy information and a shill for the UN's climate-focused sustainable development agenda, it has to talk up the "transition to a low-carbon future" while simultaneously reporting that it's not happening. But it will!

This report should be profoundly embarrassing to the Liberal government of Justin Trudeau, which has virtue-signalled itself to the front of a parade that is going nowhere, although it can certainly claim genuine leadership in the more forceful route to transition: killing the fossil fuel industry by edict or neglect.

The WEO report, yet again, projects that global fossil fuel use – and related emissions – will grow out to 2040, as oil, gas and coal continue to dominate the energy picture. But it also struggles to put a positive spin on wind and solar. Solar had a "record-setting" year in 2017. The Chinese solar business is "booming." New wind and solar additions "outpaced those of fossil fuels in 2017, driven by policy support and declining costs."

"Policy support" means subsidies worth hundreds of millions of dollars. As for declining costs, solar is still at least twice as expensive a generator as coal and almost twice as expensive as gas.

Finally, and most significantly, the report confirms what should have been obvious from the start: that the more "variable" wind and solar are introduced into any electricity system, the more expensive and less reliable it becomes.

The term Variable Renewable Energy is synonymous with Unreliable Renewable Energy, due to the terribly obvious fact that the sun doesn't shine at night, and sometimes not during the day, while the wind doesn't always blow. Therefore, the more that wind and solar are part of your system, the more technical contortions they demand from backup power and the structure of the grid. The efficient part of the system has to twist itself into a pretzel to accommodate the inefficient part.

Accommodating unreliability has led to outright perversity. The widespread adoption of wind and solar under Germany's *Energiewende* ("energy transition") has resulted in rising overall emissions, mainly from coal-fired backup facilities. Meanwhile the green Godot is battery storage, which is always on the point of turning up, but never quite does. Still, the IEA has a scenario for that: wishful thinking, as in "What if battery storage becomes really cheap?"

Supply isn't the only area where expensive and unreliable wind and solar need to be accommodated. There is also "demand flexibility." This includes having solar panels installed on your roof, or adopting – or being forced to adopt – "smart meters," which can monitor a household's electricity usage in minute-by-minute detail. According to the report, "The spreading of rooftop solar PV (photovoltaics) and the falling costs of digital technologies, combined with affordable wind and solar power options, are creating a host of new opportunities that enable consumers to take a more active role in meeting their own energy needs."

But wind and solar are not "affordable," and very few people want to take a more active role in meeting their energy needs. They just want to flip a switch.

As for smart meters, the IEA notes that many countries "have successfully rolled out smart meters on a large scale, such as Canada, Denmark, Finland, Italy, Norway, Spain and Sweden." Would such success be like the smart meter programme in Ontario, which was panned by provincial auditor Bonnie Lysyk for costing an extra billion dollars and not working as advertised, while several thousand meters were also found to represent a fire hazard? Although it mentions nothing of the absurdities attached to Ontario's Green Energy Act, the WEO report confirms that Canada has the most stringent emissions-pricing program in the world, at least out to 2025, at $35 a tonne (in 2017 US dollars), thus cementing its competitive disadvantage. Others, such as the EU and Korea, are prepared to make marginally more self-damaging commitments out to 2040 (at US $43 and US $44 respectively), but these levels nowhere near approach that allegedly required by the beyond-fantasy "Sustainable Development Scenario," which, for developed countries, is US $63 in 2025 and US $140 in 2040. In fact, those figures, like most of the IEA's projections, are not worth a solar fig.

The Sustainable Development Scenario not only solves the climate issue, but takes care of universal access to modern energy and air pollution too. Even more amazing, it achieves all this via the imposition of swathes of expensive and unreliable energy, but without the slightest impact on economic growth. How? By simply assuming that growth continues no matter what.

The report's solution to policy mayhem is inevitably to call for more – and more complex – policy. "Can an integrated approach spur faster action?" it asks. Since governments have screwed up so badly, might they screw up less if they try to do much more? At least they are assured of firm support from the IEA.

Also by Peter Foster

1979

The Blue-Eyed Sheiks: The Canadian Oil Establishment

1982

The Sorcerer's Apprentices: Canada's Superbureaucrats and the Energy Mess

1983

Other People's Money: The Banks, the Government, and Dome

1985

From Rigs to Riches: The Story of Bow Valley Industries

1986

The Master Builders: How the Reichmanns Reached for an Empire

1990

Family Spirits: The Bacardi Saga: Rum, Riches and Revolution

1992

Self-Serve: How Petrocan Pumped Canadians Dry

1993

Towers of Debt: The Rise and Fall of the Reichmanns

2014

Why We Bite the Invisible Hand: The Psychology of Anti-Capitalism

About the Global Warming Policy Forum

The Global Warming Policy Forum is the campaigning arm of the Global Warming Policy Foundation, an all-party and non-party think tank and a registered educational charity which, while open-minded on the contested science of global warming, is deeply concerned about the costs and other implications of many of the policies currently being advocated.

Views expressed in the publications of the Global Warming Policy Forum are those of the authors, not those of the Forum, the Foundation, its trustees, its Academic Advisory Council members or its directors.

Made in the USA
Las Vegas, NV
09 December 2020

12419208R00196